HAMPTON ON

Alistair Owen is the editor of *Sn*
with Bruce Robinson and *Story and Character: Interviews with British Screenwriters*. He is currently writing a feature film script for The Mob Film Co. in London.

Hampton on Hampton

Edited by ALISTAIR OWEN

faber and faber

First published in 2005
by Faber and Faber Limited
3 Queen Square London WC1N 3AU
Published in the United States by Faber and Faber Inc.
an affiliate of Farrar, Straus and Giroux LLC, New York

Typeset by Faber and Faber Ltd
Printed in England by Mackays of Chatham, plc

A CIP record for this book
is available from the British Library

ISBN 0-571-21418-5

2 4 6 8 10 9 7 5 3 1

Contents

Introduction

Christopher Hampton is telling me about the time he met Richard Nixon. The occasion is the opening of the Eisenhower Theatre in Washington D.C., the first production being Hampton's translation of Ibsen's *A Doll's House* and the first order of business a line-up to shake the presidential hand.

'I hadn't realized that the event was black tie,' Hampton says, 'or that it was in the presence of President Nixon, and I was wearing a brown velvet suit, a patterned Indian shirt and white shoes. My hair was also quite a bit longer than it is now, so I cut a pretty bizarre figure. Anyway, Nixon, who had more make-up on than the actors, went down the line shaking hands, paused in front of me and – I'm very proud of this – wouldn't shake my hand, so disreputable was my appearance. I then found myself uninvited from the post-show party at the White House and wound up at another party, smoking pot with a bunch of Native Americans in town lobbying for land rights.' He pauses. 'It was at the Watergate Hotel, three weeks before the break-in.'

It's a beguiling anecdote: Christopher Hampton as Forrest Gump. It's also a telling one: Christopher Hampton as perennial outsider. Of course, attending such an event in the first place renders him something of an *in*sider – theatrically, if not politically – but then, all success is relative. I might see him as a dauntingly confident person who has been everywhere and met everyone, but he apparently sees himself as a rather reserved man still struggling to make his mark.

'I have absolutely no sense of anyone in this country taking me seriously as a film-maker,' he tells me, in response to criticism of his second and third films as writer–director, *The Secret Agent* and *Imagining Argentina*, and in spite of praise for his first, *Carrington*. 'In the same way, although by dint of long service I think I've become an established figure, I felt pretty marginalized in the theatre to begin with. But when you reflect on it, you realize that you marginalize yourself by choosing to dwell on the margins, so you can't really moan about it. If you want to play with fire, you have to accept that it's going to burn you from time to time.'

If he does dwell on the margins, it could be because he refuses to confine himself to his core profession: that of playwright. Stage adaptations and translations, film and television scripts, even musicals, he's tackled them all – eighty-odd projects in a forty-year career – and when I try to enlist his help in identifying thematic links between them, I find myself talking to the readily recognizable narrator of his autobiographical play *White Chameleon*, a character who claims to be 'wary of every known brand of confident certainty'.

'Quite early on, I decided that there were four areas which interested me,' he begins, promisingly, 'and if you take my first four plays as the four templates, broadly speaking you can slot most of the stuff I've done since into one of those categories.'

'What *are* the categories?' I ask.

'Personal melodrama,' he says, listing them, 'like *When Did You Last See My Mother?* and *Treats*. Historical subjects, which I guess would be *Total Eclipse*, *Tales from Hollywood* and *The Talking Cure*. Character studies, and I make a vague connection there between *The Philanthropist* and *Les Liaisons Dangereuses* . . . '

'Because they both deal with extreme examples of certain characteristics?' I interrupt, wondering if we have to speak *quite* so broadly.

'Sort of,' he says. 'I don't exactly know what I mean by that. I think I know what I mean by it, but it's hard to define. Then there are political subjects, like *Savages*.'

'And *White Chameleon*?' I offer.

'*White Chameleon* is really in another category altogether,' he says. 'No, I'd link *Savages* with a different strand of my work, screenplays like *The Price of Tea* and *A Bright Shining Lie*, but I'm not very well known for that strand because on the whole the scripts haven't been made.' He hesitates, then concludes, 'It's useful for me to have the four categories, so I can say to myself, "It's one of these," or "It's one of those," but I don't think they have any significance beyond that.'

It should come as no surprise, then, that this book is struc-tured not thematically but – largely – chronologically. In other words, rather than deal with some of his work in great detail, I have decided to deal with all of it in some detail, on the basis that the more of it we talk about, the more the thematic links will – hopefully – emerge.

With that in mind, my thanks must go to Christopher for a dozen lengthy interviews and as many gourmet lunches; to Maria and Alice for arranging those interviews and lunches; to Peggy Paterson, who helped conceive the book, and Dinah Wood, who sent it out into the world; to Justin, my old friend and occasional agent; to Rosie, for always being there; and finally to my parents, whose generosity I hope one day to repay.

Alistair Owen

When Did You Last See My Mother? – Total Eclipse

When did you first start writing?

I started writing plays when I was at school in Egypt, adaptations of *The Tell-Tale Heart* and *The Fall of the House of Usher* with all the boring philosophical bits cut out and concentrating on the blood and guts. Then, when I was sent to prep school in England at the age of ten, I used to put on plays in the dormitory at the end of term. So at that stage I already knew that this was what I wanted to do.

Most boys of that age still want to be astronauts or train drivers.

I know. I don't know where it came from, really, because my parents were very sporty. There weren't any books in the house. My father took books out of the library, but the adventurous kind – P. C. Wren and Rider Haggard. The thing is, I was very small as a pre-teen, with big thick glasses and everything – the standard swot. I didn't grow until my mid-teens, when I suddenly shot up five or six inches one year.

It's interesting that the first plays you wrote were adaptations, which have played a major part in your career ever since.

That's right. I fell in love with the work of Edgar Allan Poe, which I read far too early – I was only eight or nine. At the end of the road where we lived in Alexandria there was a clubhouse of sorts for people who worked at Cable & Wireless, and it had this library. I was confined to the children's bit, and I said to my father, 'I'm not interested in these books,' so he agreed to take out books for me, and one of the books he took out was *Tales of Mystery and Imagination* – which became *the* book of my early childhood. After Egypt my father went to Hong Kong, which had no film certification, so I could go and see X-rated films like *The Revenge of Frankenstein* at the age of eleven, and I've still got an unredeemed taste for Gothic melodrama dating back to those days.

After prep school you went to Lancing College, where you wrote a novel, Peter Stone.

Yes. Lancing was in the process of a liberal unbuttoning under the new headmaster, John Dancy, and one of the things he did was to bring in a lot of young teachers. Among them was a guy called Harry Guest, who taught French, and he became very influential in my life at that point. He introduced me to a number of writers who have remained very important to me, like Flaubert and Baudelaire, Verlaine and Rimbaud, and he ran a film club that showed films like *The Seventh Seal* and *Los Olvidados*, which I remember being very impressed by. He also encouraged me to write. I'd been writing poetry and stuff for the school magazine, and he said, 'What else do you want to do?' and I said, 'I'd quite like to write a novel.' He gave me all the usual advice, like, 'Write what you know,' so I wrote fifty pages of this novel about a boy at a public school, showed it to him, and he said, 'This is terrific. Get on and finish it.' And when it was finished, I didn't have the slightest idea what to do with it. Harry said, 'Send it to some publishers,' so the mother of a friend laboriously typed up my handwritten draft, and we made copies and sent it to everyone we could think of. The only positive response was from Faber, who said, 'We don't want to publish this but keep us posted,' which was quite right, because it was enormously long and very gloomy. Towards the end of the eighties, my agent, the late Peggy Ramsay, had a terrible fire in her office, and when I called her to commiserate, she said, 'But the news isn't all bad.' I said, 'What do you mean?' and she said, 'Your novel went up!'

And after the novel you went back to plays, presumably at university.

No, before. First of all, Harry persuaded me to read French and German at university rather than English, because everyone was doing English. He said, 'You'll read those books sooner or later anyway, so what's the point of studying them now? Do French and German, and you'll have two more literatures available to you.' To which I said, 'Yes, but it'll be much more difficult.' And he said, 'Tough!' So I decided to do that.

Which has stood you in good stead.

In wonderful stead, yes. David Hare says I'm the only person he knows who's made use of his education. Anyway, I got a scholarship to New College, Oxford, and I was due to go the following October. Then, I was summoned by my housemaster, and we started this very agreeable conversation, and I realized in the middle of it that I was being expelled.

Why was that?

I'd always been quietly bolshy: refusing to kneel in chapel and that kind of thing. I said I didn't mind going and I didn't mind sitting there, but I didn't see why I had to kneel since I didn't believe in any of it. That didn't go down very well. I also spent a lot of time smoking cigarettes behind the bike sheds and going to the movies when I was supposed to be doing cross-country runs. I just didn't have the correct attitude, even for such a liberal school, and since I'd passed the exam for New College, they knew I really wanted to stay just to put on plays – which I'd done a lot of. So there I was: end of December, end of school and no clear idea of what I was going to do next. My father was very startled by this; he was in Zanzibar and thought I was safely off his hands. But, as it happened, at the beginning of the following year – 1964 – there was a violent revolution in Zanzibar and the island was incommunicado for a few weeks. So, since I hadn't quite finished my novel, I thought in a student kind of way, 'I'll finish it in Paris.'

It just seemed like a good place to finish a novel?

Yes. I'd been working in a factory, which was awful. My job involved stacking metal tubes, and I was always stacking them in the wrong order so they fell over. Eventually, I was fired for incompetence, but I'd saved £30, so I set off to France with a friend from school. We got the cross-Channel ferry to Boulogne and started hitch-hiking to Paris, but, a few weeks before, the French had passed a law against hitch-hiking, so there was a lot of sleeping in fields – which, in February, is not something I'd

3

recommend. Finally, after travelling thirty miles in two days, we found a small station and caught a train – which obliged us to change at Boulogne. So back we went, and then to Paris. I managed to exist there for a month on this £30, but my friend only stayed a week or two before going back to the safety of Surrey. We'd been paying eight francs a night to share a room in this hotel on the Left Bank, and the patron said I could stay for four francs but I'd have to share the bed if the hotel was full – which happened once or twice. My aim was not only to finish the novel but to earn enough money to get back home, which I did in various ways: I scrubbed the floor of the British Embassy church for the impending visit of Prince Philip, and I worked all night in Les Halles loading and unloading vegetables. By this time, my brother had got out of Zanzibar and was sharing a flat in Earl's Court with four or five Australians, so I went to live there and got a job tying up exam papers and sending them out to schools. And it was then that I wrote *When Did You Last See My Mother?* – quite a lot of it in the pub because it was quieter than the flat.

It's easier to see where your subsequent plays came from: Total Eclipse *is about two writers you admired, Rimbaud and Verlaine;* The Philanthropist *is an inversion of a play by a third, Molière; and so on. Where did you get the inspiration for this one?*

I knew I wanted to write something about Rimbaud and Verlaine, so in a sense this was a trial run. In those days, I did what I don't do any more: sit around thinking about what to write. Since then, I've tended to write either what I was commissioned to write or what announced itself as a good idea. In this case, the plot and the title just fell into my head, and in a casual way I thought, 'Well, the novel's been turned down, so I'll try writing a play.' I'd hardly ever been to the theatre. I'd certainly never seen a play at the Royal Court. I'd read plays by Pinter and Osborne – the new stuff, as it were – but I'd seen very little.

Were they your main influences in writing the play?

I think a careful reading of *When Did You Last See My Mother?* will show that this is someone who has read, marked, learned and inwardly digested *Look Back in Anger* – and, indeed, *Who's*

Afraid of Virginia Woolf?, which I think I'd just seen when I wrote the play. Those were the plays which were uppermost in my mind, particularly the Osborne. Osborne really gave many of us the idea that it was possible to have a serious career in the theatre without being part of some preposterous elite; that you could actually turn up and write a play about contemporary people in contemporary situations. Also, one of the main motivations for *When Did You Last See My Mother?* was to act in it.

Playing which part?

Ian, the leading role. I very much wanted to be an actor when I was at school, and that persisted into my university days. I kept auditioning for roles and never got anywhere, and then a lot of things happened in my second year. Firstly, I wrote a piece called *Mr Faustus*, an up-to-date version of the Faust story set in a university, for a one-act play competition, and that was the first thing of mine which was performed, in November 1965. Then, just as that went into rehearsal, my father fell ill, and, a week or two before it was put on, he died, so the whole experience was very strange – although I do remember standing at the back of wherever it was that they performed these things, hearing the audience laugh and thinking, 'My God, what a satisfying feeling!' Finally, at the end of term, OUDS, the Oxford University Dramatic Society, announced that they were going to put on two plays by undergraduates in a New Plays Season in the Spring Term of 1966, so that was an opportunity to do something with *When Did You Last See My Mother?*, which had been sitting in a drawer for a year.

I had a tutor called Merlin Thomas, who had replaced Harry Guest as the mentor figure in my life, and he was on the board of the Oxford Playhouse and had always been involved in university drama, and he told me that what I had to do was type up this play and hand it in. So I did, and went to the meeting at the start of the following term when the winning plays were announced and found that neither of them was *When Did You Last See My Mother?* Instead, the winners were a rather serious piece by an Algerian writer and a musical by a guy called Mike Saddler; but a couple of weeks into the term, the secretary of OUDS knocked on my door and said, 'Mike Saddler's play is too complicated and too expensive, and your play is very simple and very cheap. Can you put it together in three weeks?' So a chap called Charles O'Hagan was appointed to direct it, because he happened to be sleeping on my floor at the time; I was appointed to play the lead, because I was probably the only person who could learn the part that quickly; we held some auditions to get the rest of the cast; and three weeks later it opened at Josca's Little Theatre in Headington. Then, as the second play was about to open, the leading man got the measles, which meant that the New Plays Season of the Oxford University Dramatic Society consisted entirely of the third-place entry, *When Did You Last See My Mother?*, which wound up being reviewed in the *Guardian*.

That was a stroke of luck.

Actually, I think it was a stroke of Merlin Thomas, but it should be said that provincial plays were reviewed much more regularly in those days. The papers had stringers all around the country, and the *Guardian* theatre stringer for Oxford wrote a very good review of it, as did the *Oxford Mail*. And before I knew where I was, I was getting letters from agents saying, 'Do you need representation?' I didn't know what to do with these, so Merlin Thomas arranged for me to go and see the manager of the Oxford Playhouse, Elizabeth Sweeting, and she said, 'There's only one person you should contemplate having as an agent at the moment, and that's Margaret Ramsay. Send it to her.' So, again, I did. I also had a letter from Frank Pike at Faber, which said, 'We've been following your work in the small magazines with some interest. Perhaps you'd like to send us your play.' It turned out that there was another bloke called Christopher Hampton, who wrote poetry, and they thought that he was me – or I was he. He's still around, as a matter of fact.

He's rather radical, isn't he?

He's very radical. There was a book called *Writers Take Sides on the Falklands*, which contained – under my name and beneath my biography – an impassioned rant of several pages, basically saying, 'British soldiers deserve to be killed.' When I rang up to protest, the publishers said, 'We can't change it now. We'll put some erratum slips in,' but they never did. He also wrote a letter to the *Guardian* in praise of Edward Bond but attacking all other, less radical, writers – in particular Harold Pinter, who then rang me up. I lived in Oxfordshire at the time, and he said, 'I haven't seen you for a while,' and I said, 'No,' and he said, 'Well . . .' and I said, 'Yes?' and he said, 'Perhaps when you're next in London we might have a drink.' Then there was a long pause, and I said, 'Is this about the letter in the *Guardian*?' and he said, 'Yes, it is actually,' and I said, 'It's not me.' He said, 'What do you mean, it's not you?' and I said, 'There's another chap called Christopher Hampton,' and he said, 'You're pulling my leg. Are you *sure* it's not you?' and I said, 'If you look in the paper, you'll see it's a Cambridge address and I live near Oxford.' So he said, 'What are you going to do about it?' and I said, 'What *can* I do about it? He seems to be called Christopher Hampton,' and he said, 'I don't think this can be allowed to go on!' But it has gone on. Someone sent me something from the internet not long ago, an interview with him in which he explained that he wasn't me. I've always wondered whether, if I actually met him, he might turn out, like William Wilson in the Edgar Allan Poe story, to look exactly like me.

So what was Peggy Ramsay's reaction to When Did You Last See My Mother?

I sent her the play, then a couple of weeks later I'm sitting in my room at Oxford and there's a knock at the window. It's the porter in his formal suit and bowler hat. I open the window, and he says, 'Phone call for you.' I thought that someone else had died, but it was Peggy, who had bullied him into going to fetch me. She said, 'Your play, dear.' I said, 'Yes.' She said, 'You'd better come up tomorrow and talk to me about it.' So the next day I went to her office, this tiny room in a former brothel off St. Martin's Lane, and that was my first meeting with Peggy, who became one of the central figures in my life. She was really quite startling. At one point, she plunged her arm up to the elbow into this vast handbag and came out with a handful of £5 notes, which she then thrust at me. I said, 'It's fine. I've got a day return,' and that was apparently the right thing to do. I passed some test by not immediately trousering the fivers.

Anyway, during this extraordinary meeting, she rang up the Royal Court and spoke to William Gaskill and told him he had to do this play – and, within six weeks, he agreed. Then there was a strange period where I was still studying at Oxford but I was always going up to London. I didn't do any academic work for months on end, and Merlin Thomas was absolutely wonderful and covered for me, saying, 'This is more important.' And it was at the Royal Court that I met two more people who became central figures in my life: the actor Victor Henry and the director Robert Kidd. Bob was a stage manager who had never directed a production before, so he wasn't keen for me to attend rehearsals because he didn't want anyone looking over his shoulder. Indeed, right at the beginning, he took me aside and told me that I wasn't to speak to any of the actors, which I obeyed so conscientiously that many years later, when I met one of them, they said, 'We thought you were very stand-offish.'

Had you given up thoughts of acting by this time?

I hadn't, really. What stopped me from pursuing it was Victor's performance in *When Did You Last See My Mother?* At first I thought, 'He's an ugly little Yorkshireman and he's supposed to be playing a public schoolboy. It's going to be ridiculous,' but in fact he was marvellous. The reviews for the play were good – probably better than I've had for any other play – but the reviews for Victor himself were amazing: 'The best début since Albert Finney,' and 'The most exciting new actor since Nicol Williamson.' Every paper printed some variation on that. He really wanted to, and subsequently did – pretty definitively, I think – play Jimmy Porter in *Look Back in Anger*, and all that malign, crackling energy was there in this performance.

It was a Sunday night at the Royal Court, one of their 'plays without decor', something they don't do any more. You didn't have a set; you rehearsed for two or three weeks; the actors were paid two guineas; the writer was paid five guineas; and they had one performance on a Sunday night to a subscription audience. And after this performance, there were actually cries of 'Author!', which has never happened to me since. Frank Pike and Charles Moncrieff from Faber, who I was sitting next to, said, 'You'd better go up,' so I did, much to the horror of everyone at the Royal Court. I didn't know how these things worked, and I noticed that when it was repeated on a second Sunday night, I was placed at the back of the Circle to make sure there would be no more outrages of that kind. Then Michael Codron decided to move it to the West End – still without decor – and it opened at the Comedy Theatre in July 1966. Michael Codron's publicist deduced that, at twenty, I was the youngest writer ever to have a play in the West End, which I think I still am, and set up a whole round of interviews for me; but I was very naive and said things I shouldn't have said, so eventually she was sent to accompany me.

Were you aware of how amazing this was?

Absolutely not. I see now how amazing it was, but I didn't have a clue then. I thought it was great to have a play on at the Royal Court, but it didn't seem outlandish. At one point, as we went from one interview to another, I said to the publicist, 'Christ, this is boring, saying the same thing over and over again,' and she really tore a strip off me, and said, 'You have no idea how lucky you are!' And she was right. But it just seemed tedious on a summer's day to be trundling from one tabloid to another. None of them were really interested in the work; they were more interested in the 'dog walks down Piccadilly on hind legs' aspect of the thing. I read an article in some magazine which said, 'Can you imagine a more enviable position? An Oxford undergraduate with a play on in the West End,' but I found it very bewildering. It was the summer vacation, I'd done nothing in my second year at Oxford, and all my friends were gearing up to take their Finals. My German teacher, a man called John Cowan, who was married to a wealthy woman from Hamburg, said, 'Your German isn't very good. You should take a year off to improve it,' and he arranged a student placement for me at the municipal theatre in Hamburg, the Schauspielhaus. So, at the beginning of the following year, I set off for Hamburg, and it was just about the most miserable period of my life. I was confused, because early success is very confusing; I was lonely, because I'd split up with my girlfriend; and I was broke, because the play hadn't earned any money.

Hadn't you sold the film rights?

I sold them for £1,500, which was an enormous amount of money in those days; but on my twenty-first birthday, I took all my friends in Oxford out to dinner and bought a new suit and really went to town.

Did you write the screenplay?

Yes, I did. But I didn't have a clue how to write a screenplay, so I just tried my best to open it up a bit. Bryan Forbes was going to direct it, and he wasn't displeased with it. He recently, very kindly, returned it to me. These brown pieces of paper came through the post, together with a charming note from Bryan saying that he felt they weren't likely to make it now so would I like it back? He wanted to make two films with Victor Henry and the whole scheme fell through, which was a shame, but one of the people who bought the rights was Ronnie Shedlo, who has been a friend of mine ever since – and was subsequently one of the producers of *Carrington*.

Had you considered writing screenplays before that?

Oh, yes. As soon as the play was put on, I thought that whenever the chance came to work in film I would like to. But England wasn't a film culture at that time; theatre was what people were gravitating towards. If I'd been French, I could have gone straight into films – and I probably would have done, because I always responded more to the cinema than I did to the theatre.

Is that still the case?

It's more complicated than that. I think when a play works, which is very rare, there's nothing like it, because what makes a play work, both in the performance and in the writing, is energy. A great writer like Chekhov can transform a bunch of middle-aged Russians standing around moaning into something which tells you about the essence of life – and that's because a stupendous amount of energy has gone into the creation of those scenes. On the other hand, films are a much more reliable source of pleasure and stimulation, I would say, because you have more resources at your disposal. Just as in a novel you have passages of description or poetic meditation, in a film you can do all that with the camera, so the energy doesn't have to be quite so concentrated in the screenplay.

When you wrote the screenplay for When Did You Last See My Mother?, *did you read other screenplays first to see how it was done?*

I went out and bought *Five Screenplays by Harold Pinter* and the books they were based on. I admired the way he'd made a judgement about the books he'd adapted. The good ones, like *The Go-Between*, he'd stayed faithful to, and the less good ones, like *The Pumpkin Eater*, he'd reorganized and refined. So that was my education as far as writing screenplays was concerned.

Is that maxim – the better the book, the more faithful the adaptation – true of your own adapted screenplays?

I would say so, yes. The more usual maxim is, 'Don't adapt great books, only adapt second-rate books, they make much better movies,' but that seems unduly defeatist. It's simply that great books make greater demands, which a lot of people are too lazy to deal with. I don't see why a good book shouldn't make a good film, providing that you understand what's good about the book and translate it correctly into film terms. I think the main problem with those early screenplays was that I thought writing films was easier than writing plays. The theatre puts great constraints on a writer anyway, and you can constrain yourself even further – in other words, invent rules for yourself – and I thought you didn't have to do that with movies, whereas of course you have to do it even more to exert the required narrative grip on the audience. But in adapting *When Did You Last See My Mother?*, I just rambled on until I got to the end.

You said that you tried to 'open it up a bit'. Do you think that's the key to adapting stage plays for the screen?

I think adapting a play is a much more difficult prospect than adapting a novel. A play is such an artificial construct that it couldn't be more different from a film; the only thing they have in common is that they're dramatic forms involving actors. A film is much closer to a novel: it has those freedoms which you don't have on the stage and you're well advised to use. And, in the end, it winds up as a video or a DVD, a finished object which stands on your shelf just like a book, whereas a play happens every night and is different every time. I did open up the play as much as possible – Ian worked at this boring place tying up parcels of exam papers, and he went to the pub and he walked down the street, and so on – but I'd taken away the concentrated essence which the play exerted without replacing it with whatever it is we're talking about which I hadn't understood. It may relate to something David Lean once said to me, which is that a film consists of a series of chunks, and those chunks should be bound together with a rope, so that each scene leads into the next in a seamless and logical way; because, if you arbitrarily leap from one scene to another, or one sequence to another, the audience is not gripped or swept up or whatever it is you need to do to an audience.

Now, all this is very far away from what was in the air at the time I started writing. If you went to see a Godard film or a Brecht play, you were confronted with artists who said, 'Out the window with narrative and all that shit. I want you to think about things in a different way, and I'm going to tell you what the best way to think about them is, and we're going to look at them sideways and stand them on their head and subject every cliché to examination and replace it with a counter-cliché.' I felt that my formalist concerns, which derived from a love of nineteenth-century French literature, were all being held up to question, so I decided to keep my head down, do the work and hope it didn't get attacked on the grounds of its extreme unfashionability. At the end of the sixties, there was thought to be something slightly decadent about aesthetics, as if it wasn't acceding to the anarchic spirit of the age – although, funnily enough, in terms of politics, my sympathies are probably more anarchist than anything else.

The films you were watching at school were quite avant-garde, *though.*

Yes, but if you look at *The Seventh Seal* or *Los Olvidados* – or *Vertigo*, which was another film I was absolutely blown away by at school – they're naturalistic in narrative, just bizarre in execution. I'd been seeing two or three films a week with my parents from the age of about six onwards, and, combined with all the Victorian adventure literature which was ingrained in me, that meant I was always interested in narrative. I've always found it the hardest thing to do, though. Any fool can philosophize, but the invention of narrative is incredibly difficult. The abstract skill of picking this incident rather than that incident, this turn of events rather than that turn of events, is probably the hardest thing that any dramatic writer has to deal with.

Harder than creating characters and writing dialogue?

Well, one of the jobs of creating characters is to put them through the correct narrative developments to reveal their characters. Writing dialogue is the easiest thing. When I looked back at my novel, I realized that the bits which worked best were the bits with dialogue in. I seemed to have an ear for it, a way of phrasing lines which sat well in actors' mouths.

What are the strengths of the stage as opposed to the screen?

The thing that gives theatre its strength is that there are so many things you *can't* do, and whatever you *do* do – and there have been all sorts of fascinating experiments in the last twenty years about making theatre more visual and more visceral and more performance-orientated and so on – basically a play involves some actors and some dialogue. Pretty it up as much as you like, those are the means by which you have to exert an effect on the people who happen to be sitting there that evening – and if the play works, it will weld that group of disparate strangers into one wodge of feeling. There is no way, for example, of reconstructing the success of *When Did You Last See My Mother?*, which had to do with those particular actors at that particular time in dialogue with that particular audience. In other words, it is everything which is meant by the word 'dated'.

Is that why you didn't include it in your collection, Plays 1?

Yes. I just thought, 'This is all very well, but it wouldn't work now,' which I don't really feel about any of my other plays.

Total Eclipse, *for example, which you started writing when you were in Hamburg.*

It was then that the play really started to take shape in my mind. I didn't like Hamburg at all, and my job at the Schauspielhaus was awful. I had to read lots of stuff from their archive – mostly nineteenth-century plays you've never heard of by people you *have* heard of, like Tennyson and Byron and Swinburne – and write reports on all of them in case they wanted to première any of them. I was living in a ghastly hostel on nothing but boiled eggs, and working in a ghastly office where no one talked to you, and then I discovered that I wasn't being paid because it was a student placement. I remember going round to this colossal mansion belonging to John Cowan's wife's family, ringing the doorbell and saying, 'I don't know what to do, John. They're not paying me.' And he said, 'What do you *want* to do?' And I said, 'I really want to write another play. How about if I go to Paris?' And he said, 'OK.' And in the middle of the night – since I didn't have enough money to pay the hostel fees – I did a runner with this Belgian boy who drove a 2CV. Plan A was to go to the Italian Riviera, where he was planning to get a job as a gigolo, but when we got into the car he said, 'I've changed my mind. I'm not going to the Italian Riviera. I'm going back to my parents' house in Brussels.'

So we went to Brussels, and he also turned out to be extremely rich; it was the first private house I'd seen which had an elevator. His father was one of the chiefs of Peugeot, and this boy was obviously the black sheep of the family. They weren't tremendously pleased to see him – or, what with one thing and another, me. Firstly, I got drunk, because they gave me a generous amount of alcohol before dinner. Then, during dinner, I took a ladle full of pea soup from the butler and poured it into my plate from too great a height, so that, when I replaced the ladle and looked down, the plate was empty and there was a ring of pea soup all the way around it. Finally, I was told which my bedroom would be, so I rode the elevator to the second floor, took the first left and the second right, entered this rather feminine room and fell asleep in this vast bed, and was woken an hour later by his horrified mother, whose bedroom it was.

The next morning, I was thrown out. I was told to leave the house by ten, so I spent a day in his brother's apartment in Brussels, then I had just enough money to get the train to Paris. Luckily, a friend of mine from Oxford, Ian Huish, was teaching at the Lycée Rodin, so I lived on his floor for a while, and he got me a job translating lectures on James Joyce. And I spent the next six months in Paris, not perfecting my German, not doing any of the things I was supposed to be doing, but instead writing *Total Eclipse*. I earned enough money from translating these lectures to move into a hotel on the Left Bank, a slightly more expensive one than before, and I wrote most of the play there, then finished it in England just before I went back to Oxford.

You said that When Did You Last See My Mother? *was a trial run for* Total Eclipse. *Why were you so keen to write a play about Rimbaud and Verlaine?*

It's endlessly fascinating, just as the Oscar Wilde story is endlessly fascinating. This is the French equivalent, except that they were *both* writers of genius. When I read Rimbaud as an adolescent, I was absolutely knocked out by it. Until then, I shared the popular philistinism about modern art – 'If you can't understand it, what's the use of it?' – but I couldn't understand these poems by Rimbaud, and they were still fascinating. Then I discovered that he was my age when he wrote them, which made them even more fascinating. And, of course, his wildness and his antisocialness appealed to me a great deal at that age. The radicalism of what he was trying to do, and the purity of his eventual renunciation of it, seemed to me profoundly impressive. But by the time I wrote the play, I was exactly halfway between the ages of Rimbaud and Verlaine when they first met – twenty-one, whereas Rimbaud was sixteen and Verlaine was twenty-six – and what happened as I was working on it was that I became more and more sympathetic to Verlaine and less and less sympathetic to Rimbaud.

They both seem equally unsympathetic to me.

I'm talking about them as writers, not as people. As a person Verlaine was a terrible weakling, but as a writer he was a minor artist – and I've always been attracted to minor artists. Writers like Laclos or Horváth are, in many ways, more interesting than their larger contemporaries, Voltaire or Brecht. Verlaine had a small but unique talent. He was the writer who most understood and paralleled Impressionism, for example. And, more than any other French poet before or since, he understood the musicality of French. He had a tremendous ability to organize the language, which means that he's the writer most French schoolchildren are taught. At the same time, like most artists, he peaked at a certain point then gradually drifted downwards. He knew that he wasn't getting any better, but he carried on working until he died. I was very moved by that. Rimbaud expected his writing to achieve something more than it could, was disappointed when it didn't and chucked the whole thing in, whereas, at the end of his life, Verlaine was still writing one poem every day, taking it to the publisher and living on the proceeds. In other words, he was a professional, as opposed to the amateur genius of Rimbaud, and in the course of writing the play, I taught myself the virtues of professionalism, rather than waiting for the gush of inspiration. And I came out at the other end with a much more modest idea of what it meant to be a writer.

In fact, Verlaine's professionalism depends on his rejection of radicalism, so there's a compromise with conformity at the heart of Total Eclipse.

Looking back on it, it was my first treatment of a subject which I've dealt with over and over again: the clash between a radical and a liberal. In *Savages*, I come down on the side of the radical, Carlos. In *Tales from Hollywood*, I come down on the side of the liberal, Horváth. In *The Talking Cure*, I suppose Freud is the radical – although there's another character in it who's even more radical – and Jung is the liberal, and I come down on the side of Freud. So sometimes it's one and sometimes it's the other. It's an unresolved question in my mind. And it's because it's the kind of subject which only raises questions and never provides answers that it's so inexhaustible. It seems to me that it's the political and intellectual debate of our era.

In Total Eclipse, *then, you come down on the side of the liberal. But that doesn't stop Verlaine looking back with yearning at his radical flirtation.*

That's right. And the other thing which he does is to protect and perpetuate the radical literature in the face of a threat to it. The only invented scene in *Total Eclipse* is the final meeting between Verlaine and Rimbaud's sister, which actually took the form of a correspondence. All the scenes are dated, and that scene is dated 29 February in a year which wasn't a leap year, to tip the wink that it was made up. When dealing with historical events, I've always done the opposite of what you're recommended to do as a creative writer: stuck to the facts, because the facts are always more interesting than what you can invent. I flinch when people say, 'What the hell does it matter? Make it up,' because the point of using real events as the basis for a piece of writing is that those events are illuminating in some way, and if you start manipulating them you're betraying the language in which they're speaking to you. That's one reason why *The Talking Cure* took five years to write, because the facts are extremely inconveniently organized, and I had to be faithful to them while at the same time imposing some kind of shape on them.

Did you do a lot of research for Total Eclipse?

I relied a good deal on Enid Starkie's biography of Rimbaud. I met her towards the end of her life, and she was a very colourful figure. She always wore straw hats, and when, over lunch, I commented on her blue straw hat, she heaved up her skirt and showed me her matching bloomers. She also said to me, 'I hear you've written a play about Rimbaud,' and I said, 'Yes,' and she said, 'I hope you've pirated my book!' and I admitted that I had. In fact, there's also a book on Verlaine by François Porché, written in the thirties, and Rimbaud's teacher, Georges Izambard, wrote a memoir about him, and those wonderful Pléiade editions of Rimbaud and Verlaine have enormous amounts of biographical and textual detail; so, in the course of the three or four years I was thinking about the play, I read just about everything there was.

You said that you were talking about Rimbaud and Verlaine as writers, not as people, but in the play you do that by looking almost exclusively at their lives and barely discussing their work at all. How do you square that particular circle?

I don't know. Well spotted. I can't really explain it, except by saying that, at the time, I always found it irritating that plays or films about artists invariably showed them sitting around discussing their work, since it seemed to me, with my very limited experience, that whenever I was in the company of writers their work was the very last thing they wanted to talk about. All they wanted to talk about was their royalties. So I assumed, particularly in view of the nature of their relationship, that the last thing Rimbaud and Verlaine would be doing was sitting around discussing the ideal, or whatever. But as the years went by, I started to sneak in a bit of conversation about the work, because experience proved it to be something which is occasionally discussed – if reluctantly.

You've revised the play several times for the stage, as well as adapting it twice for the screen – once for television and once for the cinema. Why do you keep coming back to it?

I never thought I got it quite right. Also, because the play sits at the centre of the way I think about writing and is the source of a lot of my work, I'm always open to the idea of doing some more work on it. The Royal Court originally came within an inch of turning it down. I was still an undergraduate, I was coming up to my Finals, and one day Bill Gaskill and Robert Kidd turned up in my rooms and said, 'We want you to read it to us.' So I lay on the bed, the other two sat in chairs and I read them *Total Eclipse*. At the end there was a long silence, then Bill said, 'All right, we'll do it.' It ran for three weeks and got appalling reviews – which confused me, because I knew that it was an infinitely better play than *When Did You Last See My Mother?*, which got wonderful reviews. Once I'd got over the confusion, that was a good lesson: there's no reason why something should be understood the first time around. But the small number of people who did see it in those three weeks were very taken with it.

The version of the play included in Plays 1 *was the text of the 1981 revival, directed by David Hare. What prompted you to choose that one?*

In 1980, Peggy Ramsay had just begun a friendship with Simon Callow, and she said that he'd been talking to her about *Total Eclipse*: about how, as a student, he'd gone to see it three times in the course of its short run, and how he'd love to be in a revival of it, playing Verlaine. I said, 'I think he'd be wonderful in the part,' and then she said, 'Shall we get David Hare to direct it?' and I said, 'You'll never get David to direct it. He hates it.' The next day he called me, and I said, 'But you don't like the play,' and he said, 'It's always been one of my favourite plays.' Like Peggy, who told me not to write about Rimbaud and Verlaine on the grounds that I was too young and the subject was too diffi-cult, David had forgotten what he originally said, so I found myself embarking on this revival of the play at the Lyric, Ham-mersmith.

I seem to remember going to the early rehearsals, then I was out in America for a while – I was writing *Tales from Hollywood* at the time, so I was living and working in Los Angeles – then I came back, and it was due to open in about ten days. David, Simon and Hilton McRae, who was playing Rimbaud, said that the only scene which wasn't working was the last scene between Rimbaud and Verlaine, which ends with Rimbaud beating up Verlaine and leaving him. We all agreed that the actual last scene was a kind of epilogue and this scene was basically the end of the play, and David said, 'It doesn't work. It doesn't finish the play.' I said, 'No, it's never really worked,' and he said, 'Well, rewrite it then.' I said, 'You know I'm not very good at that,' and he said, 'Please just go and rewrite it.' I said, 'When do you need it?' and he said, 'Tomorrow.' So I rewrote the scene, took it back the next day and they rehearsed it – and it seemed much better. Encouraged by that, I did some more work on the play, and the version done at the Lyric – in an absolutely beautiful production by David – wound up being significantly different to the 1968 version.

How did the performances of Hilton McRae and Simon Callow compare to those of Victor Henry and John Grillo in the first production?

I think it's fair to say that the first production was angled towards Rimbaud. John Grillo was very touching as Verlaine, but he wasn't terribly experienced – in fact, he was as young if not younger than Victor – and Victor wasn't terribly nice to him, none of which helped him in the performance of the play. If Victor was feeling particularly irascible he would actually punch John in the scene where Rimbaud beats up Verlaine, and John was terrified of going on, so I kept having to talk to Victor, who wasn't very amenable to correction. There was one matinee where, because he was drunk, he did a long speech from *Look Back in Anger*, and when I went to his dressing room afterwards, quite annoyed, he said, 'Oh, you noticed!' All I can say is that he was radiant in the part. The revival, on the other hand, was more angled towards Verlaine, and was one of Simon's finest hours. Hilton was very powerful, but somehow the production moved towards the final scene of Simon sitting alone in the café, remembering nostalgically, sentimentally, and falsely – but also knowingly. It was a rather complex effect that Simon produced. Again, though, I don't think Simon was much older than Hilton at the time, so I've rarely seen the play performed with that ten-year age difference between Rimbaud and Verlaine.

What was the main difference between the first production and the revival?

I suppose it was the clear enunciation of Rimbaud's feeling that he wanted his poetry to do an un-doable job, and that when he realized it was un-doable he decided there was no point in even trying. But since his writing achieved far more than that of any of his contemporaries, the question is: what more did the bugger want? And the answer is: like all Romantics, he wanted every-thing – including the right to complain about it if he didn't get it.

In that scene in the film, Verlaine says to Rimbaud, 'You have a gift. It's no good throwing it away because your expectations were unrealistic. It's the expectations you should change.'

That's a line which was written that day for that scene. And that kind of clarification had come in the intervening years, once I'd realized what the play itself was getting at. Writing is a complicated process. If something is to work it can't reveal what it's about until you're halfway through it, and then it can lead you in unexpected directions. It's only later, when you've finished it – sometimes long after you've finished it – that you can see what it's actually about, what was going through your head at the time.

You've directed your own screenplays, but never your own plays. Why do you prefer to let someone else, like David Hare, direct them rather than doing it yourself?

Tom Wilkinson once said to me that there should be an Act of Parliament banning writers from directing their own plays, and by and large it's rare for writers to be the best interpreters of their own work. I think it makes better sense to direct your own screenplay, because by committing it to film you're making something permanent, whereas a play is endlessly provisional, because each new production is a different experience. I know that at play rehearsals I'm always wanting to say, 'No, *this* is how it should be done,' which is a fatal thing to do if you're a theatre director. Directing a play, you can't arrive with the play all mapped out in your head, or if you do you have to conceal the fact; you have to let the actors bring whatever they have to bring, then shape it all. Directing a film, you rehearse each scene, then you do it until you've got it right and then it's done, which is a process I feel much more comfortable with. A film is like a novel, it's a one-time-only thing, so there is an argument for the writer being clearer on what he or she wants than anyone else could possibly be.

Soon after its première at the Royal Court, there was a television version of the play. Did you need to open it out at all?

No. The last scene between them was shot in Burnham Beeches in the middle of the night, but most of it was done in the studio. It was directed by Peter Cregeen, with Ian Hogg and Joe Blatchley, and was very good, I think. The BBC in the early seventies was completely unlike it is now – run by constipated accountants with no sense of duty to anything higher than the balance sheet – and there was a convention of giving successful or interesting plays a television workout. They did versions of all my plays from that period except *Treats*, which was done by Yorkshire Television, and it brought the work to quite a wide audience.

When was it first mooted as a film?

There was film interest right from the start. Firstly, I sold the rights to the impresario Bill Kenwright, but for some reason I got panicky about the idea of doing the film and bought the rights back again. Then they were bought by a French producer called Jean-Pierre Ramsay, but it was a long time before the film was made. The first set of drafts were for Volker Schlöndorff, whom I'd met as a potential director of *Dangerous Liaisons*. Nothing had come of that, because he was intimidated by the Milos Forman version looming in the background, but I liked him very much. I remember a lot of sessions in this room [*the drawing room of the top-floor flat in Notting Hill which he used to call home and now uses as an office*]. Volker smokes vile little cigars and Jean-Pierre is a pipe man, so by the middle of the afternoon, large as the room is, you could hardly breathe. And we had a reading of it here, with John Malkovich, which everyone was very encouraged by. I thought the part of Verlaine was tailor-made for John, and that he would be able to produce exactly the right mix of charm and weakness and brutality and sentimentality.

The next breakthrough was casting River Phoenix as Rimbaud. I went to the Coronet in Notting Hill Gate to see *My Own Private Idaho*, walked in five minutes into the film, took one look at him and thought, 'That's the boy.' I never met him, but he looked uncannily like the famous photograph of Rimbaud, and he was preparing to play the part when he died. That obviously threw everyone for a loop. John felt that he couldn't really go forward without him and he withdrew, then Volker decided that he couldn't really go forward without John and he withdrew, so we were back to square one. We then had a series of conversations with various directors. Karel Reisz was quite interested in it and wrote me an enormously long letter about the things that he thought needed changing, but I didn't feel we were really on the same wavelength.

What did he think needed changing?

I'm not sure I can remember. Often what causes a problem is when they ask you to clarify things, character things, which are essentially part of that person's mystery and are therefore either unclarifiable or shouldn't be clarified. I don't know why Verlaine set fire to his wife's hair when she was pregnant. Why would anyone do that? All I know is that you have to confront that as part of his character and say, 'Even though he did do that he was not an irredeemable person; he was just a person prone to appalling lapses.' That pattern, of doing those sorts of things followed by all the snivelling and the abject apologies, is a central part of his character which you cannot fight. So when they say, 'Can you explain why he would have beaten up his wife?' the only answer you can give is, 'If he hadn't been the kind of person who beat up his wife and then apologized to her, he wouldn't have been the kind of person who shot Rimbaud and wound up in jail.' That was Verlaine. There isn't any way to solve that. And I suppose that's what I feel my job is: to pose these questions, knowing that you're not going to be able to answer them.

That's one of the great fallacies of Hollywood: that everything can be explained. All this appalling nonsense about 'character arcs' just reduces the mysteries of life to a series of innacurate formulae. Of course you can explain everything. Of course you can say that Verlaine was spoiled by his mother or Rimbaud wasn't given enough candy as a child. You can do all that stuff, but who needs it? I'm all in favour of things being lucid, but I'm certainly not in favour of things being explained to death. I'm not saying that what Karel was asking for was like that, but I do recall a lot of anxious questions which I felt didn't require answers. And, in fact, the next director it went to, Werner Herzog – who also wrote me an enormously long letter, in impeccable English – wanted to push it in a much wilder direction. He wanted to have more stuff in Africa, and he had a meeting with Jean-Pierre where he said, 'I want to take the actors and a skeleton crew and go to the Congo, and if you just leave us alone for a few months we'll come up with something.' Jean-Pierre began to get a bit nervous about that, and finally he said to me, 'We can't go forward with this. It's all too mad.'

It's interesting that the directors involved in the project – Schlöndorff, Reisz, Herzog and, of course, Agnieszka Holland, who eventually made it – were all European.

Well, it seemed like a quintessentially European subject. I'd love to remake it one day as a French-language film, and direct it myself.

Was the possibility of making it as a French-language film never discussed?

What Jean-Pierre and his partners wanted was an English-language film. That said, there was no particular reason for using American actors, except that John Malkovich seemed to be perfect casting, likewise River Phoenix, and we proceeded from there. When Agnieszka came in – whom I also liked very much and who had a very no-nonsense approach – she contacted Leonardo DiCaprio – another very good choice who looks slightly like Rimbaud – and he turned out to be wonderful. Watching him on the set, I was as impressed as I've ever been with an actor.

Did you base the screenplay on the revised version of the play?

Yes, but the screenplay is very different from the play, because I had the notion of organizing it in the same number of sections as Rimbaud's *Une Saison en Enfer* and giving each section the same title as that section in the poem. If you read the poem, you'll see that some sections are a paragraph long and other sections are pages long, and that helped me organize the African sequences, for example, as a series of short snapshots at the end. It was a very elaborate plan, and that was the version of the screenplay which I eventually published, but it didn't bear much resemblance to the finished product, because Agnieszka had simplified it in a fairly draconian way.

Whereas Herzog wanted more stuff in Africa, she seems to have wanted less.

I think that was a separate problem. As I understand it, they arrived in Djibouti and it instantly began to rain for the first time in several years, so they came back without the stuff they were hoping to come back with – although, during the editing, they did cut out a lot of material which they had actually shot there. The main problem with the film is that David Thewlis, who's also a wonderful actor, was pointed in the wrong direction. Going back to Verlaine, I think that while you have to confront the terrible corners of his personality, you can't use them as the benchmark for his character. If he'd been as cold and brutal as

David was encouraged to make him, it's very hard to see how anyone would have tolerated him. Clearly he was a man of immense charm who traded on his attractiveness to be hopeless, hated himself for it and, at the far end of hating himself, was pushed to acts of violence. But that range wasn't really there in the film because Agnieszka didn't really want him to be liked, I don't think, and therefore you couldn't quite understand why any of it took place at all. The curious thing is that Rimbaud, who really was like that – pretty cold and pretty brutal – nevertheless found something in Verlaine which he responded to and which brought out good things in him, but that side of their relationship doesn't come across.

It's easier to picture John Malkovich and River Phoenix together than David Thewlis and Leonardo DiCaprio. Apart from anything else they'd both have been American, whereas DiCaprio's American accent clashes oddly with Thewlis's English one.

That worried me; it never worried Agnieszka. It worried me because I think one of the reasons *Dangerous Liaisons* works is that we were careful to cast Americans across the board – except for the working-class characters, who were Scottish, which was amusing in itself. Here, it all seems pretty random: there's an American actor, and there's an English actor, and there's a French actress – a remarkable actress, I think, Romane Bohringer – and somehow the mixture doesn't coalesce. I didn't sense that at the start, even though I was included in script readings and round-table discussions with the cast. I wasn't around much during the shooting, but I was there for a week or so, and I could tell that everyone was working very well – in other words, the actors were delivering the goods. What I couldn't tell was that they were delivering the goods in different trucks.

I notice that you were one of the actors.

That was Leonardo's idea; I don't know how good it was. During the read-throughs, I generally read in the small parts, and Leonardo put it to Agnieszka that she should cast me in one of these parts. Funnily enough, I'd played the part of the judge in the television version, where it was just a voice-over, and been replaced by the producer, Mark Shivas, who was deemed to have a more judicial voice. So that was the part Agnieszka asked me to play, and it took a day, and it was absolutely terrifying. It was technically very complicated because of the shot she had devised, which required the extras who were playing the judicial commission to seize their books and candles and dive under the table as the camera passed down one side of it, and required me to bend at the knees in order to allow the camera to pass over my shoulder – in the middle of a rather complicated speech. There were eleven takes of that, the last of which was printed, because it was the one where the camera movement worked. But I can't say it was the best performance.

Another difference between the published screenplay and the finished film is that the flashback structure of the older Verlaine going about his daily business as a jobbing writer has simply become a framing device at the beginning and the end.

That tends to happen in the editing room when films aren't working: they pitch whole strands of the story. It happened in *The Quiet American*, where the device of the lead character being pursued by the policeman throughout the story, and the question of whether he will be captured and indicted, all went out the window, leaving a similar framing device at the beginning and the end. In *Total Eclipse*, they pitched a scene which was very important to me, a scene which actually happened. When Rimbaud had his leg amputated, his mother went to the hospital in Versailles, and as he woke up and reached out to her, she supposedly turned away. We actually shot the scene, and the French actress who played his mother had a powerfully expressive face, but unfortunately it got lost.

Were you present during the editing?

No, not really. I remember two or three sessions in Paris when the film was at various stages, and I know that the Americans involved, Fine Line, were very distressed by the film. Modifications were being made to it right up to its release. I think it was first shown at Toronto – or Telluride, which is about the same time – and it was even more brutal then than it is now. The sequences where Verlaine beats up his wife were prolonged, and the amputation of Rimbaud's leg was very bloodthirsty. People were walking out in droves, and this was a festival audience. The thing about Telluride, which is a lovely festival – and I had two films in it, because *Carrington* was showing as well – is that they show each film three or four times, and you turn up and answer questions at each venue. So I turned up to answer questions about *Carrington* and walked into the end of *Total Eclipse*. The credits were rolling and most people were making a hasty exit, but there was someone in the centre of the stalls applauding like crazy, and by the time the lights came up there was literally this one man sitting there – and it was John Schlesinger. I was very touched by that. He loved it.

You said that Agnieszka Holland had a no-nonsense approach. Do you think, in the end, it was too no-nonsense – to the point of being perfunctory?

She certainly didn't go for a lyrical feel, and I think the subject requires that to some extent, although it does look very beautiful: the sets and the cinematography and so on. I certainly don't dislike the film, and there are many things in it which work very well and are very powerful, but I don't think it works as a whole – which is a shame given the number of years that went into it.

{2}

The Philanthropist – Marya – Don Juan – Tartuffe – Uncle Vanya – Three Sisters – Hedda Gabler – A Doll's House – The Wild Duck – Ghosts – An Enemy of the People – 'Art' – The Unexpected Man – Conversations after a Burial – Life x 3

When you started rehearsals for Total Eclipse, *you also started a job as Resident Dramatist at the Royal Court. How did that come about?*

A few weeks before rehearsals began, Bill Gaskill said to me, 'What are you doing when you graduate?' I'd been given a drama fellowship at Bristol University, but I was too young to start it that year, and they said, 'Will you come the September after next?' So I had that to go to, but I didn't have anything in between, and Bill said, 'Well, we'd better find something for you.' And a few days later, he contacted me and said that a small grant had been secured from the Arts Council and I was going to become the Royal Court's 'Resident Dramatist'. I was the first one – anywhere, I think. Nowadays, Resident Dramatists get a grant to stay at home and write their own stuff, but my job was to do anything they could think of to throw at me, so I had to read all the plays which were submitted and voice an opinion, and go and see plays all over the country and talk to the writers, and so on. Meanwhile, *I* could also write a play.

Did you find it helpful as a writer, talking to other writers?

Yes, but it was also slightly depressing, because, having sailed in as I did, I became aware of how brutal the statistics were, and how difficult it was, if you found a writer you really liked, to say to them, 'We're not going to do this play, but please send us your next one.' I'd think to myself, 'If someone said that to me, I don't know if I'd *write* another one.' But we did manage to find people. We found Stephen Poliakoff. We found Max Stafford-Clark, who was directing a play at the Traverse, and David Hare and I persuaded the Royal Court to invite his production to the Theatre Upstairs. I even remember having a meeting with Ken Campbell, who had sent a play in – quite a conventional play, actually – and talking to him and trying to encourage him.

When did David Hare become your assistant?

After about a year. I said to Bill, 'If I'm reading twenty plays a week and meeting all these people, when do I get time to write this play? I need an assistant.' And he said, 'Well, if you can find someone . . .' David subsequently told me that they hired him for £7.50 a week. I know I took a cut in salary. I think I was getting £22.50 and I went down to £20 in order to contribute towards it. Anyway, I knew David from school and university, so he became my assistant and then my successor, and Howard Brenton became his assistant and successor.

The play you were trying to write was The Philanthropist, *which you describe in the introduction to* Plays 1 *as a study of 'compulsive amiability'. Would you also describe it as a self-portrait?*

It's more of a self-criticism – although it wasn't actually meant to be autobiographical, I just smuggled in the autobiographical stuff along the way, by using things in my own life which were relevant to the characters' lives. The idea for the play came to me from studying Molière, who was one of my special subjects at Oxford, and particularly from working on *Le Misanthrope*. It seemed to me that at that particular time – the second half of the sixties – you got on better by being blunt than you did by being placatory, therefore the way to annoy people was not by telling them the truth but by being nice to them. It just seemed like a funny idea, and when I tried it out on a couple of people they thought it was a funny idea as well, so I started working through *Le Misanthrope*, seeing what might be different and what might stay the same. The first problem was finding a milieu where a lot of intelligent people would be sitting around doing nothing, until I realized that I was already in one: could there be a more accurate description of university life than that?

Towards the start of the play we learn that, in Parliament, a mad gunman has wiped out most of the government front bench, yet the only person appalled by the news is the title character, Philip. Was Oxford really that insular?

I was exaggerating to make a point, but compared to what was going on in France, where university and society had real links, Oxford did seem very ivory-tower-ish. The notion of making Philip a philologist, for example, came from one of the papers I had to take, where you studied four texts of a hundred lines each, from *Le Roman de la Rose* through to *Le Misanthrope* – which was the most modern text – and had to know the derivation and morphology of every word. It was my particular *bête noire*, which is why one of the other characters describes philology as a subject which combines the uselessness of the arts with the boringness of the sciences.

The Philanthropist *is subtitled 'A Bourgeois Comedy', but all the characters are pretty cruel to one another – that remark being a good example.*

If you look at the plays of the day – taking a ten-year span from *Look Back in Anger* to *Who's Afraid of Virginia Woolf?* – a lot of their energy came from characters saying the unsayable. Like most of my contemporaries, I thought that the sheer drabness and conformity of life in this country in the late fifties and early sixties just had to be got rid of, so we were pretty tough with one another. On the other hand, I think my characters were much less cruel than those of many other writers, because, while I agreed that things should change, I didn't agree that you needed to kick an audience's teeth out in order to achieve that change – which was seen as a floppy, liberal way of thinking.

In fact, the character of the novelist, Braham, claims to have moved artistically from one extreme to the other – from 'earth-shaking stuff' to 'frivolous entertainments'.

This shows the difficulty of talking in terms of autobiography, because there are things I identify with in his character as well. The task of writing drama, I think, is to smuggle your way into all the characters, the women as well as the men, the bastards as well as the saints. You have to cultivate all those aspects of the human personality in order to convey the feeling of being this or that kind of person, and the effect that being this or that kind of person has on other people. One of the joys of working on something like *Three Sisters* is that Chekhov has fully realized every single character, even the off-stage characters, so you can see that all of them have both admirable sides and unadmirable sides: some are sympathetic but unbearable, while others are dangerous but weak. That's what I'm interested in, not in telling people what to do.

Like Braham, you're very fond of paradox. A line from the play which is often quoted in interviews is, 'My trouble is, I'm a man of no convictions. At least, I think I am.'

That just seemed like a good joke, but I've always enjoyed that kind of pithy remark which sums up some wry truth. This is very vague, but truth is the thing which is most telling in the theatre – truth in acting, truth in writing – and these aphorisms, containing a grain of truth elegantly expressed, can provoke a reaction in an audience in a way nothing else quite does. It's not that you strain to find them, but sometimes they occur to you and are exactly what you need.

The play starts with a wannabe playwright committing suicide following an argument with Philip . . .

I always think of it as an idiotic accident; but it was that idea, a guy blowing his head off in the first scene, which unlocked the play for me. When I started writing it, the guy just read his play, had a row and then left, and I got somewhere towards the end of the second scene and thought, 'This isn't very interesting.' The same thing happened with another play of mine, called *Death of an Optimist*, where I got a little way into it and then thought, 'There's something else I need,' except in that instance I didn't find whatever it was and the play remained unrealized – the only unfinished play I've got. The subject matter still interests me, though. It's about a man whose father has just died, and although the father was much loved by everyone and is much mourned by everyone, the son has an instinct that there was something unacceptable about him, the notion being that very happy people are somehow lethal. I started it twenty years ago, and I'm not without hope that one day I'll think, 'That's it!' and be able to finish it in six weeks.

Patrick Garland revived the play in Chichester in 1985, and then in London in 1991, with Edward Fox playing the part of Philip. Did you feel that it had dated at all?

I never felt that it had dated, and I never felt that audiences did. I would say that it's my most reliable play, in the sense that it seems to go down well whenever and wherever it's done. It's of its time, but that's different from being dated. It's also one of those plays – or one of those parts – which you don't have to cast precisely. The first actor we offered it to was David Warner, who was still quite young, because I'd envisaged that the dons were in their thirties and the students were in their twenties. But when David turned it down we came up with Alec McCowen, who was about fifteen years older, and it was a very lucky piece of casting, because Alec is a superb comedian; therefore, without neglecting the pathos of the part, he mined its potential for physical comedy – and, I think, contributed a lot to the initial success of the play, including its transfer from the Royal Court to the Mayfair Theatre. Then Alec went to Broadway and was replaced by George Cole, who played the part for two years and was much more craggily realistic; that is to say, he made the character stoical but not hopeful, and gave a very truthful performance, even over such a long period of time.

The third actor who played the part, making his début in the West End, was Nigel Hawthorne, who was extraordinary. In his autobiography he talked about how the play was a turning point for him, because he felt so close to the character and understood the part completely. He was in a strange, depressed mood at the time, and, when we first offered it to him, he turned it down. He then ran into my wife, Laura, and she said, 'I'm sorry that you turned down *The Philanthropist*.' He said, 'Oh, I imagine I was at the bottom of a long list,' and she said, 'No, you were the first choice to take over,' at which point he perked up and said, 'Oh, really?' and later in the day rang up to say that he'd do it. He combined the qualities of Alec and George: he was very truthful but also very funny – and quite heartbreaking, because he was so invested in it.

Meanwhile, I'd seen the play performed in Hamburg, in a wonderful production by a young director called Dieter Dorn, and that revealed another facet of the play, which is that if you cast someone very attractive – in this case Helmut Griem, a blond, good-looking German actor – then lots of things in the play became understandable that weren't particularly understandable before, such as why a beautiful girl like Celia is attracted to such a duffer. And that was the way it worked with Edward Fox. He's very attractive in a low-key English way, and has both an introverted thoughtfulness and an extrovert panache, which is an interesting combination. So all these actors brought different qualities to the role.

The Philanthropist, like *Total Eclipse* and *When Did You Last See My Mother?, was first directed by Robert Kidd. Presumably you had a particular empathy with him?*

Very much so. We were very close friends. Those relationships existed a lot at the Royal Court: Bill Gaskill did the plays of Edward Bond, Lindsay Anderson did the plays of David Storey, and Anthony Page did the plays of John Osborne. After Bob died, I decided not to get married to a director again – I wanted to be freer to play the field, as it were – but for the ten years it lasted, it was great. In fact, *The Philanthropist* was such a success that I've always felt I left the Court under a bit of a cloud, because they didn't really approve of big successes. But at least they did it. They subsequently developed a tradition of not doing the Resident Dramatist's play. I don't think they did David's play *The Great Exhibition*, although I might be wrong, and Howard wrote a wonderful play called *Magnificence* which they kept making him bugger around with – not necessarily to its advantage.

Also in common with Total Eclipse, The Philanthropist *was dramatized by the BBC. How close was it to the original?*

Stuart Burge, a friend of mine from the Royal Court, directed it, and it was done exactly as written for the stage, entirely in one room, except for still montages of Oxford life between the scenes. It was actually a 'Play of the Month', and I remember being invited to lunch by Cedric Messina, the rather avuncular gentleman who ran that particular fiefdom at the BBC. During lunch we were joined by Huw Wheldon, and in a teasing way Cedric Messina said, 'I gather you don't approve of Christopher's play being produced under our aegis?' at which point Huw Wheldon's eyes narrowed and he said, 'You know my views on this, Cedric. Play of the Month is for classics. This boy is hardly out of school.'

Between writing The Philanthropist, *first staged in 1970, and* Savages, *first staged in 1973, you translated four plays – Molière's* Don Juan, *Chekhov's* Uncle Vanya *and Ibsen's* Hedda Gabler *and* A Doll's House *– but, to put all that work in context, I'd like to talk about a play you worked on for the Royal Court between the productions of* When Did You Last See My Mother? *and* Total Eclipse: *Isaac Babel's* Marya.

Marya was my first toe in the water of something which then became a central strand in my work, my first inkling that my own work could be refreshed or broadened by someone else's. Babel is another fascinating minor artist, a Jew from Odessa who joined the Red Army, and the writer who tells you what it was like being in the middle of the Russian Revolution. The play is post-Chekhov, but it employs the Chekhovian strategy of throwing together a disparate group of characters and observing them with such realism that a kind of poetry arises from their incompatibility. It's about a family, the most interesting member of which – Marya – is away at the front fighting for the Reds, and the characters whom we examine are her father and her sisters. You get a kaleidoscopic picture of a society in chaos, with anti-Semitism and black marketeers and opportunism threatening to engulf idealism, and at the end, when the old father's palatial apartment is requisitioned for a young couple and their new baby, you have the tremendous hope that the revolution awoke juxtaposed with the women who are cleaning the flat saying, 'The thing about revolutions is that they always make the floor filthy.' It was supposed to be the first play in a trilogy, which gives it a slightly lop-sided feel because you can see that certain storylines were set up in order to be developed later. Babel may actually have written the trilogy, but a lot of his work was destroyed. His writing got him into trouble during the thirties, and he was so baffled by all the edicts that he stopped altogether; but even this was seen by the authorities as a kind of dumb insolence, and instead he got into trouble for not writing. Eventually, they took him out and shot him.

You didn't translate the play so much as revise an existing translation. What was wrong with the original text?

Robert Kidd went into rehearsals and realized that the text didn't sound like it should, because the two translators hired by Penguin, Michael Glenny and Harold Shukman, had translated alternate scenes, so there was no cohesion. It was the middle of term for me, and Bob said, 'Michael Glenny lives in Oxford. You'd better call him and explain what's happening.' Michael was an Oxford don, really, so I called him and said that I'd been approached by the Royal Court to do this work and I'd need his co-operation because I didn't speak Russian. Then I said, 'The good thing about this is that I actually live in Oxford,' whereupon he asked me what I did – and I was obliged to tell him that I was an undergraduate.

I remember lots of sessions with him and at the theatre. It had a marvellous cast, including Fenella Fielding and Arthur Lowe, but the rehearsals were chaotic. Bob was in terrible trouble with the Royal Court, who were of the opinion that he'd fucked it up; then it got great reviews, and he was fired. Which was typical. If your reviews were too good, you got fired. Roger Michell then revived it at the Old Vic in the late eighties, a marvellous production, designed by William Dudley, which got even better reviews. But something had happened between the late sixties and the late eighties – or even between the late seventies and the late eighties – which meant that the audience for those sorts of plays had disappeared. People were fighting for tickets at the Royal Court, but when it was done at the Old Vic no one went – just like no one went to Howard Davies's fantastic production of *Flight* by Bulgakov at the National a couple of years ago. I remember going to see Bulgakov's *The White Guard* at the Aldwych – the production by Barry Kyle, I think – squeezing into a terrible seat at the back of the stalls, and seeing actors I'd never seen before – Juliet Stevenson and Richard Griffiths – in this brilliant play with a real sense of occasion; but if you did it now, I don't know who'd go and see it.

Why do you think that is?

I just think people's horizons have narrowed. If they're going to the theatre, it has to be a play by someone they know, which they've probably already seen, with actors from television or the movies. Going to see a play you've never heard of, by an author you've only just heard of, with unknown actors, is too big a deal for people these days. So all that work which was not absolutely in the mainstream, work by minor masters like Babel or Bulgakov or Horváth, has become an endangered species.

You said that the idea for The Philanthropist *came from studying Molière. What is it about his work which particularly attracts you?*

The remarkable thing about Molière is that there's very little shading in his plays, but all kinds of things are prefigured in them – right down to sitcoms on TV. He worked out that you could spend an interesting evening at the theatre with a group of people who simply represent attitudes. All of his plays are about people who limit themselves with a series of false strategies and get their comeuppance because of it. It's a way of looking at the world which is very effective dramatically and very satisfying for the audience, because they always control more of the facts than any of the characters on stage. *Tartuffe*, for example, is an absolutely infallible play. You can't go wrong with it.

Molière's work wasn't absolutely in the mainstream, either.

Molière is not a writer of whom the English are very fond. When Bill Alexander later asked me to translate *Tartuffe*, I was shocked to discover that the RSC had never done a play by Molière. I think the English are a bit more comfortable with his work now than they used to be, but I can't say that the RSC have done many more of his plays – if any. The original motivation for doing *Don Juan* was that Anthony Page had asked me to translate *Uncle Vanya* for the Royal Court, and I said to Bill Gaskill, 'Why do people keep asking me to translate plays written in a language I don't speak?' So Bill said, 'Are there any French plays that you like?' and I said, '*Don Juan*,' which had been one of my set texts at university and, as far as I knew, hadn't been done in this country. It then became one of those things which I had on the side and worked on over a period of two or three years – I found it quite difficult, in a funny kind of way – and when I finally handed it in, Bill said, 'I don't think much of this,' and decided not to do it. It wound up being done on the radio, in a rather good production with Kenneth Haigh, and then at the Bristol Old Vic, in a production I never saw with Tom Baker, and eventually in Chicago, in a very successful production with Lou Gossett Jr. The director of that production, Garland Wright, later became Artistic Director of the Guthrie Theater in Minneapolis and commissioned me to do a translation of another play by Molière, *George Dandin*, but he died of AIDS and it was never done. In fact, it's hardly ever been done. It was inspired by Molière's personal circumstances and is about a man married to a young wife who doesn't like him at all, so it's extraordinarily bitter and rather unfunny – but also quite fascinating.

Why did you find it difficult to translate Don Juan, *since you were so familiar with the text and such a big fan of Molière?*

And since it was in prose, not verse. Most Molière plays of that period are in verse, but *Don Juan* he knocked off quickly to fill the gap when *Tartuffe* was banned – and then *Don Juan* was banned as well, because he couldn't resist infiltrating into it a lot of the stuff about hypocrisy which was in *Tartuffe*. I think the answer is that it was difficult to find the right tone for it, because, although the language is very simple, the thinking is rather literary. Don Juan has all these philosophical conversations with his servant, Sganarelle, and likewise justifies himself rather legalistically to all the people who turn up and reproach him for his behaviour.

Ironically, the character of Don Juan is rather likeable, while Sganarelle, who tries to take the moral high ground, is . . .

. . . rather less likeable. Well, that's a reflection of the way things are. The thing about the play is that Don Juan never actually gets his end away in the course of it; and when he's finally dragged off to hell, all that Sganarelle can say, the character you're invited to identify with, is, 'Who's going to pay my wages?' So the play juxtaposes aristocratic bad behaviour with working-class bad behaviour in quite a provocative way. I don't admire the play as much now as I did then, but it still seems to me a very interesting play which at the time hadn't been properly done.

Why do you think the English have this problem with Molière?

When I was doing *Tartuffe*, Antony Sher was worried about the two-dimensionality of the character, and I said to him, 'You have to embrace that. It's like a glass of water: you just drink it.' When I was working on a project called *The Florentines* with Franco Zeffirelli, one of the thousands of people I met through him was a young actor who was about to play Hamlet at the Comédie Française, and he told me how confusing he found the part. I said, 'Why?' and he said, 'Well, when Hamlet says, "Oh, what a rogue and peasant slave am I," I don't know whether he's a rogue or a peasant or a slave. It's very hard to act.' That's a very French response to an English play, and the English actors had the opposite response to *Tartuffe*. I really enjoyed working on the translation, because I was able to follow my own theory and do it in blank verse, which I still maintain is the least distracting way of letting the play come through, but the rehearsal period was rather uncomfortable. The actors kept saying, 'What's the underlying character?' and Bill Alexander kept saying, 'It's not very funny and there's no development in it,' and I kept saying, 'This is the most successful play in French theatre history, and Molière is one of the most gifted playwrights who ever picked up a pen, so don't worry about it.' The same thing happened, to a lesser extent, with *The Philanthropist*. The more you rehearse a comedy, the less possible it seems that it will ever make anyone laugh. Then, of course, at the first preview, the audience was in stitches. You just have to play the lines and trust the play.

When you translated Don Juan *and* Tartuffe, *did you adapt the plays in any way?*

Not at all. I've never adapted any of the plays I've translated. I've always attempted to be as accurate as possible.

If Marya was your first toe in the water of translation, then Uncle Vanya threw you in at the deep end. How did you set about it, given that you didn't speak Russian?

Anthony Page knew a Russian woman called Nina Froud, who was the editor of the *Penguin Russian Cookbook*, and she provided me with a literal translation, which we went through act by act. I would do the first act, then Nina would cook an enormous, wonderful dinner, and we would sit down and work through it. And eventually we had a translation which didn't seem like a traditional Chekhov translation, because what I'd gathered from working with Nina was that he was actually a much plainer writer than we're used to. We're used to thinking of him as rather lyrical and flowery, but in fact the language is very simple and concrete. For example, the first line of *Uncle Vanya*, which is always translated as, 'Would you like a cup of tea, dear?' or, 'Why don't you sit down and have a cup of tea, dear?' is just two words in the Russian: 'Tea, dear?' One of the things which struck me during rehearsals was how respectful the actors were of the text; nothing was changed. The cast was led by Paul Scofield – whom I'd seen in *King Lear* when I was sixteen and was the cause of my wanting to work in the theatre – and I remember that there was a particular line which he said in a very peculiar way; and, when I eventually plucked up the courage to ask why he said it that way, it turned out that there was a comma missing from the text.

It was a fantastic production. It only ran for four weeks at the Royal Court, and I saw nearly every performance. It made me feel that there was real value in working on those plays, that if you worked so closely on such a masterpiece you would learn in some organic way what made it work. Of course, you can say that they're very artfully constructed, but I think it's something much less obvious than that which makes them work, some technical arrangement of the words. I saw it again in *Three Sisters*: the extraordinary way in which Chekhov observes that people don't actually talk *to* each other. His genius was realizing that people say what they feel they have to say, what's on their minds, which doesn't necessarily correspond to what other people are saying. They're travelling down these tracks they've built for themselves, with no possibility of getting off them, and it's very depressing but at the same time very exhilarating, because it's so clear-eyed and unsentimental.

Is his gift for observation why, with Three Sisters, *you later returned to Chekhov?*

Absolutely – although I also relished the prospect of sitting for a couple of months with that particular play. My favourite of Chekhov's four major plays is *The Seagull*, and I'd like to do that at some point – more so than *The Cherry Orchard*, which I don't feel so personally drawn to – but I've always thought that *Three Sisters* was the most perfectly constructed, and it's the one I knew least. I'd read it, but I'd only ever seen it once, with the Cusack sisters at the Royal Court, so it was quite fresh to me. Then Vera Liber provided a very straightforward, accurate translation, so it was a great pleasure to do.

Again, you wanted to bring out the simplicity of the language?

Yes, and I also wanted to bring out the humour, because I was very mindful of all the plaintive missives from Chekhov to Stanislavsky saying, 'Don't forget it's a comedy.' Sad but not serious, he said, which is a great note, I think. It's a particular danger with *Three Sisters*, because the play starts with two of them discussing the death of their father, so it often gets off on a rather lugubrious note. In fact, they're discussing the death of their father in a very tranquil way: two people who have got over that trauma and are looking forward to the future. The whole tone of the first act is extremely light and optimistic, and if you don't achieve that then the rest of the play is like a carriage stuck in the mud. Michael Blakemore dropped in one weekend and made me read the whole play to him – which he apparently always likes to do – and at the end he said he liked its speed and lightness of tone, so that's what we went for. There wasn't a line cut, but it ran a good twenty minutes shorter than it usually does.

It was put on in record time, too. I took the commission from Natural Nylon – Ewan McGregor, Jude Law, Jonny Lee Miller and Sadie Frost – and they were very pleased with it and fully intended to do it; but, as you can imagine, none of them are right for any of the three sisters, and, in any case, they subsequently wound up their theatrical enterprise. Then Howard Panter of ATG came in on it and realized we had to get on with it, because the National announced that they were doing *Three Sisters* in the summer, so we asked Michael Blakemore to direct it and he rehearsed it in four weeks. I only went to two rehearsals, because I was busy editing *Imagining Argentina*, so I had very little to do with it. I saw two or three of the previews and discussed them with Michael, but it was really just a great bonus. *Uncle Vanya*, though, was my first experience of what theatre might be like at its best: when a production really worked and really connected with its audience, when it didn't have any weak spots and was just an effortless series of effective moments.

Is that why you continued to do translations – Hedda Gabler, *for example?*

Yes, but they were also part of my job as Resident Dramatist. *Hedda Gabler* wasn't for the Royal Court, though. Peter Gill, who'd directed a revelatory series of D. H. Lawrence plays at the Royal Court, was asked to do *Hedda Gabler* with Irene Worth at Stratford, Ontario, and invited Heathcote Williams to do a translation. But, as time wore on, no pages were forthcoming, and Heathcote eventually said that, on mature reflection, he'd decided that *Hedda Gabler* was a totally boring play and proposed something else – liable to be unacceptable to the authorities at Stratford, Ontario. So Peter said, 'I've got five weeks before the first day of rehearsals. Will you do it?' And I said, 'Yes.' I was then put in touch with a Norwegian woman called Hélène Grégoire, and we went through the same process as I had with Nina. It was slightly complicated in this instance by the fact that I was living in a bedsit in Ladbroke Square and Irene Worth was living in a basement flat ten doors down, so she took a very lively interest in what I was doing. She phoned me a lot, which was difficult because the phone was out on the landing. One day she phoned at about eight o'clock in the morning, and I came down in my pyjamas, freezing cold, and she said to me, 'Have you read *The Quintessence of Ibsenism* by Bernard Shaw?' I said, 'No, Irene. I don't think I have.' She said, 'I'm going to read you what he says about Hedda Gabler. It's very relevant.' She then launched into this reading, so I did a quick calculation in my head, put the phone down, ran upstairs and got dressed – and when I got back she was still going.

She was a wonderful woman, Irene, but in her opinion, in creating possibly the most famous female character in literature apart from Madame Bovary, Ibsen hadn't quite hit the bullseye, and she was anxious to help him out. She had a bit of a tantrum at one point in Stratford, Ontario, but she eventually understood that I wasn't going to mess with Ibsen. And she was wonderful in the role. She received a rave review in *Time*, I think, which meant that a brilliant idea of Peter's was taken up: to do *Hedda Gabler* and *A Doll's House* with the same company, but to have the actress playing Hedda play Mrs Linde in *A Doll's House*, and the actress playing Nora in *A Doll's House* play Mrs Elsted in *Hedda Gabler*. Unfortunately, Peter had now fallen out with Irene, so he wasn't invited to be the director, but the idea was that Irene and Claire Bloom, who was an old friend of Irene's, would alternate the roles, and I was asked to do *A Doll's House* on the back of the success of *Hedda Gabler*. Then, in the way of these things, Irene fell out with the producer of *A Doll's House*, who happened to be Claire's then-husband, Hillard Elkins, and Claire wound up doing both plays in repertoire on Broadway. And that's how all the work I've done on Ibsen started.

Hedda Gabler, A Doll's House *and then* The Wild Duck *came quite close together – although you later tackled* Ghosts *and An* Enemy of the People *as well. You've also translated three plays by Ödön von Horváth and four by Yasmina Reza. Does that reflect your own work of the time, or do you simply have bursts of enthusiasm?*

I don't really know what sets off these enthusiasms, but you're right, they probably do go in bursts. It's also to do with one thing leading to another: you do one play, then someone likes it and wants to do a different play by the same author. With Horváth, I thought, 'I've done the ones I like best,' but with Ibsen, there are so many great plays. Ibsen played an inadvertent part in my theatrical education, in that *An Enemy of the People* was the first play I ever saw. Then, at school, I did some sort of dissertation on tragedy, and *Hedda Gabler* was one of the set texts. And at Oxford, I saw a production of *Ghosts*, never having read it, and was absolutely dazzled by the way the narrative got a grip on you. People think of Ibsen as being old-fashioned and lumbering, and that no one can have a toothache at the start of Act One without having a full set of falsies by the end of Act Five, but I still think of him as being remarkably modern.

Modern in what sense – his themes or his techniques?

Not in his techniques, although a number of them have become commonplace – in the movies, apart from anything else. His plays are always fabulously constructed, so I've learned a lot from him in that respect over the years, but he was basically a modernist who co-opted traditional narrative techniques, like a film director who uses the horror genre or the science-fiction genre to say something interesting. There's a fascinating progression in Ibsen's work, because he began as a verse writer, with epic plays like *Peer Gynt*, then suddenly discovered the notion of bourgeois realism, probably from working as a dramaturg at a provincial theatre in Christiania. He was responsible for putting on a lot of awful French melodramas by popular nineteenth-century dramatists such as Scribe and Sardou, but he took their melodramatic techniques, like the hint which becomes a full-blown revelation, and applied them to really important themes – which, of course, was the last thing those French dramatists wanted to do; they just wanted to make a few bucks and get a big audience. His early prose plays, like *Pillars of Society*, are stodgily realistic; but with *A Doll's House*, he started using those structures to broader ends; and by the time you get to the late plays, like *The Master Builder*, his work had become more poetic again. He never wrote in verse again, but he drifted back towards poetry, and I think at a certain point, with *Hedda Gabler* and *The Wild Duck*, he reached a peak of perfection. *The Wild Duck* seems to me the perfect balance of poetry and realism. It's not performed much, because it's very demanding and has quite a big cast, with an important part for a fifteen-year-old girl. A girl called Eva Griffith played that part at the National, alongside a tip-top cast that included Ralph Richardson, Michael Bryant and Stephen Moore, and she was really good. I don't know what became of her.

The construction of his work may be straightforward, but his characters are anything but. They often behave in contrary and contradictory ways, sometimes in the course of a single scene. He's not afraid of leaving things unexplained.

But that's combined with not being afraid of exposition, of dotting the i's and crossing the t's when he feels it's necessary. So there's an interesting tension between the stuff he almost explains too much and the stuff he chooses not to explain, a tension which was obviously very carefully calculated.

You said that Ibsen started using melodramatic techniques to broader ends in A Doll's House. *What did you mean by that?*

A Doll's House is one of those plays which is periodically redis-covered because no one quite remembers how startling it is, how it grows from a conventional melodrama into a play where you can feel the new ground being broken. That extraordinary final scene, where Nora tells her husband that she's leaving him, sounded a new note in dramatic literature. I went to see the show in New York, and it was the first time that I'd been involved in a production which captured the *zeitgeist* so precisely. It hit the cusp of women's lib, and in the final act, when Nora's husband says, 'You can't ask me to sacrifice my honour. I'd do anything for you. I'd die for you. But no man would sacrifice his honour,' and she replies, 'Millions of women do,' the theatre went wild: screams of 'Right on!' and constant applause. It was much more of a success than the production of *Hedda Gabler*, which wasn't a part as perfectly suited to Claire.

Claire Bloom also starred in the subsequent film version, a project which must have been inevitable given the zeitgeist.

Yes, but unfortunately the same thought occurred to Jane Fonda, who had seen the production in New York and was very involved in that kind of politics at the time. My great writer friend of the time was David Mercer, and he called me one day and said, 'I've got a new job,' and I said, 'Me too,' and it turned out that we'd both been hired to write *A Doll's House*. So it became a horserace, like *Dangerous Liaisons*; and, again like *Liaisons*, we won because our film was cheaper. Actually, I think it was one of the cheapest films made in England since the war. At first, Hillard said, 'You can have two exteriors,' so I thought, 'I'll have one at the beginning and one at the end.' Then he called me and said, 'We scheduled two days of shooting in Norway, but now we've only got one day, so you can only have one exterior.' So there's only one exterior in the film, which is at the beginning. The rest of it was shot at Elstree on a budget of about £60,000, with the most distinguished cast you could possibly imagine: Anthony Hopkins, Ralph Richardson, Denholm Elliott, Anna Massey and Edith Evans.

I didn't have much to do with it while they were shooting, but one of the days I did go down there happened to be Ralph Richardson's seventieth birthday. I'd never met him before, but they'd planned a cake and publicity shots and so on, and he said to me, 'These things are so ghastly! Do you want to have lunch?' So he took myself and the director, Patrick Garland, to lunch at the commissary, and we'd hardly taken our seats when Laurence Olivier bowls up with a bottle of champagne and says, 'Ralph! You don't look a day over seventy!' So now I'm having lunch with Ralph Richardson and Laurence Olivier, who proceed to reminisce in the most fascinating way about working together. Olivier was at the studio shooting the television version of Michael Blakemore's production of *Long Day's Journey into Night*, and he kept saying to Ralph Richardson, 'You can't imagine how difficult the role is,' and I sat there thinking, 'Has he forgotten that Ralph Richardson was in the film of *Long Day's Journey into Night*, or is he just being provocative?' Anyway, at a certain point, Olivier had to go, to resume shooting, and Patrick also had to go, to set up for the afternoon, so Ralph Richardson and I were left sitting at the table. There was a long silence, then Ralph Richardson said, 'Tell me, did you see Larry in *Long Day's Journey into Night?*' and I said, 'Yes, I did, actually,' and he said, 'Silly performance.' So that's my memory of *A Doll's House*, that and the race with the other film.

What did you make of the other film, directed by Joseph Losey?

They had a bigger budget and bigger stars – Jane Fonda, of course, together with David Warner, Trevor Howard, Edward Fox and Delphine Seyrig – but they had a terrible time doing it.

Joseph Losey and Jane Fonda didn't get on very well, and at the wrap party the crew took Jane Fonda out and buried her in the snow, which I think she took to be a gesture of affection. I knew David Warner quite well, who was playing the husband, and he complained a great deal, saying that every scene where he appeared in an even slightly good light Jane and Delphine would rewrite so that he looked even more idiotic and insensitive. Of course, the secret of making the play work, which Patrick grasped very well, is that you have to be fair to the husband and make him as sympathetic as you can, because then you get the full impact of the final scene and realize that what she says is justified, whereas if he behaves like a pantomime villain all the way through, the scene is much less powerful.

Years later, David Mercer called me and said, 'You know how envious you always are when I tell you I'm going to some foreign film festival with one of my films?' I said, 'Yes.' He said, 'Well, I'm about to make you an offer you won't be able to resist.' I said, 'What's that?' He said, 'Belfast. November.' So the two of us went to the Belfast Film Festival, and in the same week the IRA resumed its bombing campaign – which David took extremely personally and fell off the wagon. On the evening when they showed both *Doll's Houses* and we had to appear afterwards to discuss them, David was nowhere to be seen and was eventually found in some pub or other, absolutely plastered. It was a very entertaining evening for the audience, because he decided to take the line – the opposite line to the one taken by the critics, who generally decided that Losey had made a proper film, whereas ours was just a dramatized play – that my film was much better than his film, and denounced every aspect of his film from the actors to the catering. It was hilarious; I'd never heard a writer be so vitriolic about something he'd worked on.

Was your film in the same vein as the television versions of your plays?

It was a bit freer than that. One of the things I did was move it around. The play is all in one room, and I moved it to several different venues. I also cut it by a half. The film is ninety minutes or so, whereas the play is pushing three hours. But it was basically in the same vein as those television productions, so it does seem fairly un-filmic. I happen to like that, though. I like Sidney Lumet's films of *The Seagull* and *Long Day's Journey into Night*, and I particularly like the film version of *Who's Afraid of Virginia Woolf?*, none of which attempt to conceal the fact that this is a play. They just remove some of the staginess, because in the editing you can take away that dramatic repetitiveness which often works in the theatre but not in cinema. I honestly think that cinema is at the opposite pole from the theatre, and it was only after I'd written several screenplays that hadn't been made that this dawned on me. That was my task in the latter half of the seventies: trying to figure out the difference between writing plays, which seemed to come naturally to me, and writing films, which seemed to be a great effort, something I was doing under some sort of false premise.

In the case of your screenplay of Ghosts, *there seems to be very little difference.*

Unlike *Hedda Gabler*, which I've felt able to be much freer with, you wouldn't be wise to change *Ghosts*, because it has this tremendously contained timescale. What you *can* do is use the possibilities which are already there: the business of the orphanage burning down, for example, and the open air ending with the sun coming up. It was commissioned by a producer called Eric Abraham, and I was very disappointed that the film wasn't made. It was going to be made with Vanessa Redgrave, and then there was a moment when Liv Ullmann was very interested in directing it, but it never got past the discussion stages. I wouldn't mind directing it myself one of these days; I still don't think of it as a dead project.

How free have you been with Hedda Gabler?

It's recognizably Ibsen's play; it just takes place in a fresh setting: New Orleans in the fifties. It's *Hedda Gabler* via Tennessee Williams, if you like. I wrote a draft of it, then did two further drafts with Iain Softley – whom I liked working with but who decided not to direct it – and the three drafts are very different from one another. For example, in the second draft I made the Eilert Loevborg character black, but then I was persuaded that this wasn't terribly likely; not the idea of Hedda being in love with a black man, but the idea of a black man being a threatening presence in the university, because, even if he had written something twice as good as anyone else, that wouldn't have got him advancement. Research seemed to bear that out, so we went back to the original. The producers, Myriam Cyr and Maryam d'Abo, have now asked me if I want to direct it, and I do, but I also want to write another draft before I start. One of my favourite films of recent years is *Far from Heaven*, which is pretty much what I had in mind stylistically: to recreate that idyllic, but sexually repressed, America of the fifties.

You originally translated Ghosts *for the stage, didn't you?*

I did it for The Actors Company, which was a touring group, and I seem to remember seeing it in somewhere like Peterborough. I think it's a great play, but I also think, and began to think more and more as I was working on it, that it's quite a funny play. It's always thought of as being a desperately gloomy piece, but some of the characters are quite savagely and comically drawn. Ibsen's plays were pretty aggressive towards his audience and got him into a lot of trouble.

Do you think Ibsen saw himself as Dr Stockmann in An Enemy of the People?

An Enemy of the People was written as a reaction to the terrible furore that *Ghosts* caused and his own feelings of isolation and disgust at being attacked by all shades of opinion. He was a real *bête noire* for critics of the day. Whenever he had a play put on in England, the newspapers started talking about 'sewers' and 'filthy disease'. It wasn't just that *Ghosts* was about syphilis, which was unmentionable in Victorian times; it was that the syphilis stood for the crippling weight of past mistakes and past assumptions which restricted people in the late nineteenth century, or the mid-twentieth century, or now. It's about people being dragged down by dead ideas, and it's very persuasive in that respect.

When you wrote the screenplay, in 1987, AIDS was very much in the news. Ghosts *would have been an interesting metaphor for that.*

Yes, and that was certainly in my mind at the time.

What's the main difference between your translation of An Enemy of the People *and the most famous previous one – Arthur Miller's?*

Arthur Miller did a real adaptation. He reorganized the play and emphasized the social side of it, which was obviously what he was interested in: the idea of the heroic figure standing up against – as it were – McCarthyism. I'm not saying that he didn't do a very good and very valid job of it, because he did, but the play is actually more interesting than that, because the character of Stockmann is very ambivalently seen by Ibsen. He doesn't hesitate to show that he's extremely selfish and thoughtless, and heedless of the consequences for his family, and so on. He's an obsessive, with all that implies, and when Ian McKellen played the part at the National he found that beautifully, this balance between being admirable and being exasperating.

You've translated five plays by Ibsen. Do you plan on tackling any more?

Never say never. I said after *The Wild Duck*, 'That was great. I'm not going to do any more,' but when I was asked to do *An Enemy of the People*, I read it again and thought, 'This is great, too.' I always enjoy grappling with the old bugger. When I was researching *Tales from Hollywood*, my principal source was a woman called Marta Feuchtwanger, who makes a brief appearance in the play, and she knew absolutely everyone. During the couple of days that I spoke to her, she said, 'When I was eight years old, I came back from school and I was running down the corridor and I banged into this very small man in a very tall hat. And he took me by the arm and said in a foreign accent, "Little girls aren't supposed to run inside the house." And it was Ibsen.' I was thrilled to shake the hand of someone who had met Ibsen. She was ninety at the time, and she was only eight when she met him, but she still remembered him.

The only living playwright whose work you've translated is Yasmina Reza. How did that relationship come about?

In the mid-eighties, Peggy Ramsay sent me Yasmina's first play,

Conversations after a Burial, which she'd read and thought was very promising. Howard Davies read it as well, and together and separately we tried to convince various people to commission a translation – and got nowhere, because there was, is and probably always will be an in-built resistance to foreign plays in England. Then, in the mid-nineties, I was staying in Paris, where I often go to write, and was walking to lunch one day and passed the Théâtre des Champs Elysées, which was showing this play called *'Art'*. I thought that was a rather interesting title, so I approached the poster and discovered that it was by Yasmina, then I asked at the box office and found that it was sold out – which was interesting. Anyway, I went back at curtain time, went in to see it, then went back to the hotel and called Tom Erhardt at Casarotto Ramsay and said, 'Can we get the rights to this play?' Two days later, he called me back and said, 'The rights aren't available. They've been bought by Sean Connery.' And a few days after that, the unmistakable voice of Sean Connery was on the phone summoning me to a meeting. So that was how it came about. At some point during the six and a half years that *'Art'* ended up running in London, I read *The Unexpected Man* and did that, and then *Life x 3*, and eventually *Conversations after a Burial* as well – directed by Howard Davies.

What attracted you both to Conversations after a Burial?

It's a thing which is unmistakable when you come across it – and Peggy was great at knowing how unmistakable it was – and that's a new voice unlike anyone else's. And although *Conversations after a Burial* is much more like other people's work than any of Yasmina's recent plays, nevertheless there was an original note in it. It doesn't take great genius to respond in an instinctive way to Ibsen or Chekhov, but Yasmina, like Horváth, just speaks to something particular in my make-up. I don't know what it is, but I recognize it when I see it.

The play actually reminded me of Chekhov, particularly the way the characters don't so much talk to each other as say what's on their minds at any given point.

I think that's right. And I'm sure that as an actress – which Yasmina was – those rhythms impressed themselves upon her.

Her later plays are much less Chekhovian, but the things I like about Chekhov – the lucidity and the clear-eyed, non-judgemental investigation of the way people behave badly one minute and well the next – are true of them, too. 'Art' is a simple idea, but it manages to say something quite profound about friendship – and be enormously entertaining. It's also brilliantly organized: just when you think it isn't susceptible to further development something new happens, finally reaching that extraordinary climax where Marc draws a skier on this expensive white painting. Even more extraordinary is that by the time you get to the very end, when the three men attempt to define the whole experience, Serge and Yvan simply rationalize it, whereas Marc, who's been a violent opponent of the painting all the way through, has finally understood it and become reconciled to it, which is very satisfying and unexpected and, of course, completely the opposite of what the play was said to be about by those people who huffed and puffed that it was a reactionary attack on modern art. But Yasmina isn't a writer whom the critics particularly like. The reviews of her work often make snide remarks about 'philosophy-lite'. The suggestion is that she trivializes important themes, when in fact she happens to deal with important themes in an extremely accessible way – which, for some reason, arouses critical suspicions.

It's interesting that, in the course of its run, 'Art' should have had so many different casts, featuring so many different actors, starting with Albert Finney, Tom Courtenay and Ken Stott. What do you think that says about the characters?

It's just a work which is so recognizably truthful that it adapts itself to whoever might be playing the parts. The first cast in America was Alan Alda, Victor Garber and Alfred Molina, but that didn't mean the parts couldn't be played by younger people – or even, on occasion, older people. Like *The Philanthropist*, it's very elastic in that respect.

Why did you decide not to anglicize the names of characters and places and so on?

That was a conversation we had at the very first meeting. Sean Connery and his fellow producer, David Pugh, felt we should transpose the action to London, but I thought the idea of three middle-aged Englishmen falling out over a painting was beyond the realms of wildest fiction and we should just say these people were French and lived in Paris and leave it at that – although, for the film version, the proposed setting is New York, which is rather more plausible. What we did do on both *'Art'* and *Life x 3*, although not on *The Unexpected Man* because we had English actors performing it in New York, is prepare two separate versions, an English version and an American version, because I realized that we really do speak a different language from the Americans. *Life x 3* starts with the child wanting a biscuit, but over there they don't have biscuits, they have cookies, and once you start making those little changes, you quickly find that you're doing five or six a page. So that was an interesting process.

A film version of 'Art' *was first mooted a long time ago. Why has it taken so long to put together?*

It's taken so long because I don't think that Yasmina has any great enthusiasm for the idea. Originally we were meant to write the screenplay together, but clearly she found that a less and less interesting prospect. I understand that if you have a big success in your career it can be quite oppressive, and I think she would rather move on and not dwell on it. It's still an interesting challenge, so I'd like to do it – and I'd certainly like to work with the proposed director, Sidney Lumet, who's one of the best interpreters of plays on film.

After 'Art', *there was presumably no question of setting* The Unexpected Man *in any country but France?*

No. *The Unexpected Man* is very French. It's also slightly autobiographical. Yasmina once saw a writer whom she enormously admired and followed him down the street trying to summon up the courage to speak to him but didn't, and that was where the idea for the play came from.

The Unexpected Man *deals with similar themes to* 'Art': *the idea that people define themselves against other people – even, in this case, characters in books – and the question of whether, if they then change, you have to change as well. Presumably those themes interest you, too?*

I think so – although it's not necessarily themes which draw you to a writer. Again, it was a very simple and original idea, two people letting you understand their thoughts and only speaking to each other in the last forty-five seconds of the play, and an idea which I liked very much. In the same way, I liked the idea of three different versions of the same evening in *Life x 3*, and the notion that these astrophysicists, who deal with events happening two hundred light years away, are unable to direct the course of an evening because of what this six-year-old child might do. In fact, I first read the play without really working out what it was about. That's probably why *Life x 3* doesn't hit the bullseye in terms of satisfying the public the way *'Art'* does. A certain percentage of any audience for *Life x 3* comes out saying, 'What's going on? What's she getting at?' whereas in *'Art'* you're not troubled by those questions. My theory is that the third version is the one which really happened, and the other two are possibilities which won't occur because of the constraints of civilization; and what's interesting is that the third version, which is by far the most civilized, provokes the most acute melancholy. But Yasmina is very canny about these things and isn't going to commit herself one way or the other. I think she's taken a leaf out of Harold Pinter's book and says that the play is what it is. I also think she writes quite fast, with a large element of spontaneity, so I don't know whether *she* knows why she goes in this direction or that.

Does it make any difference if the playwright is still alive, in terms of your freedom with the text?

Well, I'm not someone who looks for freedom with a text, so in a way I welcomed it. And, over the past few years, Yasmina has become much better at speaking English, so she does take a very strong interest in how it turns out.

You said that translations can refresh and broaden your own writing. What did you take away from translating Yasmina Reza?

I don't know. You'd have to analyse *The Talking Cure* and see if anything had fed into it. It covers an enormous amount of ground in quite a short space of time, so perhaps Yasmina's concision has been helpful to me. Doing a translation is so different from writing your own stuff, though. It's so technical, like taking a watch apart and putting it back together again – or, rather, it's what that process would be for someone whose job was designing watch faces. You could have a perfectly good career designing watch faces and never know what the inside of a watch looked like, but if you have to take the watch apart and look at all the screws and bits of curly metal and then put it back together again it can be very helpful. It makes you think about the intricacies of the thing.

Savages – Treats – Able's Will – The History Man

If The Philanthropist *seemed like a left turn after* Total Eclipse, *then* Savages *seems like an even sharper left turn after* The Philanthropist.

It seems to me a great piece of luck that, by the time *The Philanthropist* became as successful as it did, I was already well advanced in thinking about *Savages*, because Peggy Ramsay said, 'You've now got a choice. You're very good at writing this kind of play and you can go on writing this kind of play, or you can do something completely different. Which is it to be?' and I said, 'I've already started on something completely different, so it isn't a problem.' While I was writing *The Philanthropist*, I read a piece in the *Sunday Times* called 'Genocide', by Norman Lewis, and I reacted strongly to the image of these Brazilian Indians being bombed while performing their funeral ritual. I just felt determined to write a play about it – and, in fact, *The Philanthropist* financed the writing, because it took quite a long time, culminating in a research trip to Brazil.

In the introduction to Plays 1, *you say that the period from conception to completion was four years. Why did it take so long?*

It's the only play I didn't write in any kind of order. I think the first things I wrote were those two scenes – which eventually became one scene in the American production – where this man called Pereira gives his testimony about the genocide. Then, without knowing how they were going to fit in, I started writing those poems based on Indian myths, which entailed ploughing through books by Lévi-Strauss and compendiums of world myths. Then I got the idea that the poems were written by my central character, West, the First Secretary at the British Embassy in Rio. Then I started to feel that I couldn't deal with the Indians in isolation as I'd originally intended, because what was happening to them was related to the political situation in the country as a whole, so I had the idea of West being kidnapped by the revolutionary, Carlos – which, of course, is the central part of the play. And finally, I realized that I couldn't deal with the wider political situation unless I actually went there, so quite a lot of *Savages* was written in the British Museum reading room and quite a lot on board the Blue Star liner to Rio.

The play is partially dedicated to 'friends in Brazil'. How much help were you given by the people there?

A tremendous amount. While I was struggling to synthesize all this material, I made contact with an American guy called Ken Brecher, an anthropology postgraduate at Oxford, to whom the play is also dedicated. I went to a lecture he was giving about this tribe of Indians he'd lived with for two years, and afterwards I went up to him and said, 'You don't know me, but can you help me?' He provided me with a lot of names and addresses in Rio, in particular a famous sculptor called Poty – short for Napoleon – and his wife Celia, who was a translator. They were as helpful as could be to me and Laura, and made us realize how frightening the military dictatorship really was. We'd all go out for dinner and be speaking in English, and they'd start whispering in case someone at the next table heard them. You don't think about these things, but people were being disappeared left, right and centre.

Another person Ken put us in touch with was a Brazilian novelist called Antonio Callado, who worked for one of the papers there, so I went to see Callado and told him what I was interested in, and just like that he got us on a military aeroplane into the Xingu. I was very pleased about this and told Celia, and she said, 'You mustn't go.' I said, 'Why not?' and she said, 'Callado's been in jail already. If you use his contacts to get on the plane, then go and write this play you've been telling us about, you'll be safe back in England and he'll be put back in jail.' So I called Callado and said, 'Thanks for organizing this, but I can't take you up on it,' and he was furious. I tried to explain why, and he said, 'Don't be silly. It doesn't matter.' But I refused to go and set about working out how I was going to get into the Xingu, and in the end the only way I could think of was to buy tickets on a scheduled flight, get off at Santa Isabel – which is on an island called Bananal in the middle of the River Araguaia, where there was a tribe of Indians still being looked after by the Indian Protection Service – and walk.

Laura and I booked two seats on this Brazilian plane, where they issued you with a small box of hard rations in case it went down, and were the only people getting off at this airport, which had the caricature bloke with a big hat fast asleep in a hut. Now, Laura had been doing Teach Yourself Portuguese, so she was able to say things but not understand the replies, whereas, because I was born in the Azores and had had a Portuguese nanny, I understood what everyone was saying but could hardly speak a word myself. So we went into this hut and woke the guy up, and Laura said, 'We're looking for FUNAI' – Fundação Nacional do Indio, the agency which was supposed to be looking after the Indians but was subsequently discovered to be taking bribes to dispose of them. The guy just waved his arm, so we set off through the scrubland, and after walking for about a quarter of an hour, we came across someone by the side of the road – who turned out to be the FUNAI guy, repairing the FUNAI jeep.

He was very pleased to see us and took us to the FUNAI place, a wooden building a mile or two downriver from the Indian settlement. He said, 'We'll have lunch and then I'll take you there,' so we sat on the veranda and I thought, 'This is incredible!' There was a sinister moment when a canoe floated by and there didn't seem to be anyone in it, but then a head came up and a hand started wielding the oar before the bloke disappeared again. All the FUNAI guys, and there were four or five of them, were roaring with laughter except our friend – Garcia Lufiego, I think he was called – and I said, 'What's the joke?' and they said, 'Indian. Drunk.' Then they told a lot of stories about how Indians will drink anything, like hair restorer or paint stripper, which they seemed to think was absolutely hilarious.

That's reminiscent of the story which West is told by the anthropologist, Crawshaw, about the woman who finds it hysterically funny when her Indian servant replaces a roll of toilet paper by rolling the paper from the new roll onto the core of the old one.

That was a story I got from Ken, actually. In fact, that character was largely based on Ken and the things he told me. Anyway, here we were in the middle of nowhere, about to set off for the Indian village, when a motorboat appeared around a bend in the river and everyone started getting very nervous. It was an army motorboat with a handful of armed soldiers and a colonel on board, and the colonel was very interested in us. He said, 'What are you doing here?' and I said, 'I'm a tourist. I'm interested in the Xingu.' He said, 'Have you been taking photographs?' and I said, 'Just photographs of me with a piranha, that kind of thing.' He said, 'You have to give us the photographs, and you have to get off the island – now,' and I said, 'How?' and he said, 'Get on the boat.' There was then a tremendous row, with the FUNAI guy screaming at the colonel and the colonel screaming at the FUNAI guy, which ended with Laura and I being put on the boat, taken across the river and dumped.

We were just outside this one-horse town – exactly like a town in a western, with hitching rails and so on – and we went to an inn and said, 'Can we stay the night?' and the woman in charge was wonderfully hospitable. They had eight or nine rooms, but there were no ceilings on them, so she said, 'You must have our room,' and insisted on clearing out her room, which did have a ceiling, and remaking the bed so we could stay there. She also said, 'Please don't go out after dark, because there's a lot of shooting in this town,' and I said, 'Don't worry. We'll stay right here.' But come ten o'clock, there's a terrible banging on our door, and the colonel comes in with two armed men. I don't know what the fuck's going on, but what I do know is that he's transfixed by Laura. She's in bed, and he's looking at her, and I'm thinking, 'This could get really nasty.' Drink is called for, so cachaca is being handed around – lethal stuff: a squeeze of lime, hold your nose and jump – when Garcia arrives, having some-how found out that this was going on, and proceeds to get into an argument with the colonel about God. I don't know what the colonel had intended, but at about one in the morning he stag-gered off, and as they were leaving Garcia made a face at me as if to say, 'That was a narrow escape.'

The next day I didn't know what to do, so I went to various houses and knocked on doors and eventually found a boy who said that, for a sum of money, he'd take us across the river to the Indian reservation. This seemed like an insanely stupid thing to do, but, on the other hand, we'd come all this way and I really wanted to see it. So, at about six o'clock in morning, he took us across, told us that there was a plane going back to Brasilia at noon, then left us. And there were the Indians, all wearing T-shirts and living in a kind of concentration camp with barbed wire around it. They took us to their chief, a man called Atau, who looked about sixty but was probably only forty, and who, not to be sentimental about it, had some extraordinary quality about him. He seemed extremely at peace with himself, despite the fact that he was living in the most terrible conditions. I took various photographs of him and, I'm ashamed to say, bought his headdress from him, and then he walked us back to the airport – where we found the colonel waiting. I said, 'Good morning, Colonel. We're just going to Brasilia,' and he said, 'I'm also going to Brasilia.' Just before the plane landed, Garcia arrived, but when I went over to say good morning, he cut me dead. I thought, 'Oh, Christ, I've got him into trouble,' which I probably had, but just as we were getting on the plane he slipped a piece of paper into my pocket with his address on it.

I've lost touch with him now, although we corresponded for a couple of years, but he may very well have saved our lives. The Indian Protection Service, like everything else, was under military jurisdiction, so the colonel could have had us bumped off and no one would have known the difference. In fact, on our first day in Brasilia he turned up at the Hotel Nacional and knocked on the door of our room, so we decided to get the hell out. The whole experience was quite frightening. Amnesty International had given me the names of five or six people to contact in Rio and São Paulo, and they'd all vanished, every single one. There were posters everywhere of wanted 'terrorists', in particular one with four faces on it, and on the morning we left São Paulo, three of them had been gunned down by the police at a café in Rio; so my last image of Brazil was a guy up a ladder taping red X's across the faces of the three who were dead.

Would you have been able to write the play with such passion if you hadn't gone to Brazil?

I was already very passionate about the subject matter, but the part of the play I hadn't written when I went to Brazil was the West–Carlos scenes, and those were very much informed by what I'd seen there. A key insight came when I went into a big record shop in Rio and said, 'I'd like some Indian music, please,' and the assistant started getting out all this stuff by Ravi Shankar. I said, 'No, no. *Brazilian* Indian music,' and he said, 'What do you mean? We don't have any Indians here. They're all in Peru and Bolivia.' In other words, what seemed terrible to a western liberal was very low among the priorities of ordinary Brazilians, who had problems of their own – such as getting enough to eat. The other discovery I made was that, partly for the same reason, being a revolutionary in countries like Brazil and Argentina was a largely upper-middle-class business. The people on the left tended to be university graduates from comfortable backgrounds, which gave the character of Carlos a very interesting texture. So having first thought, 'I can't deal with the Indians without tackling the wider political situation,' and having then thought, 'I can't tackle the wider political situation without going to Brazil,' I finally thought, having been there, 'I can now see the problem from a different angle.' And all that went into the play.

The West–Carlos scenes aren't just political, they're polemical, which is something that writers often . . .

. . . shy away from. Like I shied away from it when political drama became the dominant mode of the decade. But *Savages* was different from the plays which followed in that it proposed no solutions – indeed, it suggested that there probably *were* no solutions. That's why, for example, the play got blasted in Germany, because this inconsolable voice it has was regarded as reactionary. The tendency of political plays is to say, 'If you just do this, everything will be all right,' but I saw no point in fudging things in that way.

Hence your decision to call the central character West?

You have to call your characters something, and the idea of calling him West seemed like the solution to a problem. It's supposed to be quite light, not heavily symbolic.

There's quite a lot of humour in the play. Did you see that as a way of sugaring the pill?

I was pleased that audiences laughed so much, especially in the West–Carlos scenes, because it made the play all the more shocking when it needed to be shocking. But the interesting thing is that the reviews didn't reflect that; they all portrayed it as a grim political tract, despite the fact that quite a lot of work had gone into making it slip down easily.

You said that the anthropologist, Crawshaw, was largely based on Ken Brecher, but were any of the other characters drawn from life – West, for a start?

Well, I went see a man who had been First Secretary at the Rio Embassy during the military takeover, and he was extremely helpful and forthcoming. I talked to him in his garden in Chelsea, and took note of that tone which says, 'Of course, it was absolutely dreadful, but I'm a diplomat, what can I do about it?' He was quite a bit younger than West was meant to be, but with West you get the sense of a man who's been passed over and isn't proceeding through the service as quickly as he might.

What about the British major, Brigg, who worked for the Indian Protection Service?

Again, I talked to someone similar over here and some of the things he said fed into that character – mostly the business about how you couldn't help giving the Indians diseases, because if you caught a cold they all died, but also that startling moment when the character says, 'I sometimes think the best thing is for them to get it all over with as quickly as possible.' That level of disillusionment, from someone who had worked with them for such a long time, was very shocking. The only character who's completely invented, in fact, is the missionary. I never met anyone like that, although I'd documented the type.

Just like West does.

That's right. West makes the journey I made, from benevolent ignorance to appalled knowledge – although he has to be locked up in a cellar to get that, whereas I provided it for myself. He represents the audience, really; the well-intentioned audience. *That's* why he's called West.

The odd thing about him is that he's interested enough in the Indians to have talked to Crawshaw, Brigg and the missionary, Penn, yet by the time he's kidnapped he still hasn't fitted their plight into the wider political situation.

His mistake is that he's aestheticized them. He thinks he can empathize with them, but he only sees them from his own narrow cultural perspective. He's trying to impose something on them, in the same way that the missionary is trying to make them wear clothes and stop them sleeping with each other. That was the cause and tragedy of the Vietnam War, in a sense: the Americans had no idea who the Vietnamese were and what they wanted and what had happened to them, because they were looking at everything through their end of the telescope. And all those things still apply, I think. The way we look at Iraq or Afghanistan is entirely ignorant, and until someone there figures out what's required – which isn't likely to bear much resemblance to what *we* feel is required – then you're walking through a minefield.

The play is composed of four kinds of scenes: West relating the Indian myths while the tribe performs the Quarup behind him; West on his voyage of discovery in 1970; West with Carlos in 1971; and Pereira's testimony in 1963. How close are the latter scenes to Pereira's actual confession of his role in slaughtering the Indians?

Verbatim. I stylized the language slightly, to give this terrible account a bit of distance and to balance it against these humane stories told by West, but that's basically what happened. I remember myself and Margaret Drabble sitting on a stage in Bath, during an Arts Council writers' tour, reading those scenes from the as-yet unperformed play. She was reading the priest and I was reading Pereira, and we were halfway through when the organizer suddenly leapt to his feet and said, 'Right! That's quite enough!' We were astonished. We were actually stopped from reading this piece. It's supposed to arouse people's horror and indignation, and that's what it succeeded in doing!

There's one scene that doesn't fit into your schema, in which a group of Indians who have been 'integrated' are drinking in a bar, but it does embody Carlos's definition of capitalism: a system whereby the tribes are kicked off their land and then have it sold back to them.

I cut that scene in the American production, precisely because it doesn't fit in. I just found it a bit crude.

You also mentioned that the two Pereira scenes became one scene in the American production. What else did you change, and why?

It was hard enough to mount the play at the Royal Court, on that tiny stage, but when Gordon Davidson decided that he wanted to do it at the Mark Taper Forum in Los Angeles, which has an open stage, he explained that you couldn't change the scenery at all, so that began the process of reworking. I rewrote the scene with the missionary, which I thought was too broad, and cut the scene at the end with the pilots coming on, which seemed unnecessary. Instead we had the death of West, followed by a montage of world headlines, then the lights went up on two or three dead bodies, to the sound of a recorded bird call made by an Indian. We brought Ken Brecher over to help with the Indians, whom he quite rightly decided to integrate more into the play. We cast a group of American Indian dancers, so you had a much better sense in the American production of the life of the Indians. During the scene between West and the major, for example, we had an Indian and his son sitting downstage mending an arrow, and when there was a pause in the scene, with West thinking and the major pottering about, the two Indians just got up and walked through the middle of it. We did a lot of stuff like that, which was very effective.

Would you say that the play is anti-American?

I'm no Marxist, but it was impossible not to understand that all this was happening because a number of people were making huge profits out of it – mostly in America. At the Mark Taper, we listed in the programme the ten American companies most heavily exploiting the Brazilian jungle and asked people who came to see the play to find out whether they were investing in those companies and, if so, to withdraw their money. I'd have to say that they took the play much more seriously in America; here it was largely seen as a piece of exotica. It ran for nine months at the Comedy Theatre, but that was because people wanted to see Paul Scofield, who was magnificent as West – alongside an unknown but fantastic Tom Conti as Carlos. So the word-of-mouth was good, but most of the reviews said, 'What's this about? It's about a lot of people we don't know and aren't particularly interested in.'

Nevertheless, like all your plays from this period, it was televised shortly afterwards.

I rewrote it quite a bit for TV. It was directed by Alan Bridges, with Richard Pasco as West and Michael Kitchen as Carlos, and although most of it was shot in the studio, using stock footage for the Indians, it was done in a pretty filmic way. The interesting thing is that when Paul turned down the part in the television version, the script was sent at my request to James Mason, whom I considered to be possibly the greatest British screen actor ever, and we got a response saying that he'd love to do it but it clashed with a film he was about to start – and could we therefore move the dates by three weeks. To which the BBC replied, 'We've got a quota. We can't wait.' I said, 'You can't wait three weeks for James Mason?' and they said, 'No. We need to fill the drama schedules.' Now, of course, they'd wait three years for James Mason, and even if, at the end of the three years, he said, 'I've changed my mind. I'm not going to do it,' they'd still think it was worth it.

Unlike Treats, *which is reminiscent of* When Did You Last See My Mother?, *your first four plays are all very different from one another. Was that a conscious decision?*

Absolutely. Rather than working at my craft like Alan Ayckbourn, and polishing it and trying to improve on it, I just went back to zero every time. I recognize that a lot of artists – for want of a better word – achieve their effects by pursuing a single obsession or set of obsessions, but I've never been like that. I'm interested in doing things I've never done before.

In the introduction to Plays 1, *you say that* Treats *was the short-est play you had then written and took the longest time to write. What did you find difficult about it?*

Achieving the simplicity it needed. I kept going off at tangents, but I was trying to do something very stripped down and formal.

It does have a Pinteresque quality.

Quite possibly. I wouldn't think that I'd avoided that influence, any more than I avoided John Osborne's influence when I was writing *When Did You Last See My Mother?*

Where did the idea come from?

The original inspiration came from two things. Firstly, this visual notion I had of a half-furnished room. I thought it would be interesting for the curtain to go up and reveal a room where half the possessions have been moved out. Secondly, Robert Kidd, who had been living with Jane Asher for several years, told me that he had treated her rather badly, and that being away from her for a while – he was directing a production of the Scottish play in West Virginia – had given him some perspective, and that when the play opened he was going to go home and ask her to marry him. But when he got back, he found that she'd moved out. So that was the starting point.

You were also influenced by A Doll's House, *weren't you?*

That was the other starting point. At the time, the response to *A Doll's House* in New York was very exhilarating, but after-wards, when I looked around me, I thought, 'It isn't always so easy just to walk out the door.' So I wanted to write a play in which the woman slammed the door and then came back, because she was in thrall to her own maltreatment – although, in that sense, it developed completely differently from the real-life models, since Bob and Jane never did get together again.

Although he actually directed the play, and she starred in it.

That's right. I guess they both knew I'd started from that point, and they were civilized enough about what had happened to be able to contemplate dramatizing it – and Jane understood the character very well. The casting mistake we made was James Bolam. Jonathan Pryce, who was more or less an unknown, gave a sensational audition, and I really wanted to cast him, but Jimmy was offered it because he was hot at the time.

Why did you think that Jonathan Pryce was better for the part?

Danger. Danger just poured off him. Jimmy didn't have that kind of ferocity. He had great timing and was very witty – and not ingratiating, which is the great danger with horrible characters: that the more you try and make them sympathetic to an audience, the more unsympathetic they become – but he didn't inspire the fear that the character should.

In a way, the other male character, Patrick, who was played by Stephen Moore, is a trickier part, because he lacks the fireworks of his rival.

That's right. He's like the character of Yvan in *'Art'*: the shuttle-cock in the middle. But that's the part the canny actor will go for, because you can steal the whole play – which Stephen did. Ironically, he was so displeased with his audition that he went into the pub next door and tore the script in half, and later on, when we went into the pub ourselves, I saw him sitting at a table with this torn up script and thought, 'He must really hate it!'

So how did you manage to stop yourself going off at tangents?

Noël Coward said that it's impossible to write a play with just three characters in, and I found that the only way I could do it was in a mathematical way: each character has one scene with each of the other characters, each character has one scene on their own and there are three scenes with all of them in, so you have a nine-scene structure covering all possible combinations – which means that they're all the shuttlecock in the middle at one time or another. I later used the same method with *Les Liaisons Dangereuses*, and somehow it worked better. *Treats*, on the other hand, was awfully difficult to write and very badly reviewed.

Why was that?

I don't know. Perhaps because it dealt with masochism, which isn't a very popular subject. It's a subject which *The Talking Cure* also deals with, as it happens. *Treats* actually broke the box-office record at the Royal Court, but it continued a syndrome which had started with *The Philanthropist*. There was a review of *The Philanthropist* which said, 'What a pity this isn't as good as *Total Eclipse*.' Then the reviews for *Savages* said, 'If only this was a brilliant comedy like *The Philanthropist*.' Then the reviews for *Treats* said, 'How trivial this is compared to the important subjects tackled in *Savages*.'

In retrospect, Treats *seems as weighty as* Savages – *and a lot weightier than* The Philanthropist.

Well, it's uglier. It's uningratiating. And the television version we did, with John Hurt, Kate Nelligan and Tom Conti, was even less ingratiating, because it was made more explicit that Dave had no interest in Ann except to dominate her. But those were the feelings in the air in the seventies, the sense that those ideals and aspirations which we'd been nursing in the sixties were unlikely to come to anything and that what had started as a liberating protest was turning into something else. I wouldn't make too much of this, but it occurs to me now that Dave is incipient Thatcherism and Patrick is the weakness at the heart of more progressive politics.

The same could be said of Braham and Philip in The Philanthropist.

There are definite similarities. When I was writing it, I felt that *Treats* was more similar in tone to *When Did You Last See My Mother?*, but at this distance of time, it does seem to go over ground which *The Philanthropist* had already treated. It sharpens the debate, I think, but it's in the same ballpark.

Do you think that writing Savages *taught you to be less ingratiating?*

It's always a question of matching the tone to the subject matter. I've got nothing against making an audience feel good, but the subject matter has to earn that. *The Philanthropist* was about a man with a comic failing, albeit one lightheartedly attached to the prevailing ethos of the day, so what you might call an ingratiating tone was not inappropriate for that play, whereas *Treats* was a kind of – to use a dreaded phrase – 'state of England' play, although no one took it as such.

In the introduction to Plays 1, *you describe* Treats *as the full stop on the first phase of your career. Why did you see it like that?*

I'd had five plays done at the Royal Court, and with *Treats* I had the feeling, which I'd never had before, that they were putting it on because it was by me, not because they really loved it. Robert Kidd and Nicky Wright had taken over at the Court for a short period, so Bob was obviously anxious to do the play because it was his first as co-artistic director, but I sensed very little enthusiasm towards it from everyone else. It had this weird history of terrible reviews and huge box office, then a transfer to the Mayfair which no one at the Court seemed very pleased about, and I thought, 'When I was at the Court, we were always saying that people would outstay their welcome and that the theatre was supposed to be for young talent, so this is it.'

You weren't exactly old!

I was thirty, and David Hare and I had a theory that you had about a ten-year career, so I thought I'd had my ten years.

That's pretty fatalistic.

Yes, but we were young – and we were observant. It seemed to be the case that a writer would have a flourishing career in the theatre for a while and then the theatre would turn its back on them, and we expected the same thing to happen to us. Also, after *Treats*, I had a bit of a block, which lasted a while. I'd already written *Able's Will*, but I couldn't think of anything else to write.

In Able's Will, *the title character is a writer who stops writing because, among other things, he's worried that all writers become orthodox – even if that orthodoxy is radical orthodoxy. Was that kind of thing going through your mind, too?*

For me, *Able's Will* was a kind of working out, rather like *Total Eclipse* had been, of all the worries associated with being a writer:

the fear that it's going to stop and the hope that you'll stop at an appropriate time, not go gurning on when people aren't interested any more.

There are flashbacks to Able in his early thirties, married with young children, as you were when you wrote the piece. Were you worried that family life would affect your writing – the pram-in-the-hallway syndrome?

Not really. I'd always wanted to get married and have children, and it was a very happy time in my life. So, as is often the case, whatever was going on intellectually, whatever the struggle was to do the work, wasn't necessarily linked to what was going on in my life, which was turning out rather well at that point. There was some anecdotal stuff in it about my family, which I hadn't really done before, but it wasn't what I would call an autobiographical piece.

Was it written on spec or commissioned?

It was commissioned by Barry Hanson, a friend of mine from the Royal Court who was at Thames Television, but I took longer over it than anticipated and rather missed the moment. Barry liked it but his superiors didn't, so someone suggested that I show it to a producer called Innes Lloyd at the BBC; then Innes put me together with Stephen Frears, which I was very pleased about because I'd always liked Stephen's work. So, in a sense, the most important thing about *Able's Will* is that I got to meet Stephen. It was the first time I'd really observed a director close at hand, and I appreciated the way he always included the writer in the process – even though he was very rigorous with it, and put a knife to all the passages of overwriting.

It was your first original screenplay. Did it give you an opportunity to try out some of the things you'd learned writing various unproduced adaptations?

I was just starting to work out the possibilities of writing for the screen, hence all the voice-over and flashbacks. Also, despite the fact that it's not exactly an original idea – a family gathering as someone is about to die – I was interested in breaking a bit of new ground. For example, the scene where two characters are having sex and talking at the same time, which is something you seldom see on screen but often happens in life, seemed quite bold at the time.

Equally bold – even now – is the seduction of one of the male characters by a twelve-year-old girl.

I think it would be quite hard to get away with those scenes now, judging by the BBC's nervousness about the television version of *Alice's Adventures Under Ground*, but at the time they were accepted without a murmur. In fact, the whole thing was pretty well received, but being television it was also forgotten in an instant, which seemed like a huge waste of effort.

Did you feel the same way about your television adaptation of Malcolm Bradbury's novel The History Man, *a couple of years later?*

The History Man is the only totally satisfactory television project I've been involved in – and one of the most enjoyable jobs I've ever done. It was very well acted and very well directed – by Rob Knights – and it really made people sit up straight when it came out. Michael Wearing, who'd been a stage manager at the Royal Court when I was there, was now David Rose's second-in-command at Pebble Mill in Birmingham, and they both gave us absolute freedom. The only restriction was the speed at which it had to be made. We had something like three weeks of location filming and eight days in the studio. Antony Sher, who hadn't played any big parts on TV before, had a huge chart in his dressing room so he knew exactly where he was scene by scene: which stage of the term we were at and who his character had seduced and who he hadn't. It was cited in that series *Sex on TV*, because it caused quite a lot of controversy at the time. This was when we were living in Oxfordshire, and the first we knew about it was when they refused to serve our nanny in the village post office because they were so appalled at what had happened on television the night before. People said that it was a slander on sociology departments, and there were even accusations that academics might lose their grants because of our attack on this field. The BBC were somewhat craven and never repeated it, although there were endless discussions about whether they should.

The series was in four one-hour parts. You must have relished having that much screen time at your disposal.

Yes, I did. I loved the book and could see that it would work very well on television. I don't think it would have worked nearly so well in an hour and a half, partly because there were a lot of characters and partly because that kind of character comedy needs space to develop. The better you know the characters and know what they're going to say and do, the funnier things get. I was very faithful to the book; but, because the first three quarters of it covers forty-eight hours and the last quarter the rest of term, which you have to reconstruct from the broken phrases of people at a party, I decided, in the last episode, to proceed through the term rather than put everything in one big set-piece. Malcolm used to come up here and together we'd work out what scenes needed to be invented. He found the process so enjoyable that he went on to do an enormous amount of television work himself, which he'd never done before, so to that extent I actually had some effect on his life.

The blackly comic tone is strongly reminiscent of Treats, *and Howard, the character played by Antony Sher, is very similar to Dave: shockingly adept at turning other people's weaknesses to his own advantage.*

And it is shocking when the one girl who's been standing up to him finally succumbs. For me, the defining line of the whole thing is when one of his pupils says, 'You give very good advice,' and he says, 'Mostly because it so closely resembles what people want to hear.' I really thought Malcolm had grasped something there, which was that selfishness, whether of the left or of the right, was in the ascendant at that particular moment in history, and that decent people were being done down by the slimiest kind of opportunist. Hence the caption at the end, saying that Howard voted Conservative in the 1979 general election. Malcolm thought that was a low blow, but it seemed to me exactly the kind of thing an opportunist like that would do.

{4}

Tales from the Vienna Woods – Don Juan Comes Back from the War – Faith, Hope and Charity – Tales from Hollywood

Is it true that translating Ödön von Horváth's Tales from the Vienna Woods *broke the spell of writer's block you had after* Treats?

I think what broke the dry spell was writing *Carrington* in the summer of 1977, but I was grateful that Horváth came along when he did. It was the year that the National moved out of the Old Vic, and they had these three new theatres and were desperate for product. I ran into Tom Stoppard, who had been asked to do a translation, and he said to me, 'If they like your plays, they'll commission a play from you. If they don't like your plays but think they ought to, they'll commission a translation.'

Do you think that's the case?

I've no idea. It's probably just writer's paranoia. But it so happened that the following week the phone rang and they offered me a translation. I think the play was *Les Fausses Confidences*, but, in any case, it was by Marivaux, and reading it again – because I'd read it in my student days – confirmed my feeling that Marivaux was impossible to translate, or, at least, impossible for *me* to translate. I just couldn't see how to achieve in English his extraordinary gossamer-light prose. I went to see John Russell Brown, who was the Literary Manager at the time, and I said, 'Marivaux isn't really my bag, but I've been mulling something from the same period: *Les Liaisons Dangereuses*.' A week or two passed, then he called me and said, 'We don't think that's a good idea, but we do have this play by Ödön von Horváth: *Tales from the Vienna Woods*.' I'd heard Horváth's name when I had that job at the Hamburg Schauspielhaus, and I'd read another of his plays, *Faith, Hope and Charity*, and thought how modern it was, so I was interested straight away; and when I read *Tales from the Vienna Woods*, I thought, 'This won't be any less difficult than the Marivaux, but it's fantastic.' I really fell upon it, because I was in a bit of a depression and not quite sure where to go next and uncertain about the one idea I had, and of all the translations I've worked on, it was one of the most involving. The National had this marvellous plan – the kind of plan they can't afford now, except for the occasional grant to bring over a production from Japan or Germany – to invite distinguished foreign directors. That threw me into the path of this formidable figure, Maximilian Schell, who, because he was unfamiliar with English actors and was of a collaborative frame of mind, wanted me to participate in the rehearsals and wanted, on his part, to participate in the translation. He was very particular about it being accurate.

Unlike Russian, German was one of your languages, so presumably you didn't work from a literal translation?

In typically, wondrously bureaucratic fashion, they omitted to ask me whether I could speak German and commissioned a literal translation anyway. Then there was my friend Ian Huish, who was the senior German teacher at Westminster and specialized in Horváth – and has done some translations of his own – so we got the National to stump up for him to come to a few rehearsals and follow it from the German text, and he gave us his take on the whole thing.

Why was it no less difficult than the Marivaux?

Horváth didn't write much about himself and he wasn't a theorist, but he did write an infamous document called 'Gebrauchsanweisung' – 'Instructions for Use' – discussing the style in which his plays should be performed. He says, 'Every word must be spoken in good German, or at any rate as if spoken by someone who normally speaks only in dialect and is now forcing himself to speak good German,' and what I inferred from that was a kind of Pinteresque formality of working-class speech. I came to think that it wouldn't have been such a problem if I'd been Irish, because an Irish writer would have had the same colourful turns of phrase naturally available to him; but when the English write in dialect it has a class connotation, whereas in Vienna everyone has a Viennese accent, from the Emperor to the chimney sweep. There are degrees of it, but basically accent is not a matter of class, it's to do with the colour of the language. Horváth, as a foreigner, a Hungarian writing in German, was very sensitive to this, so his Viennese plays are different from his Munich plays, and both are different from his later plays, which are in regular high German. *Don Juan Comes Back from the War* was far easier to translate, because it's just regular German, but the turns of phrase in *Tales from the Vienna Woods* are very particular, and Max was onto that like a bloodhound from day one.

How much did he participate in the translation, and you in the rehearsals?

I was there all the time except for ten days in the middle, when I suddenly had to go to Hollywood and came back to find that Max had retranslated the play and was insisting that the actors speak large chunks of it in pidgin English. One of the characters says, 'Und konsequent,' which means something like, 'What will come of that,' but Max was having the actor say, 'And consequent.' I said, 'What's this "And consequent" stuff? You employed me because I'm a playwright and I speak the language. What are you doing making all these changes?' and he said [*German accent*], 'And consequent? And consequent? I hear it all the time!' We subsequently made a film of it and he took a co-credit on the screenplay, which he was perfectly entitled to do, but there was no dialogue in the film which wasn't in the play; it was just rearranged and refocused.

I got on pretty well with him, but he was very unpopular with the company because he directed in the German manner, which meant that he would yell from the stalls, 'I tell you to take your hat off on this word, not that word!' I also remember him striding down the centre aisle of the Olivier, probably after the revolving stage had broken, saying, 'If this is not repaired, I will make such a stunk in the newspapers!' He had this wonderful method which was known as 'I pay.' If he asked for something and the theatre said, 'I'm afraid we can't afford it,' he'd say, 'Don't worry! I pay!' Of course, he never did pay, and he always got it, so it was a very expensive undertaking. It was one of the first plays into the Olivier, and it was mounted on a scale which, apart from Trevor Nunn's musicals, hasn't been seen at the National since. There was a hugely elaborate set, there was a cast of about forty, and there was a live orchestra playing in the pit; but it was also a huge success, an extraordinarily good production, and the first unknown play to really take off there. In fact, the Horváth estate wanted to give me the exclusive right to translate his plays and said that they would stop anyone else from doing them, but I said I was absolutely opposed to any restriction of that kind, which bewildered them because they thought they were making me a great gift. But I never wanted to be *the* Horváth translator; I was just glad to have introduced a writer whom few people knew about – certainly in English-speaking countries. I feel that was a real achievement.

In the preface to Faith, Hope and Charity, *he says, 'As in all my plays, I have neither prettified nor disfigured.' Would you say the same about your plays?*

I take that to be my main task, to describe things as they are, and it's actually a very difficult task. It's an abiding problem that you don't want to caricature people but some people insist on behaving like caricatures, and it's a problem that you have to think your way out of, because it's too easy to make fun of people's weaknesses or eccentricities. In *Tales from Hollywood*, when Horváth first talks to his girlfriend and tries to explain what kind of writer he is, because she's never heard of him or read any of his plays, he says, 'I know the people, how terrible they are, and still I like them,' whereas caricature always implies something judgmental.

The preface continues, 'I have also tried to be as disrespectful as possible towards stupidity and lies,' and lies are what Tales from the Vienna Woods *is all about: the way nostalgia and sentimentality allow people to ignore the way things really are.*

That's right. Everyone's always bursting into song and embracing each other and slobbering about Vienna. It's a terrifying moment when they start playing 'Deutschland über Alles' in the nightclub and people stand up and salute. The play was written in 1930, so it's very prescient, but it's also very unpreachy. It simply says, 'This is what it was like,' but you can see exactly what's going to happen a few years down the line: how people lazily adopt prejudices instead of thinking carefully about things, and how that leads to inhumanity. The epigraph of *Tales from the Vienna Woods*, which I imagine is a line of Horváth's, says, 'Nothing gives as strong an impression of infinity as stupidity,' and that's a wonderfully true notion, I think.

Of the three Horváth plays you've translated, Tales from the Vienna Woods *is by far the most complicated.* Don Juan Comes Back from the War *and* Faith, Hope and Charity *are very spare by comparison.*

I think he was finding his voice in the early plays, then there are four plays in the late twenties and early thirties which represent what we think of as mature-period Horváth: *Italian Night*, about the Nazis and a Republican group in Munich both hiring the same room on the same night; *Tales from the Vienna Woods*; *Kasimir and Karoline*, an enormously complicated play, which Howard Davies and I have always wanted to do, set in a fairground during the Oktoberfest; and *Faith, Hope and Charity*, a deliberately small play – although there are a lot of characters in it – in which he refined his method to a kind of shorthand. *Tales from the Vienna Woods* is probably the best, though, and the peak of his career, really. It was done in the big theatre in Berlin, with Peter Lorre and Carola Neher in the leading roles, whereas *Faith, Hope and Charity* closed in the middle of rehearsals in 1933, and he never had a play put on again. His later plays, like *Don Juan Comes Back from the War*, have a totally different style, in which he's taking semi-mythical themes and running them through his sensibility – and, you sense, writing them very quickly, in a fairly desperate state, not expecting to have them put on. But there's something about that sensibility I find very sympathetic.

Why did you choose to translate one of his later plays next?

Peter Hall's plan was to do a *Don Juan* season. They were going to do *Don Giovanni*, then they were going to do Molière's play, also in my translation, and then they were going to do the Horváth, but it all went wrong and they wound up only doing the Horváth. It was one of those brave schemes which just crumbled. I was keen to do it, but I wouldn't have chosen it myself – although it is an interesting contrast to *Tales from the Vienna Woods*. I think of it as the male flip side of Wedekind's *Lulu*, except that *Lulu* is so unwieldy that it never quite delivers the goods, whereas this is more crafted and somehow works. It's a version of *Don Juan* where he's the pursued rather than the pursuer, which may be how Horváth felt at the time. He loved women – and women loved him – and the idea of writing a play with one man and thirty-five women must have seemed irresistible. And, in fact, it's by far the most performed of his plays. I suppose it's the simplest to mount, but people are also very taken by this idea of putting on a play with lots of women in it. We more or less followed Horváth's scheme and did it with about twelve playing the thirty-five.

A man who comes back from the front with a genuine desire to mend his ways, but who isn't allowed to, seems very symbolic of Europe between the wars.

Horváth eventually – very successfully – took to writing novels, and *Don Juan Comes Back from the War* is a companion piece, in a way, to a book called *A Child of Our Time*, about an unemployed veteran who, for perfectly understandable reasons, drifts into being a Nazi. The difference is that, in *A Child of Our Time*, the character comes to his senses, and the book ends with him murdering this Nazi dwarf and throwing his body in the river, whereas *Don Juan Comes Back from the War* is about a society in such complete breakdown that all the normal ways of conducting your life go out the window. But they both have the same kind of resonance.

Horváth not only shares his love of the ladies with Don Juan, but also his wanderlust – or exile.

Horváth never lived anywhere, he just drifted for years from one hotel to another. He supported himself during those years by writing film scripts, and by and large that took place in Berlin, so I guess he was there quite a lot at that time, but he was always an outsider. He'd been to school in Germany for a sufficient amount of his childhood to be able to pass as German, but he wasn't, which makes it even stranger that he chose to stay there when almost every other writer of his temperament got out.

His character admits in Tales from Hollywood *that he has 'a taste for the bizarre and the ridiculous', and I imagine that Germany in the thirties would have provided those things in abundance.*

That was my diagnosis in *Tales from Hollywood*, and I'm sure it was right. A side of him absolutely loved that kind of thing, and the solemnity of the Nazis, combined with their complete stupidity, must have tickled him in some reprehensible way. There's a story I ought to tell you about Horváth, which is very characteristic. He was buried in Paris, because that's where the tree fell on him, but in 1988, which was the fiftieth anniversary of his death, the Austrian authorities decided that he should be given a state funeral in Vienna. His French translator – thank God it wasn't me – was deputed to go and reclaim his body from the cemetery, and when he arrived they said, 'He was in a cheap coffin and the whole thing had rotted . . . But here he is,' and handed him a carrier bag with a bunch of bones in it. He went home, very freaked out, and called the Austrians, who said, 'Will you bring him back for the funeral?' He said, 'But he's in this carrier bag,' and they said, 'That's fine. Bring the carrier bag.'

So he goes to Charles de Gaulle, where he has terrible trouble checking in, gets on the plane, where they make him put the bag in the overhead compartment, and eventually arrives in Vienna, where no one is at the airport to meet him. It's pissing with rain and the carrier bag is starting to get wet, but he knows he's supposed to be staying at the Hilton; so he gets into a taxi, goes to the Hilton, gives his name at the desk, and they look down the list and say, 'I'm very sorry, but we don't have a reservation for you and the hotel is fully booked.' Now he doesn't know *what* the fuck to do, so he says, 'But I'm here with the remains of Herr Horváth!' and they say 'Ah, Horváth! We *do* have a reservation.' And the story goes that he took this bag of bones upstairs, installed it in the room and then ran for it. There was another tremendous cock-up on the day of the reinterment, which I've forgotten the details of now, but it seems that to the very end Horváth was embroiled in grotesque and ludicrous happenings.

How was Don Juan Comes Back from the War *received, compared to* Tales from the Vienna Woods?

For some reason, the play works much better in performance than it looks as if it will when you read it, so, after a rather troubled rehearsal period, the whole thing went like a dream. Daniel Massey was wonderful in the part and the play got great reviews – almost better than *Tales from the Vienna Woods* – and one of my enduring theatrical memories is of Dan sitting against the tombstone at the end with the snow falling. But, because of the way it was looking in rehearsals, it had been scheduled for very few performances – which was extremely frustrating.

You didn't have much luck with Faith, Hope and Charity, *either.*

No. Between 1977, when *Tales from the Vienna Woods* opened, and 1989, when we did *Faith, Hope and Charity*, there was, as I said, a real change in the theatre, and the audience for those out-of-the-way plays had disappeared. We did it at the Lyric, Hammersmith, with Julia Ormond – it was the first thing she was in, and we decided to take a chance on her, and she was absolutely great – but no one came to see it.

A story about a woman who's just trying to make ends meet in a repressive society couldn't have been more relevant at the time: the Thatcherite eighties.

I certainly felt that. It's like an Edward Bond play or a Fassbinder film. Fassbinder's films – his middle-period, top-quality films – are unimaginable without the influence of Horváth, and *Faith, Hope and Charity* is like a Fassbinder film written in the thirties. He wrote it as a result of a challenge by a friend, who showed him a paragraph in a local paper about a suicide and said, 'This is the kind of thing you should be writing about.' In fact, most of his best plays have a woman at the centre, or say that the only decent, clear-minded people are women – although he doesn't sentimentalize them.

The grandmother in Tales from the Vienna Woods *is anything but. She deliberately allows a baby to catch pneumonia, and when confronted with the crime her reaction typifies something which runs through that play: the more in the wrong someone is, the more self-righteous they become.*

I think that's a very accurate and lifelike observation. He certainly understands things like that.

Between Treats *in 1975 and* Tales from Hollywood *in 1981, you wrote nothing but translations and screenplays. That's quite a long time for a playwright to be . . .*

. . . not writing a play. Well, it was exactly five years from the time *Treats* was on to the time I started work on *Tales from Hollywood*, and during those five years, I worried a lot about whether I should be writing plays; but, of course, when I came to write *Tales from Hollywood*, I was able to *use* the energy of not having written for five years. V. S. Naipaul says in an introduction somewhere, 'For five years no novel suggested itself,' which is absolutely what the process is. It's no good – or at least it doesn't work for me – sitting down and thinking, 'I must write a play.' It either happens or it doesn't.

So how did Tales from Hollywood *suggest itself?*

Ken Brecher, who by then was second-in-command at the Mark Taper Forum, called me and asked if I'd like to take part in their big project for 1982, which was the 150th anniversary of the founding of Los Angeles. The theatre was commissioning six plays to celebrate, and the only requirement was that they be set there. He then read me a list of suggested topics, one of which was European émigrés in California, and I said, 'Stop.' I'd always been fascinated by notions of exile and homesickness, because of my childhood experience of being a kind of émigré everywhere we went, and I'd also read a book by Nigel Hamilton called *The Brothers Mann*, which I'd thought would make a very interesting subject for a play; so I said I'd specifically like to write about German émigrés in Hollywood during the Second World War, and the Mark Taper said, 'Fine.'

In the same way that Horváth may have stayed in Germany because he relished the absurdity of it, you seem to find Hollywood endlessly . . .

. . . fascinating. Well, it is. The medieval codes of behaviour are absolutely incredible. It's more subject to the quiverings of status than the court of Louis XIV. Funnily enough, although it's a company town in quite a narrow way, I got to know it through working in the theatre, rehearsing *Savages* at the Mark Taper. My longest stay there has been ten weeks, with my family, researching and writing *Tales from Hollywood*, followed by another six or seven weeks the year after, again with my family, during the rehearsals and up to the opening. But my film work in Hollywood has been more in the nature of smash-and-grab, apart from the short stint of post-production I did on *Imagining Argentina*. As I'm not a car person it's not really my town, but I look forward to going there for meetings, and they've been very good to me over the years, especially in terms of paying me for stuff. In fact, I feel bad that they've paid me for a lot of stuff which they then haven't made, which I think is a complete waste of money – but they don't seem to mind.

You said that you disliked manipulating historical events, but in order for Horváth to be the narrator of the play, you had to make him sidestep the falling branch which killed him.

When I started it, the play was going to be about Brecht and the Manns and so on, but I needed a linking device, and the idea of making Horváth the central character solved everything. It just went off like a firework in my head, in the same way that finding out about Otto Gross, a minor character in *The Talking Cure*, unlocked that play for me. In a curious way, you have to wait for the piece of work to tell you what to do. You can work out a structure or a list of scenes – in the case of *Tales from Hollywood*, I drew a giant plan of when everyone arrived in America – but you have to allow the characters to take you by surprise and say, 'You ought to go this way.' It's difficult to talk about this subject without making it sound like a load of bullshit, but unless you stay open to what happens when you're writing the words on the page you're certain to wind up with something unsatisfying. Something I could never have invented, though, was the discovery that Heinrich Mann's wife, Nelly, was actually Jewish – which made the fact of her anti-Semitism even more psychologically interesting and meant that the rest of her behaviour, the drinking and the suicide attempts and the self-hatred, all fell into place. As a writer, that's the kind of thing you're looking for.

To what extent is Horváth, as depicted in the play, a version of yourself?

To a great extent, I suppose. I do feel he was a kindred spirit, and in the extension I gave him beyond his lifetime most of the experiences he has are mine: the business about writing a film of *Edward II*, for example, and even the business at the end about cracking his head open on the steps of the producer's swimming pool, which actually happened to me on my first visit to Hollywood.

And, in turn, echoes the opening of Sunset Boulevard.

That's right. Also, I was thirty-five when I wrote *Tales from Hollywood*, and I was very conscious that Horváth died when he was thirty-six.

He's like a lot of characters in your work – Philip in The Philanthropist, *for example – in that he's a watcher, not a doer.*

That's the writer's position. I've always tried not to write autobiographically, because writers who can only find material in their own lives tend to find that the material dries up sooner rather than later, but there's a spiritual autobiography in many of the plays to do with the writer's life. It's the only life I have, I know no other, so, however various I try to be, there are inevitably certain themes which keep cropping up.

The clash between a liberal and a radical, for example, who in this case take the shape of Horváth and Brecht. In fact, there's a scene where Brecht says, 'It's not enough just to interpret the world any more, you have to change it,' and Horváth replies, 'People are being told what to do all day, they want to be told what they are,' which sums up their positions.

David Hare advised me to cut those lines on the grounds that they were obvious, and I can see his point, but those stark alternatives were really what the play was about. We'd just been through a decade when it was very much the thing to announce your intention to change the world in the plays you wrote, which is one of the reasons why I wasn't writing much during that time. It wasn't that I was unsympathetic to what those plays

82

were saying, it was simply that it didn't suit my temperament to write them, and I imagine that if Horváth had had a row with Brecht, that's exactly what Horváth would have said in his defence. In fact, if you read Brecht's letters and diaries, thousands of pages of opinions on every subject you can think of, the one name he never mentions is Horváth, which I take to mean that he was the one writer Brecht was scared of.

He certainly isn't scared of Thomas Mann, who's even fonder of sitting on the fence than Horváth.

The case of Thomas Mann is very complicated. His personality was that of a man who had made the immensely difficult decision not to be gay but understood that a lot of the power in his work came from that very repression, and was therefore profoundly aware that not giving way to impulse was often the only way to achieve what needed to be achieved. On top of which, he was being told that he was a genius from the age of twenty-five – which he saw no reason to disbelieve – so he took himself immensely seriously, which is something that people used to beat him about the head with. I feel that he was a really admirable character, in the sense that he did a great deal for other émigrés from his position and realized that he shouldn't jeopardize that position. Also, he had the exasperating quality of almost always being right. He was the first person to broadcast publicly about the concentration camps. He was the first person to say, 'We shouldn't assume that this isn't the fault of the German people, because in a way it is.' And when McCarthyism started, even though he'd become an American citizen and intended to spend the rest of his life in America, he said, 'This is wrong,' and went back to Switzerland. But in the play, I presented him in the way he was actually seen, which caused outrage when it was first done in Germany. There was a huge piece in the *Frankfurter Allgemeine Zeitung* called 'Defaming the Dead', and the Brecht estate let it be known that if theatres did this play they wouldn't be likely to get any Brecht plays in the future. This is something which writers often suffer from, that the way your characters are presented is taken to be . . .

. . . the way you think about them.

83

Exactly. But the reason for Brecht coming on every five minutes and making jokes about Thomas Mann is that that was the way Brecht felt. One of the great problems of the intellectual life is that there's so much jealousy and backbiting, so much envy of other people's success and dislike of other people's opinions, that the sensible ideas which all these people have in common don't make the impact that they should. That's how Communist movements, in particular, have fallen in on themselves. They splinter into so many small, warring cabals that they either don't get anywhere or they fall prey to the ruthlessness of men with very simple ideas: put me in charge, I'll kill a few million people and then you'll be all right – or, rather, *I'll* be all right.

How was the play received?

For a start, the actors weren't terribly enthusiastic. They said, 'There are good things in it, and we'll do it,' but I think they were hoping for extensive rewrites which they never got. They got some, but not many. Then, by the time it was put on, almost a year later, the other five plays either hadn't been delivered or had been delivered and disliked, so, rather like the story of the three *Don Juans*, the only play put on to celebrate 150 years in the history of Los Angeles was a play in which character after character came staggering onto the stage saying, 'I can't bear another minute in this shithole!' And it was taken rather personally. It was very badly reviewed by the *Los Angeles Times*, who said the play was 'as shapeless as California itself'. Fortunately, at the same time as it was being mounted in Los Angeles, it went into the National Theatre, and there was a modest feeding frenzy about who was going to direct it, so at least I knew that *they* liked it.

You said that the Mark Taper got some rewrites, but not many. What were they?

One thing I did rework was Horváth's relationship with the blacklisted writer, which I didn't think was as sharp as it was meant to be. The scene I particularly remember rewriting was the scene on the beach towards the beginning of the second act. Until then I'd been skirting around the edges of it, so I decided that what they should be having was an ideological discussion.

What she says to him is a variation on what Brecht says to him, except that Brecht says it in terms of art and she says it in terms of . . .

. . . politics. That's right. I didn't want to give Horváth too easy a ride, really, so I needed to have someone attack the same argument from a different angle, a more sympathetic angle, and I think that in that argument you side with her rather than him – in so far as you side with anyone, since I try not to do anything but ask the questions.

Who was involved in the directorial feeding frenzy at the National?

David Hare liked the play very much and wanted to direct it, but I chose to go with Peter Gill, because I had a longstanding promise to give him a play. We had a terrific cast, too. Ian McDiarmid was great as Brecht. Billie Whitelaw was wonderful as Nelly. And Michael Gambon gave a *tour de force* performance as Horváth. At the beginning of the play, he strolled onto the stage – this vast sky-blue expanse with a ripple effect across it, designed by Alison Chitty – walked down to the front, looked around at the audience and then said, 'Hello,' as if he was just talking to a couple of people. It was brilliant the way he did it, without a hint of self-consciousness.

What did you make of the 2001 revival, directed by John Crowley?

I loved it. In fact, I was so pleased with it that it gave me the impetus to go off and write *The Talking Cure*. I was delighted with how well the play had lasted and how well the production worked, in terms of its size and scale. The Mark Taper has 750 seats, and the Olivier has 1,100, so to do it in the Donmar, which only has 200-odd, required a radically different approach. I also thought Ben Daniels was very good as Horváth – and Phil Davis was a brilliant piece of casting as Brecht. He's a terrific actor but he's mainly a director now, and he told me he hadn't done anything on stage for years.

There was also a television version of it, wasn't there?

Yes. It was directed by Howard Davies – his first television production – and had a very starry cast: Jeremy Irons as Horváth, Sinead Cusack as Nelly, Jack Shepherd as Brecht and Alec Guinness as Heinrich Mann.

I saw it a long time ago, and the scenes which stick in my mind are the ones where Brecht argues with Horváth.

I didn't think those scenes worked very well on television, because they're essentially discussions about the theatre. It wasn't as powerful or amusing as Brecht coming onto the stage in the theatre and complaining about the kind of play it is. But, given that it was so poorly received on its first outing, its afterlife has been very satisfying. Several of the notices for the revival seemed to imply that it was my best play.

It does bring together many of your favourite themes.

Yes. And, as I said, I think a lot of that was due to the fact that I hadn't written a play for five years. It had all dammed up and just flowed out, in a way that I feared I'd lost after *Treats*.

Tales from Hollywood, *like* The Philanthropist *a decade earlier and 'Art' a decade later, won the Evening Standard Award for Best Comedy. Would you describe it as a comedy?*

It was slightly surprising to win Best Comedy for it, but I suppose formally it's a kind of comedy. You could describe it as tragedy replayed as farce – except that the farce in question, which was the House Un-American Activities Committee, destroyed a lot of people's lives. A lot of my plays begin as comedies and mutate in the course of the evening, because my instinct is that you have to welcome the audience in and make sure they're sitting comfortably before you can give them an adequate punch on the jaw.

{5}

*Ned Kelly – Edward II – The Great Gatsby – The Ten-
ant – A Temporary Life – The Moon and Sixpence –
Agatha – The Last Secret – The Honorary Consul –
The Florentines – The Price of Tea*

Your first screenplay, the adaptation of When Did You Last See
My Mother?, *wasn't made. Your second, a rewrite of* Ned Kelly,
*was made – but without your name on it. How did that come
about, and what was it like working with Tony Richardson?*

It was absolutely unforgettable. Tony Richardson, of course,
was this legendary figure who'd set up the Royal Court, but I
hadn't met him. At our first meeting he said, 'I'm voting for the
Oscars. It's very boring; I have to do it every year. I tell you what:
I'll go and buy some champagne and you can do it. You can vote
for anyone you like except Vanessa.' So he handed me this thing
and off he went, and I voted for the Oscars while he was buying
champagne. Anyway, he said he wanted to shoot this film in the
autumn and he'd had a lot of trouble with the script. I can't
remember who the original script was by, but then he'd commissioned a script from Edward Bond, and then he'd commissioned
a script from David Storey, and he pointed to this heap on the
floor and said, 'They're all dreadful! You've got to do better.
And you've got two weeks.' I was supposed to write it in the
south of France, where Tony owned this big farmhouse with a
lot of outbuildings which he'd bought using the proceeds of *Tom
Jones*, and I was met at Nice airport by his driver, a sinister thug
called Jan whom I'd seen at the meeting when Tony called him in
to open the champagne – which he did by inserting the cork in
the door and slamming it. He drove this open-top Mercedes at
about 100mph, and at one point *en route* there had obviously
been some appalling accident – there were smashed vehicles all
over the place, and blood and glass and lights and police – and
Jan put his foot on the accelerator and weaved his way through
all this, roaring with insane laughter at the mayhem on the road.

That was pretty much the experience of writing *Ned Kelly*, actually: one long car crash. I don't know whether it was my youth and inexperience, but I wasn't able to strike up any kind of rapport with Tony. He didn't seem to take much interest in what was in the script and what wasn't in the script. He had a constant house party going, with all kinds of people passing through. I was given a small cottage in the far corner of this little square, and the main difficulty was finding time to write. The first evening I was there, Tony said that after dinner there would be games, but he knew there was nothing more awful than being made to play games when you didn't want to, so I was perfectly free to do what I liked. He then described this horrifying-sounding game – which was, in fact, charades – and I said, 'No, I think I'll get on with my work. I don't really want to do this.' He said, 'But you must! Don't worry, we'll give you something easy,' and the first title they gave me was *Martin Chuzzlewit*. Then someone in our team suggested that we give the other team *Total Eclipse*, and Tony said, 'You can't do that! Nobody's ever heard of it!' At the time it seemed like he was being wilfully sadistic, but that may just have been my youthful sensitivities. At the end of it all, I finished the script the night before I was due to leave. Tony ran his eye over it and said, 'Can you go to Australia in the summer?' and I said, 'Absolutely,' and was then sped back to the airport by Jan. And, of course, I never heard from him again. In fact, I never even *met* him again.

Was any of your work used in the finished film?

It certainly was. My brother and I went to see it at the London Pavilion, paying for our own tickets, and a good chunk of it, I'm ashamed to say, was taken from my script – but, in an uncharacteristic act of mercy, Tony hadn't given me a credit. It was credited to Tony himself and an Australian writer, Ian Jones, and they'd obviously taken my script and worked on it. They'd given it a kind of ballad structure, with a 'Ballad of Ned Kelly' strung through it like a Frankie Laine number, but nevertheless my brother kept saying, 'That sounds like one of your lines.' I never knew Mick Jagger was going to be in it, because Tony would never tell me. He said, 'It's such interesting casting,' and I said, 'Who is it?' and he said, 'That's for me to know and you to find out.' But, years later, accidentally upgraded to the Concorde, I was thinking I had an empty seat next to me, when, at the last minute, someone was hustled on – and it was Mick Jagger. I thought, 'I won't bother him. The poor bugger must spend his whole life fending off strangers,' so I said nothing and just read my book. Then lunch arrived, and the first course was fruit, including a bunch of absolutely tiny blackcurrants, and Mick Jagger picked up these blackcurrants, turned to me and said, 'What are you supposed to do with these?' To which I replied, 'I once wrote a movie you were in.' And we then had a very nice conversation for the rest of the trip. So that was *Ned Kelly*.

Did you learn anything from working on it?

Absolutely nothing – except to be circumspect, really; to keep my head down and my mouth shut in these circumstances, which were evidently rife in the industry.

Something confirmed by your next film project, Edward II, *an experience so bizarre that, as you said, you gave it to Horváth in* Tales from Hollywood.

That's right. Ian McKellen had just made his name in two great productions of *Richard II* and *Edward II*, and the director Douglas Hickox had the notion of doing a film based on *Edward II*. This was the late sixties and London was full of independent producers with projects of one sort or another, so I was hired, again for two weeks, to write the screenplay. The production of *Edward II* was a revelation for me, because I'd read it but I hadn't seen it, so I didn't know how well it worked on stage. In writing the screenplay, I tried to do what Kenneth Branagh did to *Henry V*, which was to make it filmic; but it was based pretty closely on the play, and the dialogue was the dialogue of the play, and so on.

I was then told to report to a house in Eaton Square and was shown into the basement, where I found this producer glowering at me. As I entered the room, he left it; then he came back in with a big black folder, which he hurled across the room and said, 'What the fuck do you think that is?' I picked it up and said, 'Goodness, it's my script.' He said, 'Script? You wouldn't even get that on fucking television!' He then went into this screaming diatribe, and it was clear that he'd neither read the play nor seen it, because he was appalled to discover that it was in verse, and even more appalled to discover that the King of England was gay. He said, 'Have you any idea what kind of shit you've dropped me in? People are coming from the coast. How can I show them this piece of shit?' In the middle of this tirade, Douglas was shown into the room, but the guy kept yelling at me. Finally, Douglas piped up and said, 'I don't think you're being very fair to Christopher,' whereupon the guy said, 'You can shut up. You're fired as well.' It's curious, because I wasn't at all upset. I didn't feel as if I'd failed some important test; I just felt that the producer and I were coming from such different universes that this kind of thing was inevitable.

Presumably you didn't feel that way about Jack Clayton, for whom you wrote one screenplay, The Tenant, *and rewrote another,* The Great Gatsby?

When Jack called me out of the blue and asked if I'd like to do a screenplay of *The Great Gatsby*, I said I'd give my right arm to do it – which would have been fine, since the other arm is the one I use for writing – because, at the time, F. Scott Fitzgerald was one of my favourite novelists, and, at least in its plot, *The Great Gatsby* is pretty much the perfect novel. Of course, that's probably why you ought to leave it alone, but to me it seemed like the job of the decade. Then, about a month later, Jack called me in the middle of the night – because he hadn't worked out the time difference in California – and said, 'I'm afraid there's a problem.' I said, 'What's that?' He said, 'Robert Evans has never heard of you.' I said, 'That's all right. I've never heard of him.' He said, 'He's the boss of Paramount and he doesn't want you. He wants a name writer.' So that was a terrible blow. I hadn't actually started writing it, but I had done what I later did with *Schindler's List*, which is work out exactly how I was *going* to write it, so it was very disappointing to have it taken away from me. Eventually, Francis Ford Coppola wrote the screenplay, which was good but very long, and the ending was rather botched, I think. But, because Coppola was then unavailable, Jack hired me himself, under the counter, for a couple of weeks, and I rewrote the ending, I rewrote most of the scenes between

Karen Black and Scott Wilson – Myrtle and the garage owner who kills Gatsby – and I rewrote a lot of the voice-over, because Coppola – as I might do myself now – had tried to skew it away from the point of view of the narrator, Nick Carraway, and Jack wanted to restore that.

I think the film is pretty good, but Jack had a tremendously difficult time making it. Something which often happens with the studios is that by a process of attrition you wind up doing precisely the opposite of what you wanted to do. For example, he was quite happy to cast well-known actors in all the other parts but he really wanted to cast an unknown as Gatsby, largely because of that one scene where everyone is talking about him and this man is sitting at the head of the table saying nothing – and that man is Gatsby, which ought to be as much a surprise for the audience as it is for the reader, according to Jack. Instead, he was coerced into casting a well-known actor as Gatsby – Robert Redford, whom he actually liked very much – and casting unknowns in all the other parts. Also, an interesting thing happened to the film which I've never observed quite so clearly since, although people often talk about this phenomenon. The first cut I saw was something like three hours and ten minutes, and I thought it was absolutely magnificent, but then Paramount made Jack cut it to two hours forty – and it seemed tremendously long at two hours forty, whereas it hadn't at three hours ten. Cutting that half hour just buggered the rhythms, which is very strange.

I watch the film whenever it's on TV, but it never recovered from the initial critical drubbing it got. At the opening in London, I was sitting right behind Jack, who was extremely nervous, and that thing you dread happened, which is that the film broke down. Beforehand, someone had given him a red rose, and when the lights came up, Jack had gone but there were rose petals all over the floor. There was then a huge party at the Savoy, where he drank a lot of brandy and got very irascible with someone from Paramount – which ended in a punch-up, as I remember. He was an extremely sympathetic and very quiet man, but he did have this volcanic temper. On another occasion, in the headquarters of Gulf + Western, who owned Paramount, he famously picked up a metal chair and smashed it through a glass table in order to get the attention of the head of Gulf + Western, Charlie Bluhdorn. Jack subsequently asked me to write this thing called *The Tenant*, which was a straight-up-and-down horror film, from a French novel by a Polish émigré cartoonist called Roland Topor, about a man who starts to imagine things because he's so lonely and unhappy.

A bit like Repulsion *with a man?*

Exactly. That's why it was extremely careless of Jack to leave the script lying around at Paramount, because one day Roman Polanski walked in, picked it up and said, 'I know this novelist. He's a friend of mine,' and they said, 'Jack Clayton's doing it,' and he said, 'No, I'll do this' – and nine weeks later they were shooting it with a completely new script by his regular collaborator, Gérard Brach, and produced a film about as diametrically opposite to what Jack and I had in mind as you could possibly imagine. It wasn't bad, but it was extremely peculiar. The funny thing is that I probably thought about *Repulsion* quite a lot when I was writing it, but Polanski's film wasn't a bit like *Repulsion*. Jack was a master of menace and unease, though, and the one film like that which he did make, *The Innocents*, was very scary and beautifully shot. It's a tragedy that he didn't make more films than he did. He got a terrible dose of glandular fever when he was making a film called *Something Wicked This Way Comes* for Disney, and he hardly did anything after that – except two terrific films with Maggie Smith, *The Lonely Passion of Judith Hearne* and *Memento Mori*. He was extremely fastidious, Jack; everything was very carefully thought through.

You worked with several major directors who boasted an extremely fastidious style: Jack Clayton, Fred Zinnemann, David Lean. Is that because it suits your own style?

Not particularly, but its necessity was borne in on me by working with them. Also, they were fastidious about different things. With Fred, it was the way each event prepared you for the next event – what I used to call the 'narrative juggernaut' – whereas David was particularly interested in the arrangement of scenes, like an editor. I think Jack worked more on instinct than they did. They were better at intellectualizing – although 'intellectualizing' is a word which David would have been horrified by – exactly what they wanted and why, whereas Jack was more in the Stephen Frears mould: 'There's something wrong with this. I don't know what it is, but there's something wrong with it.' Which is fine, as long as they're right. Exasperating, but fine. I've found that directors who are trying to do something profound often can't express it very easily, because what they're trying to do isn't easily expressible, but you'll also find that they're more reliable than the ones with the glib answers. I wouldn't say that Jack was inarticulate, but he wasn't very clear in conversation, yet it was he who taught me to pay attention to every detail, whereas before I'd slightly blurred my way through writing films.

In fact, you've described your adaptation of David Storey's novel A Temporary Life *as your first proper screenplay. What made that one so different?*

It was the first screenplay I wrote which did exactly what I had in mind. The plays usually managed to shape themselves into the right form, but the screenplays always tended to slip out of my grasp, so I was really pleased with this one when I'd finished it. I wrote it very quickly and with great enjoyment.

What did you have in mind when you wrote it?

I liked its anarchy, its uncompromisingness. Outsiderdom was one of the real themes of the age, although I can see now that it was at the fag-end of that age, and whatever it was that started with Jimmy Porter was very much what one felt growing up at the time. There was such a lot of pressure in the late fifties and early sixties to cut your hair and put on your tie and shine your shoes and shut the fuck up, and this seemed to be a particularly strong example of someone turning their back on all that. Lindsay Anderson, who directed David's plays at the Royal Court, was thinking of doing it with Malcolm McDowell, which would have been terrific. I thought Lindsay's *This Sporting Life* was *the* great British film of the sixties, which was one of those rare periods in British cinema when our usual insularity has been turned to advantage. I also thought Malcolm was perfect for this part, but for some reason Lindsay withdrew, and I think the decisive factor was that David didn't really like it – that is to say, he didn't really like the book, and was very ambivalent about the idea of it being perpetuated as a film. Many years later, when Michael Wearing was at the BBC, he thought he'd do it on television, and I remember having the same weird quarrel with David all over again: him saying, 'You don't want to do this. It's not very good. I never got it right,' and me saying that it was much better than he thought it was.

How did you set about adapting the novel? Did you keep it beside you all the time, or did you read it and then forget about it?

I kept it beside me, because I liked it so much that I didn't think there was any point in straying from it. David's dialogue is so good that you improve upon it at your peril. In fact, one of the things which David said to me, rather dismayed, was: 'You've been so faithful!'

But you followed it up with a much less faithful adaptation – Somerset Maugham's The Moon and Sixpence.

The Moon and Sixpence is one of the freest adaptations I've done, because I didn't really approve of Somerset Maugham's take on Gauguin. I approved of his narrative skill but not of his attitude to the Gauguin character, Strickland, which was the attitude of a moderate man's dismay in the face of something extreme – so I decided to do two things. The first was to make the end of the screenplay resemble far more closely the life of Gauguin, because for me the interesting thing about Gauguin was that after a lifetime of contempt for all known forms of human society he really did find a cause in Tahiti and subsequently in the Marquesas, defending the rights of the indigenous people against the brutalities of the colonialist regime. In my view, it's no coincidence that this is the period of his work which now we know and respond to best, because some new element came into his life and infused the painting, and I wanted to deal with that.

The second thing I did was take certain elements of Somerset Maugham's life and merge them with the character of the writer, Ashenden, in order to involve the character in the story rather than have him be a colourless narrative voice – which is what he was in Albert Lewin's film in the forties. In other words, the screenplay tries to move the novel in the direction of these artists' lives, so that, because success is very important to Ashenden, whereas Strickland literally doesn't give a damn, it becomes a story about a businessman who turns into an artist, and an artist who gradually turns into a businessman. I recently met with Somerset Maugham's grandson, who asked if I'd contemplate a slightly more sympathetic – or, at least, slightly less *un*sympathetic – portrayal of his grandfather, although he understood that I was just trying to impose a dramatic shape on the material, not say that Somerset Maugham was a bad man. I don't see Strickland as a very sympathetic character either, except in his dedication to his vocation and in this fascinating conversion which came over him at the end of his life. Before that, he's a monster.

It's obviously a project you're very fond of. Has it ever come close to being made?

I first adapted it for Maximilian Schell to direct, whom I'd just worked with on *Tales from the Vienna Woods,* and his notion was to do it with Richard Burton and Michael York. It was all announced and everything – although I was a bit worried that I hadn't been paid – but then the whole thing collapsed because some German tax-shelter money – a phrase which now strikes dread into my heart – never materialized. So *no one* was paid. Then, a few years ago, the producer Serge Silberman, whom I'd met while writing *Nostromo,* wanted to work with me on something else, so I gave him *The Moon and Sixpence,* which he liked very much. He paid quite a lot of money to some lawyers in South Carolina, who seemed to own the remake rights to the MGM film, but we were then contacted by the Royal Literary Fund, who said that they owned the British and Commonwealth rights. By this time, of course, we'd done all the recces, we'd decided to shoot in Paris, Hamburg – standing in for London – and Hawaii, and we'd cast Alan Rickman, Jeremy Northam, Irene Jacob and Timothy Spall. And we're still trying to sort it all out. But it's a film I'd love to make.

You've only worked uncredited on three screenplays: Ned Kelly, The Great Gatsby *and* Agatha. *What was your brief on* Agatha?

Again, I was hired for two weeks – the last two weeks, in fact – and my job was largely technical. Kathleen Tynan had written the original script, but she'd been replaced by Arthur Hopcraft. Then, when they snagged Dustin Hoffman to play the journalist, he'd brought in his own writer, Murray Schisgal, to write his dialogue. And by the time the director, Michael Apted, put in a call to me, they'd all fucked off, the plug was due to be pulled in two weeks and the script was an incoherent mess. I went and watched a rough assembly of what they'd got, and it looked ravishing because it was shot by Vittorio Storaro, and it had two enjoyable performances – from what appeared to be two completely different films – by Dustin Hoffman and Vanessa Redgrave, but the plot didn't really make sense, so my job was to connect the dots until it did.

Trying to do this in two weeks was daunting enough – they provided me with a make-up room at Shepperton, where I sat in one of those absurd dentist's chairs looking at a mirror and writing dialogue as fast as I could – but it soon became clear that the actors all had their own agendas. Vanessa Redgrave and Helen Morse had decided that there was a feminist angle to the story and were anxious to play that up, whereas Dustin was more interested in pressing the comedy button than anything else; so I was bounced from Vanessa's trailer, where you'd have to pop twenty pounds into a bucket to support the firemen's strike before you could go any further, to Dustin's trailer, where he'd be playing backgammon with his stand-in and saying to me, 'We don't want all this boring stuff about politics. We need to entertain. This is purely an entertainment piece.'

Dustin had a particularly lethal trick, which was to offer me a lift from the studio in his Daimler. We'd drive in stately fashion with the lights on in the back and pages of script being thrown around, and the moment I dreaded was when the Inn on the Park hove into view, because he'd often say, 'Drive on!' and you'd see the hotel sailing by and find yourself lost in central London, driving around for what seemed like hours on end. There was one morning where I was with him until four o'clock in the morning, then had an hour's sleep on his sofa before going back with him to the studio. But it was very good fun, and I was dazzled by his inventiveness. I liked him very much, but I imagine he could be pretty difficult to work with if you were a director.

In other words, you were writing for Dustin Hoffman first, Vanessa Redgrave second and Michael Apted a distant third?

That's about right. Apted was busy most of the time, and in any case he was a wreck because he'd had such a punishing time of it. The key to the whole thing was a scene between Vanessa Redgrave and Timothy Dalton, who was playing Agatha Christie's husband, but unfortunately I couldn't have a scene with him because he was off doing some other film, so there were certain aspects I wasn't able to deal with. In the end, Warners did pull the plug and Dustin sued them – and lost – because he wanted to shoot the scenes they hadn't had time for. The last thing I remember was going down to Shepperton and putting a lot of dialogue on a scene where you just saw the backs of people's heads, in order to make sense of some particularly complicated piece of business. All this was done for very little money, and when it was over I got a magnum of champagne from Dustin and a couple of tickets to the Twentieth Congress of the Fourth International from Vanessa.

The most ambitious film project you worked on during this period was a screenplay for Fred Zinnemann, The Last Secret, *about the so-called Lienz Cossacks, who fought for the Nazis and were shipped back to Stalin's death camps by the British when the war was over.*

That was an unapologetic epic, and I really enjoyed doing it. I'd love to have seen the resulting film. The story dealt with things which were unknown at the time, and that was very interesting. Who knew then – indeed who knows now? – that six weeks after the end of the war, British soldiers were banging people on the head, throwing them into cattle trucks and sending them to their deaths? That was not what the war was fought to achieve. The Cossacks did fight for the Nazis, but I think they were living in a time warp. They belonged to a kind of nineteenth-century guard of honour, and thought that if they fought for Hitler he'd give them back their native land. They followed this weird guy called General Kraznov, who was a novelist and a romantic – and a White Russian *par excellence*.

It was adapted from a book, wasn't it?

Yes, it was. With Fred's previous film, *Julia*, he'd basically lifted a few pages from Lillian Hellman's autobiography and blown it up into the movie, and he proposed that we use the same method on this. In fact, there were two books: *Victims of Yalta* by Nikolai Tolstoy, who was later sued and bankrupted by Lord Aldington over some allegations he made in a subsequent article, and *The Last Secret* by Nicholas Bethell. Fred met both authors and thought we'd be safer with *The Last Secret*, so I read the book and zeroed in on one particular incident. Then we interviewed all the witnesses we could find and constructed the screenplay from that. We had a very emotional day with a guy called Davies, the Welsh liaison officer who was obliged to carry out the deception of the Cossacks. He was a bank manager in Ebbw Vale, and at one stage we went all the way down there to find that he'd changed his mind and wouldn't see us, but Fred eventually managed to persuade him. We also had an extraordinary day with General Sir Horatius Murray, who was the retired Commander-in-Chief of NATO forces in Europe and the one guy who defied the order and told the Cossacks to head for the hills. He was living with his wife in a bedsit in Harrow-on-the-Hill – to Fred's amazement, who said that this was the only country in the world where someone who had given his nation such distinguished service would wind up without even a proper pension.

Finally, in a big hotel in the middle of the golf course at Carnoustie, a woman called Zoe Polanska told us how her entire class had been sent from Odessa to Auschwitz, sterilized – but not exterminated, because they weren't Jewish – and then moved to Dachau, from where she escaped, made her way to Italy, encountered this group of 50,000 Cossacks, assumed that they were also going back to Russia and discovered that that was the last thing they wanted to do. So that gave us a central character who was alone among this vast number of Russians in actually wanting to get back to Russia – and, in fact, never did get back, because she was so badly injured during the evacuation that they had to take her to hospital, where she fell in love with a Canadian doctor, married him and wound up living in Scotland. She sat there and wept and told us all this, and at the end of the day I said to Fred, 'I don't know what you think, but I think this is the story,' and he said, 'Absolutely.'

It was the first of those David Lean-style experiences: we wrote it and we rewrote it and we re-rewrote it until we got it to Fred's satisfaction. Even when the locations had been found and the casting was underway – Fred cast Nastassja Kinski, who was then about nineteen, as Zoe, and was going to cast Robert De Niro as the Russian liaison officer, Butlerov – we continued to work on the screenplay pretty much every day. When we were on location in Austria waiting to start shooting, we always had an 8.30 meeting in the hotel conference room and Fred was always waiting impatiently for us to arrive, but one morning he was five or ten minutes late. Everybody was very puzzled by this, then he came in and said [*German accent*], 'Pack your bags.' We all looked at him, amazed, and he said, 'They called me at one o'clock in the morning and cancelled the movie.' So we got into the cars and went to the airport and that was that. About six weeks later, he called me and said, 'We've been working for a long time on this, and I don't think you were paid enough.' I said, 'I was paid what the contract called for.' He said, 'I've spoken to Twentieth Century Fox, and I've convinced them.' And a couple of weeks after that, I got a cheque for $10,000 – which was quite a lot of money in those days. I can't imagine anyone else in the film business being as scrupulous as that. He was a man of enormous decency and integrity.

Why was *the film cancelled?*

There was a change of studio head at Fox, and the knee-jerk reaction of anyone who takes over a studio is to cancel all the previous guy's projects – and, once cancelled, they're not very easy to resuscitate. When the whole thing was over, Fred sent me a six-page short story by Kay Boyle and asked if I'd like to write a script based on it, but I couldn't really see how to do it and turned it down. That became his next film, *Five Days One Summer*, but it wasn't particularly successful and he never made another one. Whereas, I suspect, *The Last Secret* would have been very successful – or, at least, would have made an impact. Fred's entire family was killed in the concentration camps, so he felt this project would connect with that part of his past. Also, one of the few jobs he got during his early years in Hollywood was as an extra in *All Quiet on the Western Front*, which was a film he often referred to and enormously admired. At the beginning of the process, Alan Ladd Jr, who was then head of Fox, and his right-hand man, Jay Kanter, came to London and sat in a screening room in Soho and watched this incredibly bleak Hungarian television documentary about the subject; and when it was over, there was an enormously long silence, then Alan Ladd turned around and smiled at Fred and said, 'I'm so glad you're getting back into light entertainment!'

Did working with a major director like Fred Zinnemann make you all the more eager to write films, or did working for a year on something which didn't get made have the opposite effect?

I was very frustrated that the film wasn't made, but I'm afraid it made me more open to writing them. I could see the film so clearly in my mind, in a way that doesn't really happen with plays. In the theatre it's mainly words in your ear, whereas with cinema you're writing in pictures. I remember saying to Fred that we should end the film with this image of thousands of horses, and his eyes lighting up. I also remember looking for war-damaged locations in northern Italy, where there had been a huge earthquake, and Fred's mood getting better and better as we toured these ruined towns: 'This is wonderful! We don't have to build anything!' And I vividly remember standing at the top of a mountain pass in the Apennines, with Italy on one side and Austria on the other, and Fred saying, 'I think we'll do the opening scene here, and I think we'll put the camera here' – and he was looking straight at a sheer wall of rock. I said, 'Yes, and you can use this fantastic view here and you've got that fantastic view there,' and he said, 'The scenery is irrelevant. We're not doing a travelogue. We want to see the people.'

That was Fred's way. He was very impatient with anything which deviated from the thunderous advance of the narrative. We used to go to the cinema a lot – because I practically lived with him for a year – and one day we went to see *Days of Heaven*. At the end I said, 'Well, I thought that was wonderful,' and he said, 'No, it is so pretty you cannot follow the story!' He was very pernickety, Fred, and distrusted the audience more than I do. For example, I'd started the script with swarms of people marching down a road in the middle of Europe, and a caption saying something like, 'May 8th, 1945'. He said, 'Who are these people?' and I said, 'They're refugees,' and he said, 'You cannot expect the audience to know that. You have to explain it.' He believed in explaining everything. He didn't want there to be any hint of ambiguity. I still joke with Laura about things passing the Fred Zinnemann test, in terms of how fully and lucidly they're explained. *Memento* is the kind of film which would not have passed the Fred Zinnemann test, I think. Towards the end, his script was an absolute forest of notes. He had different coloured pencils for different sorts of notes, and he was always sitting in his office doodling with the blue pencil and saying, 'Is this quite clear?'

Not long ago, you received your first screen credit in several years for The Quiet American, *just as, after all these uncredited rewrites and unproduced screenplays, you received one for another Graham Greene adaptation,* The Honorary Consul. *What are your memories of that film?*

I had a bit of a shock when I read *The Honorary Consul*. At the time there was a production of *Savages* going on somewhere in Denmark, and I was invited to the opening and the last few days of rehearsal. On my way out, I bought this new Graham Greene book at the airport, started to read it on the plane and realized that he and I had both been writing about the kidnapping of an obscure consul in South America, which I found absolutely extraordinary. Cut to a few years later, and I get a call from Richard Lester, who said, 'Norma Heyman and I want to make a film of *The Honorary Consul*, and we thought you might like to write the script.' So I agreed to do it and worked with Dick and Norma for a while, then Dick decided *he* didn't want to do it. By this time, Richard Gere, who had just made *An Officer and a Gentleman* and was a very big star, was attached, so there was a lot of to-ing and fro-ing about who would direct it. Then *The*

Long Good Friday came out, and John MacKenzie seemed like a good idea. John is on record as saying that he didn't think the script was very good, which he certainly never conveyed to me, but at any rate I did some more work on it with him.

Then John and Norma went to Argentina to find locations, and narrowly avoided being interned when the Falklands war broke out, so it was clearly out of the question to shoot there. I remember going to a meeting in Los Angeles to discuss where we should shoot it instead, and Paul Bluhdorn, the son of Charlie Bluhdorn – the head of Gulf + Western, who still ran Paramount then – said completely out of the blue, 'We could always shoot it in Costa Rica.' John frowned and said, 'Why Costa Rica?' and Bluhdorn said, 'Because we own it.' They eventually settled on Mexico, but I wasn't present for any of the shooting. I was working for Franco Zeffirelli at the time, and now and again I'd get a call from Vera Cruz, but Franco's villa was so exquisitely designed that all the phones were in cupboards, so I'd have to stand in a cupboard to dictate changes over the phone.

John had a terrible time making the film. As soon as the rushes started coming in, Paramount started calling him at three in the morning and saying, 'Why has Richard Gere got a faggot accent?' At first he couldn't understand what they were getting at, then he realized that they meant he had an *English* accent – because the character was meant to be half-English. Then the editing process was pretty brutal. There were lots of drafts of the script, as there always are with films which actually get made, and from the first draft to the shooting script, the philosophical side was minimized and the action side was maximized – but not to the extent that it was in the finished film. They threw out anything which smacked of sensitivity or reflection. Then the composer was fired and Paul McCartney was brought in, who picked out something on the piano which was orchestrated by Stanley Myers. Finally, Paramount did a cunning thing: they changed the title to *Beyond the Limit*, they put out an extremely misleading trailer and they opened the film in seven or eight hundred cinemas simultaneously – it was one of the first films they opened wide, actually – and it made its money back on the first weekend. In fact, it made a considerable profit. All in all, it was pretty educational.

Not for Graham Greene, though.

No. He gave a long interview to the *Guardian* in which he denounced the whole enterprise, but if you read the article carefully it became clear that he hadn't actually seen the film. I kept asking, 'Can I meet Graham Greene?' and I kept being fobbed off, and the reason we were never introduced is that he had worked closely with a director called Peter Duffell on a previous version and was very annoyed when the thing was taken away from him – in the same way that I was very annoyed when Phil Joanou was taken off *A Bright Shining Lie.* You just think, 'Why are they doing this?' Michael Caine recounts in his autobiography that he was in the Savoy Grill and he saw Graham Greene, and Graham Greene said to him, 'Dreadful film, but you were very good.' But I was talking to Nicholas Shakespeare about *The Quiet American,* and I said, 'I don't know if Graham Greene would have liked it. He certainly didn't like *The Honorary Consul,*' and Nicholas said, 'Yes, he did.' I said, 'What do you mean?' He said, 'I did a series of interviews with him, and he said that *The Honorary Consul* was one of the best adaptations of his books there had ever been.' So there we are. I think *The Honorary Consul* was very close to Greene's heart, because in addition to the political aspect, which is also there in *The Quiet American,* it contains a great deal of his late thinking about religion – all of which I chose to ignore, because it was of no particular interest to me.

Whenever I see it, I rather enjoy it. I don't think Richard Gere was ideal casting, but he's perfectly good in it, and Michael Caine is wonderful in it. It doesn't have much atmosphere, though, and that's one thing you can't do to Graham Greene. *The Quiet American* has different problems, but it benefits from being shot in Vietnam, because Greene is like Conrad: you have to find a visual equivalent for that atmospheric prose, otherwise they're just stories which don't resonate in the way the books do. In that sense, the thing I was most pleased about with *The Honorary Consul* was my original opening. I was thinking about how to begin the film, and I decided to use the scene from the book where the doctor and the policeman meet on the banks of the river, then walk across the water on these floating logs and arrest an Indian who's sitting on a raft beside a dead body. It was a very atmospheric opening and no one had any objection to it, so they ordered $20,000 worth of logs, brought them overland to the location and took them out into the middle of the river – where they promptly sank. So now the opening scene of *The Honorary Consul* is just Richard Gere looking rather plaintively across the water, which is the only thing they could shoot because they didn't have any logs left.

The Honorary Consul and The Quiet American *are very similar stories: both involve a love triangle between a young man, an older British man and a foreign girl, both are set in an exotic location against a backdrop of political turmoil, and both deal with a conflict between a liberal and a radical, just like much of your own work. Is that why you're so drawn to Greene's novels?*

I just think that there's no other writer who's taken the central historical themes of his era and evaluated their moral aspects in such a lucid and entertaining way. Michael Caine's character in *The Quiet American* is equivalent to Richard Gere's character in *The Honorary Consul*, someone who's forced to take sides in the end, and I think the theme of a man anxious to distance himself from whatever happens to be the urgent cause of the day, but gradually finding that he can't go on maintaining that distance, is a very attractive theme for an audience. Rather like West in *Savages*, that character represents the audience, because he knows nothing about what's going on and runs through a whole gamut of emotions as he discovers the truth – which is always much more complex and much more dirty than you ever imagine it could be. In other words, you put the characters through all these hoops and see what they're made of in the end. At the end of *The Quiet American* the character makes a particularly courageous choice, whereas the character in *The Honorary Consul* is more morally removed and doesn't really want to get involved. To that extent, *The Quiet American* was easier to adapt than *The Honorary Consul*, but you're right, it is just a set of variations on the same theme – including the girl in the middle, who, in *The Quiet American*, prefers the older man, and, in *The Honorary Consul*, prefers the younger man, for clear reasons.

You've mentioned working with Franco Zeffirelli on a project called The Florentines. *What was that about?*

Franco approached me in the early eighties with the idea of doing a mini-series about Leonardo and Michelangelo, set against the democratic experiment in Florence at that particular time. They were the two most distinguished Florentine artists of the day, but for different reasons they had both left the city; and when the Medici were driven out, Leonardo came back from Milan and Michelangelo came back from Rome and they were asked to paint frescos at either end of the new democratic forum, the Sala Del Gran Consiglio. It was the only time that the two of them encountered each other, and although Michelangelo was the younger man he felt he was the greater artist and was very contemptuous of Leonardo. Leonardo was the character who interested me most, and Michelangelo interested Franco, and we had a fascinating conversation where he explained that, in his opinion, they represented two different kinds of homosexual: Leonardo was quite comfortable with being gay and looked for youth and beauty in a straightforward way, whereas Michelangelo was more tortured and masochistic and drawn to brawny working-class types. It's unprovable, but it seemed a very persuasive analysis of these two characters and, together with the underlying material about art and society, a very interesting basis for a television drama.

After a year, we had an eight-hour script, separated into four parts named after the four elements – one was called 'Earth', one was called 'Air', one was called 'Fire' and one was called 'Water' – and I was pretty pleased with the result. Franco put together a budget of something like $35 million – mostly from RAI Television, who'd financed *Jesus of Nazareth* – and we were going to ask Paul Scofield to play Leonardo and had a meeting with Robert De Niro about playing Michelangelo. Franco then called me from Los Angeles in great excitement and said, 'We don't want to make this for television. We have to make this as a movie,' and we subsequently spent God knows how long boiling the script down to three hours. In the end, I resigned and Robert Bolt was brought in. He did a version in three weeks, for which he was probably paid twice as much as I'd earned in the past year; then Franco did a version, and emerged with a script which I'd say was two thirds mine and one third his, with an opening sequence by Robert Bolt; then that was that, because at the time he couldn't raise the money to do it as a movie. But he kept asking me to come back and work on it, so eventually I introduced him to Martin Sherman, who did another version – and now all three of us are discussing getting together to come up with a definitive version.

Did you have a good working relationship with Zeffirelli?

I'm very fond of Franco, but I don't think his worst enemy would accuse him of being decisive. He's a designer of genius and a very talented theatre director, but let free among the infinite possibilities of cinema he can't always decide between possibility A and possibility Z. It wasn't particularly easy to focus on the work we were doing, either, because he held a ceaseless artistic open house at this beautiful villa in Positano. I took my children there for the summer and he had everyone from Placido Domingo to Gregory Peck trooping through, and sometimes things like that are more valuable and interesting than the work itself. My first meeting with him was rather endearing. He took me to the London première of the film he'd just finished, *Endless Love*, which was absolutely appalling. We watched it in one of those big cinemas in the West End, and after a while the audience started to get very restive, and then they started to laugh and catcall, and at the end Franco turned to me, shrugged and said [*Italian accent*], 'Well, we do better next time.' Which I thought was extremely stylish.

Your next foray into television led to one of the few unproduced original scripts in your résumé: The Price of Tea.

That was my big project for 1984. It was commissioned by Granada, and the director was a woman called Eva Koloukhova, a Czech refugee who had advised on one or two programmes and then directed a very good television film, *Enemy of the State*, about an émigré who'd escaped from Czechoslovakia and wound up in Cambridge. The original brief was to write a film about the American journalist who won a Pulitzer Prize for her stories about a ten-year-old heroin addict and was then discovered to have made the whole thing up. But I said, 'I'm not very interested in that, because her motive was ambition,' so Granada said, 'Well, is there anything else you'd like to do?' and what I wanted to do was something along the lines of *Savages*. I'd been following what was going on in Sri Lanka, the civil war between the Tamils and the Singhalese, and I wanted to write something with a female central character, which was of growing interest to me after *Carrington*; so I had the idea of a journalist for *Vogue* going to Sri Lanka on a luxury trip to write about the best hotels, and instead becoming embroiled in this civil war. Because of an encounter she has on the plane out with an executive from a tea company, she becomes convinced that the tea companies are disreputably involved in the situation, so someone who was going there for a completely frivolous purpose is radicalized by what has happened.

What was the situation, exactly?

The situation was that the Tamils, who were a minority in Sri Lanka, were favoured by the British and were therefore resented by the Singhalese – the classic colonial divide-and-rule – but at independence, in 1947, the Singhalese majority imposed its will and the Tamils suddenly found themselves to be second-class citizens. The worst victims were the plantation workers, who had been imported from Tamil Nadu, in India, in the late nineteeth and early twentieth centuries, and who, for some scandalous reason I could never discover, at the moment of independence were declared stateless. These workers were picking all the tea for the tea companies but were living in incredibly squalid conditions; their children weren't educated but were made to go and work full days in the fields from the age of seven or eight; and they were all working under draconian rules which said that if they didn't fill so many baskets of tea a day and if the baskets of tea didn't weigh so many pounds then they weren't paid anything – and they were in hock to the companies anyway. Whenever there was ethnic unrest in Sri Lanka, they were the ones who were set upon, because they had no means of fighting back, whereas the Tamils in the north-west and north-east, who were citizens of Sri Lanka, were well organized and had their own communities.

That was the background to the film. I spent a fascinating few weeks with Eva in this beautiful country, interviewing a lot of Singhalese in Colombo and a lot of Tamils in the north, then I came back and struggled with the script. I finally found it centring on a Sri Lankan doctor, who had set up various communes in and around the jungles of the north and then gone around the tea plantations saying to these destitute Tamil workers, 'Leave, and I'll give you two hectares of land and enough money to plant your crop for the year.' About 40,000 people left the plantations to take up this offer, and when the trouble started, in 1983, almost the first person to be arrested was this doctor, who was dragged off the largest of these communes and taken to prison in Colombo. A week later there was a riot in the prison, and when the riot died down he was found to have been killed – no one else, just him – and it seemed a fair bet that someone was behind the removal of this thorn in the side of the tea companies. So the plot of the film imagined the journalist stumbling upon all this, meeting the doctor and realizing that he's in danger, and the crucial plot point involved the fact that when all this blew up it came out of nowhere, and anyone in Sri Lanka who was a journalist was able to file stories with the *Guardian* or whoever. The script called for her to write an account of what the tea companies were doing without knowing whether the story is a hundred per cent true but thinking that, since the doctor is in danger, if she files it and it gets some international attention then it might have a positive effect and save someone's life – in which case, why would it matter whether the story was true or not? In other words, it turned into a backwards investigation of journalistic ethics.

Were you pleased with the screenplay?

I think there's a sense of strain, to do with marshalling all the things I'd discovered into this plot, but I was quite happy with it at the time, and I still look at it as one of the ones that got away. When I finished it, I went for a meeting with David Plowright, the Head of Drama at Granada, and he said, 'Our flagship programme is *World in Action*. We can't make a film which says that it doesn't matter whether journalists tell the truth or not. Can you change it?' I said, 'No. That's the heart of the story,' and he said, 'Then we won't be able to do it.' So I thought,

'Fine,' and sent it to the BBC – who snapped it up in a second. Christopher Morahan was going to direct it, and he started making arrangements to shoot it in Kerala, in south-west India, where he had just made *Jewel in the Crown*. This was a couple of years later, because it took all that time for it to bounce to and fro, and in the meantime Mrs Gandhi had been assassinated, and the Indians said, 'We can't give permission for you to make a film about ethnic violence. It's too provocative.' So they withdrew their permission, and it was never made. I decided not to write any more original scripts for television after that – although, of course, that's not a problem these days, because they no longer *want* anything original for television.

The Portage to San Cristobal of A.H. – Les Liaisons Dangereuses – Dangerous Liaisons – The Ginger Tree

Les Liaisons Dangereuses *wasn't your first stage adaptation of a novel. A couple of years earlier you'd adapted George Steiner's novel* The Portage to San Cristobal of A.H., *about a group of people bringing Hitler out of the jungles of South America to face an international court. How did that come about?*

Bernard Miles, who ran the Mermaid Theatre, called me and said, 'There's this novel by George Steiner, do you know it?' I said, 'I do, actually,' because I've always been interested in the Holocaust, and he said, 'I think it would adapt very well for the stage, let me know what you think.' So I pulled it off the shelf and read it again, then called him and said, 'Yes, it would,' and did it right away, in about a week. The director was John Dexter, whom I knew as a frighteningly energetic figure at the Royal Court, and it was fascinating working with him. And Alec McCowen, who played the part of Hitler, was sensational, although he had to be talked into doing it. But the play has had no afterlife at all. It was done once in America, at a theatre in Hartford, Connecticut, and a review in the *New York Times* said something like, 'Of all the cheap exploitations of the Holocaust I've ever seen this is undoubtedly the most disgusting.' It was as terrible a review as you could possibly imagine.

Not surprising, given that the play ends with a long monologue in which Hitler uses other nations' crimes against humanity to justify his own.

I wasn't surprised; it's a difficult one for audiences to swallow. There's a real problem about how you deal with this whole subject, which is like a huge black hole in the middle of the twentieth century. You can't avoid it, but it's extremely delicate. The only screenplay I've been offered to direct apart from my own which I've wanted to do is an adaptation of a novel called *See Under:*

Love by David Grossman, dealing with both a child learning about the Holocaust in Israel in the fifties and perhaps the most insane of all the things the Nazis did, Treblinka, where three quarters of a million people went into the camp and only twelve came out. It's a complicated and ambitious book, from which Martin Sherman has distilled a still complicated but very graceful script; and I talked to Jonathan Pryce and Jeremy Irons about doing it, and they both wanted to, but you just can't get that kind of film financed now. I think it's an unavoidable subject, though, even for post-war gentiles like myself.

You once said, 'I find it hard to write about the present except in the disguise of the past,' which is true of Portage *to some extent – and certainly applies to* Liaisons.

That sounds about right. In any given era it's very hard to work out what's of lasting significance and what's of passing interest only, and those questions are immediately answered when you write something set in the past. It seems to me that the desire to be up-to-the-minute, certainly in writing plays, is a formula for being of no relevance at all by next Thursday. Experience has taught me that it's a great advantage to be a little bit ahead, because then if you get delayed it doesn't do you any harm and the thing lands on more welcoming soil. It's been suggested that one of the reasons why *Liaisons* spoke to people is because it hit the apex of Thatcherism, and I said myself in interviews that this was a government in the process of institutionalizing selfishness and here was a play which addressed that point – and issued a warning about it. So if I'd written it when I originally wanted to, in 1976, perhaps it wouldn't have struck such a chord. I have no way of knowing, but that's my instinct.

The idea of sexual promiscuity without thought for the consequences also happened to coincide with the rise of AIDS.

I think *Liaisons*, the novel, belongs to that group of work which is so great that you're always going to find some relevance in it. In *Three Sisters*, you're very struck by Tuzenbach saying, 'It could be we'll be remembered with respect. After all, there are no invasions any more,' because it's ironic to hear that now. But I guess there was nothing in Chekhov's mind except that it was what that character might say at that point. As far as writing about the present is concerned, to put it at its simplest, I think the present is inevitably confusing, and a way to analyse one's feelings about it is to find some analogue in another society or age.

When did you first come across Laclos's novel?

At Oxford. Merlin Thomas gave us a representative piece of work from each period of French literature, so that we could make an informed choice about which period we wanted to study, and the eighteenth-century book was *Les Liaisons Dangereuses*. I thought it was the greatest novel I'd ever read; I couldn't believe how powerful and insightful it was. Laclos had taken this very complicated form, the epistolary novel, and produced a compelling page-turner. The popular novels in France at that time were Samuel Richardson's *Pamela* and *Clarissa*, the prototype epistolary novels, but they're very clumsily constructed and there's no variation in the tone of the letters – and, half the time, you think that these characters must have been writing for twenty-five hours out of every twenty-four – whereas Laclos saw the dramatic potential of the form and devised a complicated mathematical structure with lots of highly individual voices. Merteuil, for example, is an absolutely unprecedented character in literature. There had been motiveless evil men, like Iago, but a woman of this formidable and cold-hearted kind he invented more or less single-handedly. What's puzzling is that he only wrote this one novel, but in the end I decided that was also to his credit: he realized he only had one novel in him, and then didn't bother anyone any more.

Laclos was writing at the same time as Sade, wasn't he?

Yes, he was. In fact, I wrote an essay on that. The period of literature I specialized in was from 1780 to 1920, which was known as 'the modern period', but the early part of that period was generally thought to be Voltaire and Rousseau, neither of whom I was particularly interested in – whereas I was interested in *Les Liaisons Dangereuses*. I was interested in the fact that, during the pre-Revolutionary decade, many of the most considerable writers of the time were writing pornography, and I was also interested in the correlation between revolution, which tends to be something frenziedly puritanical, and its polar opposite. So I asked if I could write an essay on the late eighteenth-century pornographers, authors like Sade and Crébillon *fils* and Restif de la Bretonne, and Merlin Thomas was rather tickled by the idea – at which point I had to obtain a letter from the Vice-Chancellor authorizing me to read these books, most of which were locked up, and not only locked up, but locked up in separate cabinets. I never came to any satisfactory conclusions about why this should have been the case in pre-Revolutionary France, but I still find the fact of it very interesting.

Would you describe Liaisons *as pornographic?*

Well, first of all you have to define pornography, and if you define it as writing where, independent of any literary merit, the purpose of the writer is to excite an erection in his male reader – or a moistening in his female reader – then there's very little of that in *Liaisons*. There may one or two slightly risqué passages, but the sex is mostly in the head. It's really a discussion – a very rigorous and quite harsh discussion – about the differences between sex and love, which is a subject that has always interested me. They're two distinct universes, I think, and the catastrophe in *Liaisons* happens when those two universes coincide; when Valmont, almost without knowing what's going on, finds himself falling in love and doesn't know how to deal with it. The whole house of cards comes tumbling down because this one decent impulse spoils the symmetry of his life.

In other words, it makes you think in a way that something more arousing wouldn't.

Yes – although I cherish a compliment by Alan Clarke, a director I admired enormously, who saw the film at a screening in Los Angeles and said to Stephen Frears and me, 'Congratulations. It's a three-erection movie.' But the film is probably sexier than the play, because there are things you can show which aren't necessarily appropriate on stage.

Why do you think the National Theatre turned down the idea in 1976?

I mentioned it to two or three theatre managements, but nothing came of it. I think the main thing which worried them was that the two main characters never meet. They'd say, 'What will you do about that?' and I'd say, 'Well, I'll *make* them meet!'

So how did you set about making them meet?

First of all I constructed a huge grid which traced the characters through the novel: where they were spending their time when they were writing the letters. Then it was like shaking a kaleidoscope: I had to reorganize the grid so characters could be in the same place at the same time without disrupting the plot. It was quite complicated but good fun.

Complicated, presumably, because the letters are part of the plot?

Yes, as I became very aware. Stephen encouraged me to make the letters a visible thread in the film, but in the play they were pretty much subtracted altogether. That's why the play ends differently from the film – and the novel – because in the play there's no incriminating evidence and therefore Merteuil gets away with it. At the end of the novel, she gets smallpox and goes blind, and loses her fortune in a trial and is forced to flee the country in disgrace; then there's a footnote which says, 'As a matter of fact, even worse things happened to her which I can't tell you about,' which is really Laclos winking at you and saying, 'I'm only giving you a moral ending because I have to.' But, not being subject to those pressures, I thought I might as well let her get away with it.

You mentioned the mathematical structure of the novel, and when we were talking about Treats *you said that your mathematical approach to that play worked better when you applied it to* Liaisons. *In what way did it work better?*

It was mathematical, but in a completely different way. What I did was to construct the play in six groups of three scenes, with each group containing a general scene which covered quite a large area of the novel; a more specific scene which covered a couple of letters; and a snapshot which covered just one letter – although they weren't always in that precise order. Also, in order to give a sense of acceleration, each group was slightly shorter than the one before, until, by the end, they were really zipping along. It's a structure which the audience shouldn't be aware of, but it took a lot of planning and worrying for it to emerge.

The other aspect of the adaptation was the language. How did you deal with that?

The language in the play was my third attempt. My first attempt was a pastiche of eighteenth-century English, so I read a lot of Fielding and Smollett. It was great fun to do, but ten pages in I thought, 'This is distancing us from the immediacy of the novel.' Then I decided that the thing to do was make it absolutely modern, with the characters telling each other to go fuck themselves. So I started on that and thought, 'This isn't right, either.' It seemed trivial, in a curious way. Eventually, I had the idea of bringing eighteenth-century formality to twentieth-century language, and as soon as I began writing the first scene in that style I thought, 'This is going to work.' But, again, it was trial and error. And it was trial and error conducted at some speed, because I'd spent so long on *The Price of Tea* that I only had seven weeks to write this.

The play had a rather bumpy production history, didn't it?

There was opposition at every turn, really. Howard Davies wanted to work with me and was attached to the RSC, and the RSC had offered me an open commission to write something for the Barbican, so I gave them both *Liaisons*, much to their dismay. I remember Howard calling me and saying that he was rather disappointed with the play but that Trevor Nunn and Terry Hands both thought it was very good – although they didn't think it was right for the Barbican – and that I might want to consider the possibility of one of them directing it. But I said, 'No, you must do it,' and at the end of the conversation he said, 'Oh, all right then.' So the play had twenty-two performances in Stratford, at The Other Place – a shed in the car park with a tin roof – then another twenty-three at the Barbican, in The Pit – where it was the hottest ticket – and then it just stopped. It was eventually resuscitated by an American producer, Frank Gero, who was so determined that the play should have a life that he actually bought it from the RSC. We couldn't get Juliet Stevenson to come back – or Lesley Manville, who played Cécile, or Fiona Shaw, who played Mme de Volanges – but we did resuscitate it. Then Alan Rickman didn't want to do the play in a big theatre. We'd been offered the Wyndhams, which is a lovely theatre, but Alan said he couldn't go there, because it was too big. And finally the Ambassadors came up, which was acceptably small, and the play wound up running for five years.

How involved were you in the casting of the play?

Very. In the case of *Liaisons*, Alan Rickman was my idea – or possibly Laura's – and Lindsay Duncan was Howard's. Likewise, with *The Talking Cure*, Ralph Fiennes was my idea and Jodhi May was Howard's – although one I completely approved of. All the actors in *Liaisons* were ideally suited to their roles. Juliet is an amazing actress, but I don't think she's ever been better than she was as Mme de Tourvel – and the others seemed to me equally definitive.

Were you equally involved in the casting of the 2003 revival, directed by Tim Fywell, with Jared Harris as Valmont, Polly Walker as Merteuil and Emilia Fox as Tourvel?

Not really. The offer to revive the play came from ATG, with whom I'd got on very well during *Three Sisters*, and I gave them a list of actors I thought might be good, but they didn't really follow it up. I thought Jared Harris was a very interesting idea when they put it to me, and indeed I thought he gave a very interesting performance, more in the slouching Malkovich style than the classical way Alan did it. But whoever did it was going to get clobbered, I've now decided. Apart from the fact that it wasn't a very smart time to open, right before Christmas, and the fact that the Playhouse Theatre is completely out of the way – and was covered in scaffolding until the play opened – I think that unless the revival had been absolutely of the highest calibre, with a suitably high-profile cast, people were bound to say, 'It's not like it was in 1985.' I suppose I should have foreseen that reaction, but I was quite happy to go with that cast and I feel they were very harshly treated. The last time I saw the production was on Boxing Day, and although the audience obviously wasn't very big, they really seemed to like it.

Were you disappointed that you couldn't cast Alan Rickman et al. *in the film?*

Yes, I was. I also felt very guilty about it – and I felt even guiltier when I read that Alan Bennett had insisted on Nigel Hawthorne starring in *The Madness of King George*. But I wasn't in a position to insist, and the evidence that I'd accepted that fact was that it was I who cast John Malkovich and Glenn Close before Stephen came on board – because I had to, since Milos Forman was forging ahead with his version.

You presumably cast Malkovich and Close in your role as co-producer – the first time you were credited on a film as anything other than screenwriter.

The business of being a co-producer was in order to maintain some control over the film. I didn't want to hand it over to be made as a big studio picture, because I had no faith in it not being emasculated if we went down that route. And, as chance would have it, if we had accepted any of the studio deals, the film would certainly never have been made, because they would have cancelled it as soon as they heard that Milos was on the rampage. Legend has it that the crucial moment in the history of the film came at a shareholders meeting of Lorimar, where a man called Merv Adelson said, 'Are we out of our minds? We've paid a lot of money to buy the rights to a property which is out of copyright, and we're proposing to make a film in competition with a director who's won two Oscars, at a time when the company is going bankrupt.' To which Bernie Brillstein apparently gave the immortal response, 'Well, if our company is going bankrupt, what the fuck difference does it make?' I don't know how true that is, but that was the story which was told to me. It's really a miracle that the film was made. By any rules which you can devise, it ought not to have been. There was a good fairy watching over the whole thing, just as there are some projects where there's a bad fairy and you lurch from mishap to disaster to oblivion.

Having cast Malkovich and Close, was it a conscious decision to cast Americans as the rest of the aristocrats – and, on the other hand, Scottish actors as their servants?

That was a way of amusing ourselves. Our first idea was to cast Irish actors, and we offered the part of Azolan to Stephen Rea, but he wasn't available, so we thought of Peter Capaldi instead. Michelle was Stephen's casting, and she was brilliant, but we had no idea whether she was going to say yes or not, because she was also offered Merteuil by Milos – so that was another tense little drama.

What did you think of the Forman version – Valmont?

I think of it as the sixties version, really: a 'Boys will be boys' and 'Sex is good fun' and 'No harm done' kind of approach. Milos said that he'd been shocked when he saw the play by how different it was from the novel, which he hadn't read since he was young. He then went back and read the novel again and found that, on the contrary, the play was a very accurate rendition of it – whereupon he decided to make a film based on his *memory* of the novel. Of course, the problem is that if it doesn't matter who sleeps with whom the stakes are low to non-existent and therefore there's no story, no drama. So the film looks ravishing – and if you read David Thomson, he says that it's a much more interesting film than *Dangerous Liaisons* – but it bears no relation to the original. One of the many extraordinary strokes of luck relating to our film of *Liaisons* is that Milos and I turned up at the same restaurant on different dates and thus never met, because if we had met and had got on, God knows how we would have resolved such a fundamental philosophical difference about how to approach this particular material. I don't think we would have. I think I'd have been fired.

Stephen Frears, on the other hand . . .

I thought it was splendid material for him; the ambivalence and the insolence of the characters fitted him very well. I just couldn't persuade anyone else of that, so I had meetings with Volker Schlöndorff and Wolfgang Petersen and Mike Nichols and Alan Pakula – and Louis Malle, who almost did it – and I know it was also offered to people like Polanski. In fact, at one point, it seemed like Lorimar would go with anyone *except* Stephen.

Before writing the film you worked on David Lean's unrealized version of Nostromo. *Did you learn any lessons from that which you could bring to bear on* Liaisons?

I did learn a lot from David, so I was probably thinking about the way a film works in much greater detail than I'd ever thought about it before. For example, David always paid an extravagant amount of attention to the way each scene flowed into the next. There was a montage sequence in *Nostromo*, which occurred when the rebel army marches into the town and the church bells start ringing and the various protagonists in various places all hear them and react to them, and we spent a week to ten days just discussing the order this sequence should take. To me, it seemed like a perfectly good sequence in any order, but by the time we got it right, it had an extraordinary inevitability and said that this was the end of an era and that the characters had come to this point of their development – all in one sequence which would only have lasted about forty seconds.

Now, Stephen read the script for *Liaisons* on 1 January – I put it through his letterbox with a note saying 'Happy New Year' – and we started shooting in May, and although there were no radical changes during that time, what work we did was all to do with the same thing: making the film flow properly. For example, the entire opening sequence came out of a long conversation we had very late on. The script originally started with the scene in Merteuil's salon, but I somehow wanted to set up her and Valmont as rivals, and the idea emerged of showing the two of them getting dressed. I'd either read somewhere, or the costume designer, James Acheson, had told me, that the process of getting ready for the day was so elaborate, and involved so many people, that these aristocrats weren't ready to have their breakfast until half past three in the afternoon. So Stephen passed me on to Jim, and I said, 'What did they actually do?' and he told me lots of stuff which I then went on to use.

Likewise, the whole ending was a matter of endless discussion. There were so many different versions of it that the actual ending was something of an afterthought. I had written that it should end with a caption, 'From then on, her soul was written on her face,' which is a wonderful line from the novel. But when Glenn saw that, she said, 'I can act this,' so the final scene was done at the end of a day when we'd finished a bit early, in one take, with Philippe Rousselot on the lighting board artificially cheating down the lights – and even, when he saw a tear coming out of Glenn's eye, slightly cheating them up again. And when we saw it we thought, even though it wasn't written as such, that it was the end of the film. We did shoot Glenn being guillotined, but when we saw it in the screening room Stephen and I looked at each other and both burst out laughing, so obviously that wasn't a good idea.

From the opening shot of the film, where a woman opens a letter and the title is superimposed over the paper, to its final scenes, which has the villainess almost literally booed off the stage by the audience at the opera, the film seems more consciously theatrical than the play.

You may be right. I remember that when David Puttnam came to a screening, he said, 'Cut the scene in the opera. It's not the right tone.' Stephen and I didn't agree, so we didn't cut it, but it's interesting that he had that reaction. Certainly the end of the film is more melodramatic than the end of the play, because, in keeping with my theory that films are more like novels than they are like plays, I wanted to go back to the novel in writing the film, whereas the play pulls back on the melodrama in the novel. That's why, when we did the play in Paris, I rewrote the final scene, because the translator, Jean-Claude Brisville, convinced me that French audiences would be horrified by this radical change. In the rewrite, Mme de Volanges and Mme de Rosemonde discuss all the terrible things which have happened, in particular the smallpox which Merteuil has developed, and the scene ends on that wonderful line: 'Now her soul is written on her face.' Then Merteuil came on, veiled and dressed in black, turned to a huge distorting mirror at the back of the stage and lifted the veil – and you saw this hideous face.

In other words, the final scene of that version of the play is more like the final scene in the film version, more emotional?

Lindsay injected some of that emotion into the original version of the play as well, because she discovered something powerful in rehearsal which people playing that part have stuck to ever since: that, rather than being triumphal, the last speech is like whistling in the dark, spoken with a mouthful of ashes by someone whose triumph is completely hollow. Lindsay decided that that was what she wanted to convey in the speech, which played completely against the tone of it but made it work much better. But the open emotion of the film, and the revealing of Merteuil's adoration of Valmont in that extraordinary scene – again, done in one take – where she bursts into the room and smashes everything up after hearing the news of his death, makes it clearer that she's cut her own throat.

When, in the scene before the duel, Merteuil says to Valmont, 'Vanity and happiness are incompatible,' you feel that she could be talking about herself as much as him.

I don't think that line is in the novel; it's just something I feel. People who are driven either by vanity or by ambition are doomed to a miserable life, because there's nothing you can do to fix those particular qualities. You're absolutely damned by them, and you just have to hope that they go away.

The end of the film ties the deaths of Valmont and Tourvel together in a much more direct way than the play, making it clear that he commits suicide and redeeming him to an extent which the play doesn't.

Alan had always given a suggestion of suicide in the play, and there are certainly a couple of moments where he could have killed Danceny and chooses not to, but John decided to make that explicit in the film, and came up with this idea of dropping his own sword and turning onto Danceny's – which I was perfectly happy with. There are thousands of differences between the way Alan approached the part and the way John approached it, but the main difference is that John's was the more romantic approach. John subscribed more to the notion that Valmont was destroyed by love, whereas Alan fought a rearguard action against that possibility. Alan's theory was that because this man had had a lifetime of behaving in a certain way, he would resist behaving in any other way and not give way to these impulses, whereas John felt the opposite, that he was entranced by the wonder of what had happened to him and was indulging himself in love in the same way that he had indulged himself in everything else in his life. I think both approaches are valid.

I've always found it easier to believe in the idea of Valmont being desperately in love with Tourvel than the idea of him being desperately in love with Merteuil, something which is even more noticeable in the film because we're shown the development of Valmont's relationship with Tourvel rather than being told about it after the event.

But that's the point: his whole relationship with Merteuil is the playing out of a habit. He isn't really in love with her, and that's what she comes to realize – which is why she has to destroy him.

In the film, the way the camera moves in relation to the actors, and the way they move in relation to each other, emphasizes this idea of a deadly game played with military precision.

There's a wonderful moment – and I remember Stephen saying at a screening, 'I'm rather pleased with that' – at the end of, if you break it into three acts, the first act. It's the scene where Valmont is sent back to the country by Merteuil, and at the end of it she walks out of this vast room by one door and he walks out via another and they both disappear at the same time – followed by a fade to black – and it's a marvellous piece of visual punctuation. The decision to devote so much of the film to close-up was also inspired, because of all those moments – which are very subtle in the play, and easily missed – when Merteuil registers her horrified understanding of Valmont's naive enthusiasm, like the scene where he inadvertently utters the phrase 'It's beyond my control,' and she files that away in order to throw it back at him later.

We've talked about the visual sequence at the start of the film, but there's another one in the middle, where the characters are gathered in the salon and Merteuil sees Valmont looking at Tourvel in a way which confirms his love for her.

That scene was a source of particular anxiety to me, because it's the only time when Merteuil and Tourvel are together and is therefore the fulcrum of the film. I kept saying to Stephen, 'We've got to get those looks absolutely right,' but it worked wonderfully in the end.

It's unusual to find the writer present throughout the making of a film. Directors often prefer the exact opposite.

Yes, they do. But Stephen is different, and I knew that from *Able's Will*, when he used to pick me up every day and drive me to the location where we were shooting. With *Liaisons*, the routine was that I would bang on his door in the morning – because he always got up at the last minute – and then we'd drive to the set in the same car and he'd put questions to me about the scene. He'd obviously done his preparation, but there were often last-minute things which he wanted to clarify, and the advantage of my being on the set was that if something came up I could deal with it. For example, in the scene at the end, where Mme de Volanges and Cécile visit Mme de Tourvel, a semi-circular tracking shot brings them to her bedside, and when the tracks were set up and the shot was rehearsed, Stephen looked at it and said to me, 'I think she has to say a line of dialogue.' I said, 'What do you mean?' He said, 'The shot needs punctuation. When the women stop by the bed, Michelle has got to say something.' So I said, 'What?' And he said, 'You're the writer.' What happens now is that they stop by the bed and Michelle says, 'I'm dying because I wouldn't believe you,' and Stephen was right: it completes the shot and allows you to go on, things which didn't occur to me when I was sitting writing the script.

There was a lot of that, and there was also a lot of pleading, because one thing which made Stephen very uneasy was long scenes. Every scene of more than a page had to be rigorously defended and every word thoroughly considered, and if it wasn't contributing to the flow it had to go. He was quite anxious to get rid of the scene where Tourvel turns up and catches Valmont with the courtesan, Émilie, because it came so late on and was two or three pages of dialogue, including long speeches, and it was a question of convincing him that it was worth the space it was taking. John and I had to plead with him to give it a go and cut it if it didn't work – and, of course, it works very well, especially as John does this particularly brilliant thing in the middle of it, where he can hardly stop laughing.

For those reasons, you'd think that any director with common sense would always have the writer on the set – except that some writers get very panicky and protective about their material and have too rigid an idea of how the lines should be delivered or what the actors should do. An actor will often do something which you didn't envisage, something which may contradict what you had in mind, but experience has taught me that, until whatever happens in front of the camera happens, you can't predict whether it will be more interesting than what you originally intended. If it isn't, and you're there, then you can say, 'Why don't you try this?' and propose what you had in mind in the first place. But it may be that the actor is doing something less ordinary than whatever it was you had thought up, and I think a lot of writers don't respond very well to that, which is why directors don't like having them on the set, because they don't want someone sulking behind the camera saying, 'Well, that's not how *I* imagined it.'

The reintroduction of the letters in the film, at Frears's sugges-tion, allowed for some visual comedy, almost slapstick, around their delivery which the play lacked. Do you think it helped?

It's quite interesting to analyse that. The turning point in the play, when the audience start to rethink what's happening in front of them, is the scene where Valmont sneaks into Cécile's room and gets into bed with her. In the theatre, people found that scene very funny to start with, but when he got into bed with her and, as it were, penetrated her, you could feel that they weren't quite so comfortable with that – although the next thing you see she's having a wonderful time and badgering him to do it again. In the film, we had to cut the second half of that scene, because it was so graphically done. He got into bed with her and he raped her, and at the first preview twenty-five people walked out. Warners were very alarmed, and at first Stephen and I said, 'We're not going to change it,' but the more we looked at it, the more it did seem, because of that slapstick of hiding the keys and so on, too ugly a note to introduce that early, and we cut it – not under pressure but because we felt we ought to, although John was very upset and felt we should have left it in. So I think there is a lighter tone in the first half of the film, but both it and the play work by starting in that light mode and tightening the screws later on.

Were you at all surprised by the way in which the play seduced the audience in the first half and turned on them in the second?

The effect of what you write is always a surprise. For example, with a comedy you hope that people will laugh, but it's a surprise where they laugh and how much they laugh, because they don't laugh in the expected places. In this case, I was aware of that device, but I hadn't quite realized the extent to which it would work. During that scene between Valmont and Cécile, a hush would descend in the theatre as it turned ugly, and you could sense the audience assessing the extent of their collusion. As I said, it was always my idea to beckon the audience in so I could punch them in the jaw, but they wouldn't come close enough for that punch unless they wanted to.

But doesn't the fact that, a couple of scenes later, Cécile is having a wonderful time, absolve Valmont – and the audience – of any guilt?

It makes it more morally complex, and you have to sort out your own reaction to it. I suppose, talking as we were about pornography, that it's the closest Laclos gets to a pornographic standby, namely the reluctant virgin who then can't get enough of it – which was a metaphor I used to describe myself after directing *Carrington* and is certainly an observable phenomenon in life. That's the reason why *Liaisons* is so interesting, because it veers between a kind of moral shock and an acknowledgement that these things are present in all of us and not sufficiently considered.

It's interesting that when Cécile tells Merteuil about the rape, Merteuil conditions her to accept this kind of treatment, which might nowadays be termed a cycle of abuse.

That's right, and one of my favourite moments in the film is when Glenn Close says, 'You'll find the shame is like the pain: you only feel it once,' because she does it with a tremendous melancholy, which is fantastically strong.

Given your belief that films are closer to novels than to plays, would you say that the film of Liaisons *is closer to the novel than the play is?*

I think so, yes. But I wouldn't like to give the impression that I prefer the film to the play, because I don't. When the play opened in that small room in Stratford, with 150 people in the audience all holding their breath, the experience was more intense than anything you'd ever get in cinema. On the other hand, it's easier in a film to suggest the outside world. I didn't want mud-filled streets and starving peasants, but the scene where Valmont plays that pantomime of going to the village tells you more about the state of society at the time than anything in the play – although the play has the same line about how 'Fifty-six livres to save an entire family from ruin seems like a genuine bargain.' Film is kinder to the supporting characters as well, like Uma Thurman as Cécile or Swoosie Kurtz as her mother. You can focus on them for tiny moments, in a way that you can't on stage.

In your introduction to the published screenplay, you thanked 'anybody who lobbed in a suggestion' – including the preview audiences, a process I've heard you disdain.

Liaisons was the first time I'd been through this process, and the film had very high scores from the first screening – so Warners were delighted. They asked us to make that change to the rape scene, which we did, and to tone down the death of Tourvel at the end, which we also did – there was a rather disagreeable scene of her scratching at the wounds on her back, which we cut – but apart from those, maybe, forty seconds of cuts, we hardly made any changes between the first preview and the release print. In general, though, the preview system is, I think, not a helpful one. I don't see how someone trundling in off the street for a free show, someone who isn't interested in films in general or yours in particular, is going to make much of a contribution. They can say that they liked the film or they didn't, and you can sense by standing at the back where it's working and where it isn't, but you don't need them making suggestions about what you ought to do. The only suggestions which you should act on are informed suggestions, made by people who have been think-ing about the film for a long time. For example, we had a lot of difficulty orchestrating Valmont and Tourvel's relationship in the first third of the film, and the to-ing and fro-ing between them and Merteuil, but the editor, Mick Audsley, made an adjustment to the order of the sequence where Valmont talks about going for walks with Tourvel and the scene where Merteuil is reading his letter, which solved the problem in quite a clever way.

I read that you became so absorbed in the film that you ceased to exist outside it, which sounds rather unusual for you.

I fell in love with the whole process of film-making at that time, and being in love with the process of film-making requires the exclusion of almost everything else in your life, so it doesn't necessarily improve your character – although once you're made aware of that, as I was by my wife and daughters, you can try and do something about it. I don't see that you can do anything else as a director because it's such an all-absorbing job, but as a writer I've usually been able to detach myself from the work at the end of the day. And if I don't want to detach myself from it, I'll go away somewhere for a week and finish it without distractions, as I did with the last fifty pages of *Atonement*. I didn't expect to finish the script in that week, but I did. I don't know how sociable you would have found me in the evenings, though.

You won a clutch of awards for Liaisons – *including Olivier and Evening Standard awards for the play, and BAFTA and Writers Guild of America awards for the film – but the most high-profile was the Academy Award for Best Adapted Screenplay. Were you surprised to be nominated for, and win, an Oscar?*

Yes, I was. I really was.

What was the actual ceremony like?

I'm afraid the word which immediately springs to mind is 'hideous'. Of course, it was great to win an Oscar, but the business of waiting for it to happen was such a strain, I found: sitting in the auditorium for three hours before they get round to your category, which is one of the last to be announced, and then having to get up on stage and say something coherent, in front of a camera monitor which is blinking red at you to get off almost before you've started and a man wearing white gloves who draws his finger across his throat – which hardly makes addressing an audience of a billion any easier. And then, when you do get off the stage, the press just wants to take photographs of the famous actor who gave you the Oscar. But there were things I liked about it. I remember pulling up to the Shrine Auditorium behind a double-sized white limousine and thinking, 'I wonder who's in that,' then seeing a six-foot Roger Rabbit getting out of the car in front of me. I also remember walking up the red carpet and hearing lots of cheering from the crowd and seeing three bearded chaps in full eighteenth-century drag waving a banner which said 'Dangerous Liaisons' – which was rather wonderful.

Did it make any difference to your screenwriting career?

I made a big mistake: I thought it *was* going to make a difference. Two things were different: one was that my salary shot up, which was very pleasant, and the other was that for a period of a few weeks I was bombarded with every conceivable idea, book, script – whatever anyone was doing. And from all this, I foolishly selected *Imagining Argentina*, which was a novel that I actually read on the plane on the way back from Los Angeles after the ceremony. It haunted me, and I thought, 'I know it's a difficult subject, but perhaps because I've got the Oscar people will pay attention.' Which, of course, was idiotic. It took fourteen years, including buying the bloody rights myself, to get it off the ground, and even then it was fraught with every possible difficulty. So I don't think it makes a hell of a lot of difference.

Between the play of Liaisons *and the film, you made your last foray into television with* The Ginger Tree. *What do you remember about that?*

The Ginger Tree was a four-part mini-series for the BBC, and I'm afraid I only agreed to do it because I wanted to spend some time in Japan. It was based on a novel by a Scottish chap called Oswald Wynd, whose family was caught in Japan during the war and put in prisoner-of-war camps, and the book itself was based on the real story of a Scottish woman, who married a dashing young army officer she'd only met a couple of times who was serving out in the Far East. The book begins with her long journey to find him in Hong Kong, but he turns out to be a complete bastard, and, in this unhappy state of affairs, she meets and falls in love with the Japanese military attaché there. This continues while her husband is trapped in another Chinese city during the Boxer Rebellion, in 1904, so when he comes back and finds her pregnant he knows that it's not his baby and casts her out without a penny. She's rescued by the military attaché and put on a boat to Japan, only to find herself set up as his concubine and the baby taken away from her, because in his culture your son isn't brought up by your concubine, he's brought up by people in some other town who are assigned to do this. Of course, she's absolutely appalled by this and breaks with the guy, and winds up alone and abandoned in Tokyo before the First World War. So she goes to work in a big department store, which were just getting going in that period, and starts to import western clothes, which become immensely fashionable. She also institutes a search for her son, and carries on looking for him all the way through to 1941, when her ex-lover, who's been trying to prevent the Japanese high command going to war, turns up, tells her that she has to get out of the country, puts her on another boat, then goes home and commits suicide. On the way back, when the boat is in Singapore harbour, various Japanese officers come on board, and one of them asks to interview her; in the course of this interview, she realizes that it's her son, and he tells her that he's a Kamikaze pilot. It's quite a good story, really.

Anyway, I embarked on this bloody thing, and it took a year, mostly because of the impenetrability of the Japanese. Although NHK put up no more than twenty-five per cent of the budget, they were the tail which wagged the dog, because they kept making objections all the time. They never told you what the objection was; they just told you there was an objection, and, on the one hand, the BBC couldn't understand what it was all about, but, on the other, they felt that they should try, so there were endless meetings here and in Japan about what should be done. It went right down to small details. They suddenly said, 'Her son can't be a major in the army,' and I said, 'But that's the climax of the film!' By this time, I'd learned a little bit and I realized that, because the Japanese are quite prejudiced against foreigners, his rank was too high for a half-caste. So I said, 'Suppose we make him a lieutenant?' and they said, 'That's fine,' but they never said, 'Make him a lieutenant.' I couldn't care less whether he was a lieutenant or an Eskimo, but they wouldn't tell you what would have solved the problem.

Then, the day before shooting begins, I'm asleep in bed at three o'clock in the morning when the phone rings. It's Alan Shallcross, the producer, who says, 'The Japanese have fired Ross Devenish.' I said, 'What do you mean?' He said, 'They claim he insulted someone.' I said, 'Then who's directing it?' He said, 'The Japanese assistant director.' I said, 'Does he speak English?' And Alan said, 'No.' So the first six weeks of shooting were directed by this Japanese guy who didn't speak English, and that was when the real agenda was revealed, which was that they wanted to shoot the whole thing in High Definition. No drama series had ever been shot in HD before, and Sony were putting money into it to do this. That's why Ross was fired, because NHK wanted a director who knew about the cameras, and, if you see it, half the scenes are shot in corridors or on staircases to show off the depth of focus. The BBC finally found Tony Garner knocking around TV Centre and said, 'Get on the plane and go out there,' and he took over and shot the rest of it, but he came to it out of nowhere and could only do so much to help. Samantha Bond was absolutely heroic. She was quite young then, and she somehow held the whole thing together and was very good in the part. But according to her, it was chaos. I wasn't there at all; I was just at the end of a phone, responding to cries of distress.

And, apart from adaptations of your plays, you've written nothing for television since.

'Never again' was the phrase which crossed my lips at the time. It was a nightmare, and under the circumstances I'm amazed it came out as well as it did. My favourite bit was researching the history of the department stores, and the third episode, which is largely in Japanese and deals with the way the stores functioned, has a kind of Arnold Bennett social realist quality that I like. But after all that, a year's work and God knows how many drafts, it went out on the night and that's it. Occasionally, I meet someone who saw it and liked it, but that's about all. So I don't think television is a very friendly or responsive medium to the writer, especially now that they've abandoned the notion, widely held in the sixties and seventies, that writing for television is a worthwhile and important thing to be doing. It was claimed that writers like

David Mercer and Dennis Potter actually made a difference to people's attitudes, and I think they did, but now there's an entirely craven corporate ethos prevailing. What the fuck do these people think they're doing?

{7}

White Chameleon – Sunset Boulevard – Dracula – Alice's Adventures Under Ground

Before embarking on White Chameleon, *you'd always avoided autobiography. What prompted you to dramatize this part of your life?*

It's strange how the origin of these things is often so different from the end result. In this case, it started with a bright idea by Richard Eyre when he first took over at the National. He knew about my childhood in Egypt, so he proposed that I write a play about the Suez Crisis and that David Hare write a play about the Hungarian Uprising, and that both plays be done in 1991, the thirty-fifth anniversary of those events.

Because the Hungarian Uprising happened at the same time as the Suez Crisis, and the Russians used the distraction caused by Suez to put down the Hungarians?

Exactly. In 1956. So David went to eastern Europe, and I started reading books and looking at newsreels about Suez. But David couldn't draw together his material into a play, and the more I studied mine the more I thought, 'I'm not very interested in writing about Suez, because everyone knows that it was a callous and stupid adventure, all about flexing muscles which Britain no longer had, and what else can you say except that?' And, of course, the more I thought about that, the more I remembered my own relationship with Egypt, which seemed to be something I kept coming back to and was interested in exploring. I thought that it raised larger issues than just personal issues – issues which, as it happens, have fed pretty consistently into my work – and I could see that it would make a viable play. So I put that idea to Richard instead, and when he eventually read it he said that he liked it very much and wanted to direct it.

Did you find it more difficult to write than your other plays?

I did, actually. Writing it took a lot out of me, even though my memory is that it didn't take more than a couple of weeks, and watching it took a lot out of me, in a way that I don't think any of my other plays have. But there was something positive about being affected that deeply, so the whole experience was a very valuable one. It seems to me that, every five years or so, you have to have some galvanizing experience within your profession to give you the energy you need to go on with it, and the filming of *Liaisons* was one of them and this, five years later, was another. If you produce a lot of work, as I've tended to in recent years, you're always doing it half in the hope of having one of these energizing experiences, but you can't plan in advance what's going to affect you deeply and what isn't.

So there were emotional difficulties; what about technical difficulties? You're usually scrupulously accurate when dealing with factual events, for example.

This was a different process, and the process, very simply described, is that I wrote down every single thing I could remember from those five years. Then I looked at that for a long time, then shapes began to emerge and certain events began to present themselves more insistently than others, until finally I was left with a core of interesting fact.

In your afterword to the published play, you wrote, 'Although I have tried to remember and portray myself as a child as accurately as possible, the other characters in the play have undergone inevitable modifications.' Why did you want to be truer to what you did and felt than what the people around you did and felt?

You have to make decisions. It's a huge change, for example, to take out my brother and give the impression that I was an only child. But I *felt* as if I was an only child, because the company my father worked for, Cable & Wireless, would only pay for my brother, who was at boarding school in England, to visit us once every three years; so, by the summer of 1956, when he arrived for his holidays in Egypt, I'd been living on my own with my parents for some time. And when I learned that the outrage in Ismailia in 1952, when the British army massacred fifty Egyptian policemen, had occurred on my birthday, it was the cue for me to invent Scene Two, which didn't happen like that – although I do remember my father coming home and saying that this event had taken place. So it's a distillation of my personal history and how it intersected with historical events, but my parents are portrayed more or less accurately – and so is Ibrahim.

One of the epigraphs in the published play was from Camus: 'Even if a writer does happen to put himself in the picture, it is only very exceptionally that he talks about what he is really like.' Were you trying to warn readers that there was a limit to how accurately you could remember and portray yourself?

I did make a conscientious attempt to show what I was like, but afterwards I thought, 'I've no idea whether I was like this or not,' so I put that quote in to muddy the waters a bit. I'd always been interested in that remark by Camus: don't trust writers, particularly when they're talking about themselves. Special pleading, I suppose, was what he was warning against, and I certainly tried to avoid that.

Did you go back to Egypt before you wrote the play?

I went back with the designer, Bob Crowley, and it was quite extraordinary. I wanted to show him the house I lived in, and the only way I could think of to find it was to get on the tram and get off at the Cleopatra Station, but the bastards had moved the station two hundred yards down the line, so when we got off I was absolutely bewildered and wandered about with Bob for some time. We eventually did find the house, and the reason it was so hard was that what looked like a four-storey apartment block had been built in the front garden. You're told that if you go back and visit places from your childhood they're always much smaller than you remember, but when we went around the side, to where the entrance now was, this place seemed much larger, and I was very puzzled by this until I realized that it had been a semi-detached house and they'd demolished the boundary between the two houses. They'd turned them into a school, and the block in the front garden served as the classrooms, but it was a girls' school, and various horrified matrons appeared and shooed us out, because it would have been wrong for the girls to see infidel men wandering about the place.

1 Simon Callow as Verlaine and Hilton McRae as Rimbaud in the Lyric
Hammersmith production of *Total Eclipse*. (© Nobby Clark)

2 Leonardo DiCaprio as Rimbaud and David Thewlis as Verlaine in the Fine
Line film *Total Eclipse*. (Courtesy of BFI Stills, Posters and Designs)

3 Alec McCowen as Philip and Charles Gray as Braham in the Royal Court production of *The Philanthropist*. (© John Haynes)

4 Paul Scofield as West and Tom Conti as Carlos in the Royal Court production of *Savages*. (© John Haynes)

5 James Bolam as Dave and Jane Asher as Ann in the Royal Court production of *Treats*. (© John Haynes)

6 Ian McDiarmid as Brecht and Michael Gambon as Horváth in the National Theatre production of *Tales from Hollywood*. (© Donald Cooper/ Photostage)

7 Lindsay Duncan as Merteuil and Alan Rickman as Valmont in the RSC
production of *Les Liaisons Dangereuses*. (Joe Cocks Studio Collection
© Shakespeare Birthplace Trust)

8 Glenn Close as Merteuil and John Malkovich as Valmont in the Warner Bros.
film *Dangerous Liaisons*. (Courtesy of BFI Stills, Posters and Designs)

9 Tom Wilkinson as Christopher's Father and David Birkin as Chris in the National Theatre production of *White Chameleon*. (© John Haynes)

10 Jonathan Pryce as Lytton and Emma Thompson as Carrington in the PolyGram film *Carrington*. (Courtesy of The Ronald Grant Archive)

11 Bob Hoskins as Verloc and Patricia Arquette as Winnie in the Fox Searchlight film *The Secret Agent*. (Courtesy of The Ronald Grant Archive)

12 Antonio Banderas as Carlos and María Canals as Esmerelda in the Myriad/Arenas film *Imagining Argentina*. (Courtesy of UIP)

13 Ralph Fiennes as Jung and Jodhi May as Sabina in the National Theatre production of *The Talking Cure*. (© Ivan Kyncl)

We were just retreating from the house, walking down the narrow road beside it, and I was pointing out things to Bob which were referred to in the play, like the shop across the street where I used to buy eucalyptus-flavoured sweets, when this man of about sixty stepped out of the shop, looked across at me and said, 'Christopher!' And it turned out to be the proprietor of the shop, whom I hadn't seen for thirty-five years. I found that extraordinary, and very touching. I was very moved by the whole journey, actually. Bob and I stayed at the Cecil Hotel, where my parents used to go in dinner jacket and ball gown and dance the night away, and when we went to check in, they said that both of the penthouse suites were available. I said, 'How much?' and they said, 'Seventeen dollars,' so we each took one of the penthouse suites, which had a view of the harbour. The hotel still had this elaborate lift, but it was falling to pieces. The whole of Alexandria was falling to pieces. The great movie palaces where I saw all those American movies of the fifties were still there, but semi-collapsed. This great cosmopolitan city had just vanished.

You were born in the Azores, then moved to Aden, then lived in Alexandria. Is this where your facility with languages comes from?

I suppose so, except I felt like a dunce at the so-called British Boys' School – which had very few British boys in it but conducted all its lessons in English – because at the age of eight, every child in the class could speak five languages. They could speak English and Arabic, of course, but they could usually speak French, Greek and Italian as well, because the city was teeming with those nationalities and children's minds are so receptive to language. My Lebanese friends, Eddy and Freddy, lived with an extended family in a big apartment at the other end of the street from our house, and they'd all speak French, like a Russian family, even though they came from Beirut and lived in Alexandria. It was like a Chekhov play.

You've described the play as pro-Arab, which is certainly true, but more than that it's simply pro-tolerance.

Yes, but in retrospect I do feel particularly warmly towards the

Egyptians. I liked them very much, for their courtesy and their tenderness. I'm aware that there are paradoxes about them; I think their attitude towards women leaves a huge amount to be desired. Nevertheless, the sense was that you were growing up in a much more considerate and civilized society than I felt to be the case when I came back to England.

You were also better educated.

Oh, much. I was years ahead when I arrived. My father had some ghastly catalogue of prep schools and he just picked one out with a pin, so I was sent to this prep school in Reigate which was absolutely on its last legs – in fact, it closed down the year I left. I also remember going to a school in Plymouth for a few months when I was about six and finding it very bizarre and bewildering. Having been to a French-style school in Alexandria where one was taught very rigorously, I was suddenly in a school where you had prayers first thing in the morning, then sat in the classroom and listened to the radio and then – in a freezing cold country where it rained all the time – went out into the playground and threw beanbags around for twenty minutes. I sensed that I was English, from hearing the way I spoke in the way the other kids spoke, which was not an everyday experience for me in Egypt, but on the other hand I thought, 'God, get me out of here and back to some kind of rational education system.'

Is it fair to say that you felt like an outsider in both countries, for different reasons?

Yes, but mostly to do with what was going on politically. In other words, the Egyptians were quite anti-British – although less anti-British than you'd expect them to be, under the circumstances – and in England, if you breathed a word about the folly of Suez – which I knew in my gut was wrong, even if I was just parroting what my father said – you were hauled up for being unpatriotic. The scene with the burning of the *tarboosh* actually happened to my brother in front of the whole school, but I co-opted it because it's such a dramatic incident. In fact, although I did have that talk with him about being unpatriotic, my headmaster was quite a bit more sympathetic than my brother's.

The title of the play, which derives from the chameleon in your garden in Alexandria, is presumably meant to be ironic, since 'Chris' manages to stand out from the other boys in both Egypt and England – almost changing to the opposite colour from his surroundings, in fact.

That hadn't really occurred to me, but you may well be right. I suppose what was in my mind when I wrote the play was that, as a result of these experiences, I did try to blend in as best I could thereafter, because it was so distressing being singled out and bullied all the time. My parents got very upset at one point, because I started to talk English with an accent, which is how all my friends talked. Like a Yorkshireman going up to Oxford in the forties, I tried not to stick out in Egypt like a sore thumb. But, as you say, none of these strategies really worked, so I think the key lessons I learned around the time of Suez were to keep my mouth shut and, conversely, not to accept the generally agreed line on anything.

Your father's attitude changed when the RAF tried to bomb his Cable & Wireless station but succeeded in hitting a nearby Presbyterian church and killing the verger. Yet rather than showing the reaction of 'Christopher's Father', you have 'Christopher' describe it, which seems quite a muted way of dramatizing such an important event.

Its dramatic function seemed to be as a fact rather than an event. If I'd dramatized it, it would have meant introducing another character, and stringing that character through the play, and I didn't want to do that – although there's actually a screenplay of *White Chameleon* where he does see that event happen. My father came to an arrangement with the armed guard on the front gate that he could leave via the back gate when he wanted to, so he went off to work and a day or two later they tried to bomb the office. There was a smouldering pile next door, and this old guy had died. My father was a very straight-down-the-line, patriotic, conservative man and he was extremely shaken by this, but it was probably naive of him to suppose that in these circumstances the RAF gives a bugger who's down the far end of the bombs they drop.

Why did you employ the device of having the same actor play both the narrator and his father?

The narration was always planned as a kind of meditation by someone much older than the character portrayed in the play, who is necessarily unselfconscious and fixed on whatever goals a child would have. And, in many ways, I thought I'd become rather like my father, so doubling those parts didn't seem at all fanciful. I also thought that it would offer some interesting opportunities for the actor to slide from one persona to the other, and Tom Wilkinson dealt with that very well. David Birkin was marvellous, too, and actually did look rather like me. You can't remember exactly what you were like at that age, of course, but he seemed to be pretty close. I'm still in touch with him and I'm not sure whether he wants to be an actor, but he was very talented and very confident. When children have no fear they can be miraculous on stage, and I think it's difficult for actors to retain that immediacy as they get older. It's the same with writers: the person who wrote *When Did You Last See My Mother?* was a completely different person to the person who wrote *Total Eclipse*, because self-consciousness had intruded – or a consciousness that I was engaged in some sort of public activity rather than something I was just doing for myself, which was the case when I started writing.

How did your mother feel about the play?

I felt quite trepidatious about my mother's reaction. When she went to see it, I sat with her, and when the curtain went up and Tom Wilkinson came on, she started crying. The whole way through the first half she was shaking with sobs, and I thought, 'My God, this is awful.' At the interval I said, 'Are you all right? Do you want a drink?' and she said, 'I'll be fine. Just leave me here.' My brother was there as well, and he and I were heading for the bar when a couple came forward and said, 'We lived in the house before you, and knew Ibrahim very well,' so they went and talked to my mother while we went and had a large scotch. And by the time we got back, she'd completely recovered, was fine all the way through the second half – which, of course, is much more moving and troubling – and even went to see it once or twice more. At a certain point, I was emboldened to say to her, 'Do you remember that day when you were sitting in that little room on your own, crying? What were you crying about?' and she couldn't remember – or said she couldn't. Perhaps she genuinely couldn't recall this moment which, for me, was an inviolable memory of my childhood, and it's interesting how memories like that can accrue without the other people involved in them thinking they were significant moments at all.

Another significant moment is when an acquaintance of Chris's parents administers a beating to his half-Egyptian son and Chris watches it with guilty fascination, which Christopher highlights as evidence that he was 'born to be a writer'. Were you also using it as a metaphor for the British attitude towards their colonial subjects?

I added the notion, in retrospect, that it was the kind of thing which a writer would be simultaneously appalled and fascinated by, but it was certainly one of those moments when, as a child, you realize that terrible things go on in the world which no one can do anything about. They're irreparable outrages, which can occur without causing any fractures on the surface of existence, and once I became aware that they surrounded us, I became interested in ways of making other people notice them. In this case, the man I was depicting subsequently abandoned his wife and son – after Suez, I think – and the son was eventually brought to England; but the wife was just left in Egypt.

There's a scene where Chris asks Ibrahim what 'colonialism' means, and Ibrahim replies, 'Means you talking to the wrong people,' which seems an odd attitude for an Egyptian servant to have.

Well, Ibrahim was an old reactionary, really. He was very opposed to anyone having anything to do with politics – although he had this bizarre fantasy that I was going to be prime minister. After I'd written the play, I learned that Ibrahim was actually Libyan – a fact which we had never bothered to discover – and that, after we left, he took his family – or families; I wasn't able to gather whether he'd managed to get both of his wives out of the country – and went back to Libya.

Interestingly, White Chameleon *was put on, as per Richard*

Eyre's original idea, in 1991, and happened to coincide with . . .

. . . the Gulf War, yes. It actually began after I finished writing the play, but I was certainly aware that trouble was brewing, just as much as it had been in the early fifties. But very few people made anything of that. In fact, the play passed off without making any particular impact. Audiences went to see it at the Cottesloe for a few months, and that was that. Nevertheless, it was a very special event for me. It was my first play for quite a long time, and easily my most personal. And it was a beautiful production, extremely well acted. So it didn't really trouble me that it didn't run for ages. I found it immensely satisfying, and I went to see it a lot while it was on.

And you also wrote a screenplay of it.

Norma Heyman and John McGrath were going to produce it, and we managed to get quite a long way down the line. I had a nice meeting with Julie Christie about playing my mum, and I'd asked Jeremy Irons to play my dad. We had a budget, and we went looking for locations in Tunisia and Morocco. But I wasn't able to come to terms with not shooting it in Egypt. You couldn't get insurance to film there, because this was just after all those tourists had been gunned down in Luxor, but I couldn't imagine filming it anywhere else. I know that's woefully unimaginative of me, but having survived the possibility of *Imagining Argentina* not being made in Argentina – for which there was enormous pressure – I now know that Argentina is such an important character in the film that its whole atmosphere depends on it having been made there. In the case of *White Chameleon*, we looked all over Tunisia to find what we wanted, but it just looks different, so at some point I would really like to venture back to Egypt and do it.

Your next theatre project after White Chameleon *was a musical adaptation of* Sunset Boulevard – *another example of doing something you'd never done before?*

I'd always wanted to do an opera – in fact, I'm about to do one with Philip Glass, based on J. M. Coetzee's novel *Waiting for the Barbarians* – and I thought *Sunset Boulevard* had the perfect opera plot. I first had talks with the English National Opera and a composer called David Blake, and we all got very enthusiastic about it, but then I said, 'Hang on a minute. I'd better find out about the rights.' One of the many people I'd met when I was writing *Tales from Hollywood*, to get some idea about life as an émigré in the thirties, was Billy Wilder. So, presuming upon our meeting, I wrote to him and said, 'We're very interested in doing an opera based on *Sunset Boulevard*. What's the rights position?' And I got a letter back promptly, written on elegant blue paper, saying, 'As a writer yourself you will not be surprised to learn that I have no rights whatsoever in *Sunset Boulevard*. You must apply to Paramount. Good luck!'

Which is exactly what Gloria Swanson had to do, when she tried to turn the film into a musical.

I didn't know that at the time, but that's absolutely true. Andrew Lloyd Webber has a tape of it, and it's an extraordinary item. Anyway, I applied to Paramount and they said that the rights were already spoken for, so that was that. A year or two later, Andrew invited me to lunch at the Carlton Towers Hotel. I knew Andrew through Tim Rice, and they actually asked me to write the book for *Jesus Christ Superstar*. They played me the demo tape, and I said, 'It's two hours long. Where's the book going to go?' and they said, 'We just want some linking material. We'll cut you in,' but I said, 'I think you'll find that people are familiar enough with the plot without my help' – blithely talking myself out of several million quid. Then, over this lunch at the Carlton Towers, Andrew offered me *Phantom of the Opera*, and I said, 'That's a dreadful idea. I don't think that'll work at all. But,' I said, 'there's something else I've been nurturing, which is an opera or musical based on *Sunset Boulevard*, but some bastard already has the rights' – at which point he smiled and pointed at himself.

Finally, after several more years, he called me and said, 'I'm going to do *Sunset Boulevard*. Would you like to write the book?' So I went to see him, and I said, 'I don't want to write the book, firstly because none of your musicals have books as far as I can see, they're all through-composed, and secondly because what I really want to do is write the lyrics.' He said, 'I've already asked Don Black to write the lyrics,' and I said, 'Then I don't quite know where that leaves me,' and he said, 'Well, you'd better have a meeting with Don.' So I had lunch with Don, whom I liked enormously, and I said, 'Look, I'd prefer to work on the lyrics as well as the book,' and he said, 'Fine, we'll work on the whole thing together.' And that's what we did – and had a wonderful time.

Andrew is always tremendously impatient – once he's made the decision to do something he wants to do it – but I was particularly busy writing all kinds of things – probably *A Bright Shining Lie* or *The Custom of the Country* – so we all used to go down to his house in the south of France for the first week of every month. We did it in six sessions, February to July, and it was very enjoyable. Don taught me the rules and regs of writing lyrics, and Andrew supplied us with the tunes in roughly the places he felt they should go, and I was enormously impressed with both of them. One evening I said, 'We need a hymn-like song about the dawn of silent movies,' and Andrew said, 'Right,' and pottered off after dinner with a thoughtful gleam in his eye – and the next morning he played us 'New Ways to Dream', the song Norma sings as they project one of her old films, which he had composed more or less overnight.

How much of Sunset Boulevard *was there in* Tales from Hollywood?

Sunset Boulevard was certainly in my mind when I was writing *Tales from Hollywood* – not least because of meeting Billy Wilder, who granted me an entire morning. We met in his office at Paramount, and I said, 'It's very kind of you to see me,' and he said, 'It's very good to talk about this. Most people want to talk to me about Marilyn Monroe's tits, and after half an hour what can you say?' In fact, he's enshrined in a lyric in *Sunset Boulevard*. All the songs were written with Don, but some of them are more him and some of them are more me, and one of the ones which is more me is the one called 'Sunset Boulevard'. In it, Joe Gillis says, ' . . . after a year/A one-room hell/A Murphy bed/A rancid smell/Wallpaper peeling at the corners,' because Billy Wilder talked about how he shared a room at the Château Marmont with Peter Lorre and they had a Murphy bed. I'd never heard the expression before and didn't know what it was, but it's one of those beds which folds up into the wall, and they were so poor that they had to draw lots for it. He hadn't actually fled from Hitler, he'd come earlier because he knew that Hollywood was where he wanted to be, or needed to be, to write the kind of movies he wanted to write, but he was still pretty desperate. He told me the famous story about a group of screenwriters who are standing in a room chatting to each other in Hungarian, when another one comes in and says, 'Boys, boys! Remember you're in Hollywood! Speak German!' He was an endless fund of these hilarious anecdotes. When we met he was editing *Buddy Buddy*, and he said to me, 'The patient is on the operating table. We don't hold out much hope!'

Horváth also has a one-room apartment with a Murphy bed, but unlike Joe Gillis he seems happy with that lifestyle.

Horváth isn't as discontented as Joe Gillis about things like that, but of course he's got a whole range of deeper concerns. He has a lot of guilt, really, as does Joe – but Joe's is of a more superficial kind, to do with selling out and leeching off Norma.

Do you think there's an element of self-criticism by Wilder in the character of Joe?

No one who's worked as a screenwriter in Hollywood could possibly fail to recognize themselves in Joe Gillis. Wilder had years of that kind of life, not knowing how to pay next week's rent and doing bits to make ends meet – and he was one of the successful ones. So of course there's self-criticism in *Sunset Boulevard*, in the same way that there's self-criticism in *Tales from Hollywood*.

Did it give you pause, writing a new version in a different medium of a classic film, with a figure like Billy Wilder . . .

. . . looming over you? Funnily enough, it never bothered me at all. I intended to be as faithful as possible, so I didn't think he was going to disapprove. And, in the end, he came to London and gave us his advice – very specific advice, like the fact that the doctor's arrival after Norma's suicide attempt didn't come at the right moment – all of which we listened to. They were the notes of a real professional – think about doing this precise thing at this exact point – rather than all that vague waffle you hear from studio executives.

It's quite common to adapt plays for the screen, but comparatively unusual to adapt films for the stage. What problems did it present?

You have to decide what is un-doable. For example, un-doable, I decided, was one of the most famous scenes in the film, where all those people come to play bridge with her. What are they called?

The waxworks.

The waxworks, that's it. Buster Keaton and so on. I just thought, 'There's no way you can do that, because the joke is that it *is* Buster Keaton and the others. But, in a way, because a play is so much constructed of dialogue, if you take a film which has a lot of dialogue – and good dialogue, at that – it's easier to adapt for the stage than it would be to adapt a play for the screen. In any case, Billy Wilder's films are arguably quite theatrical, because he comes from that great Austro-Hungarian playwriting tradition.

If the film is quite theatrical, was the play at all cinematic?

We wanted to refer to the world of movies without using obviously cinematic devices, but, in fact, Trevor Nunn did use quite a lot of fades and irises, so the whole thing was redolent of cinema.

Why did you want to do it as a musical? It's a form which has always baffled me.

A lot of people are baffled by musicals, because a lot of musicals are so dreadful. They're often sentimental or unambitious or compromised in some way, and therefore you can't understand why anyone would like them. It means that people tend to think of them as a kind of sold-out or inferior art form, which I don't think they are, properly done. If you see a really good musical, like *Cabaret* or *A Little Night Music* or *Evita*, it's very satisfying. I certainly enjoyed working on one. It was a rather enormous and scary object to sit astride, but once it lumbered into gear it was great fun to do.

Nevertheless, despite winning Tony awards for its book and lyrics, it didn't run and run like many of Lloyd Webber's other musicals.

It had just over 1,500 performances in London, and 997 performances on Broadway – which was rather vexing – but it never broke even, because it cost an absolute fortune. In fact, it was the most expensive musical ever mounted. The technical problems were immense. The main, glorious room, designed by John Napier, went up in a lift, and all through the previews it kept jamming and being set off by cab radios and so on. Then, after the Los Angeles production opened, Andrew closed the London show for two weeks and re-rehearsed it, because we'd realized that it was a mistake to minimize in any way the blackness of the story. It wasn't only to do with the text, it was to do with the look of it, so we soured it up a bit, and it was a much more cohesive show.

Did it amount to an extensive overhaul?

It wasn't enormous, but it was significant – and it's interesting that, although it wasn't very well reviewed on its first appearance in London, it subsequently got great reviews all over the world – as good, I think, as Andrew has ever had. And, if you talk to him on a good day, he'll say that it's his favourite of his musicals.

If you eventually soured it up a bit, were you previously aware of having . . .

. . . unsoured it? Well, I was aware that we'd gone for both light and shade. We hadn't sentimentalized it, but the scene at Paramount at the beginning, and the scene in Schwab's Drugstore, which doesn't really exist in the film, where everyone is merrily discussing how dreadful it is working in movies, we made tougher. Also, more of that part of the show was musicalized – like the Sheldrake scene, which became wittier and sharper than it had been. But the scenes in the house we left pretty much intact.

You said that you had an unredeemed taste for Gothic melodrama stretching back to your childhood fascination with Poe, and Gothic melodrama would be a pretty good definition of Sunset Boulevard.

Oh, it is. That's why I love it so much. The final shot of the film, with that face coming down the stairs, is high melodrama. And at the end of the show, we projected a huge photograph of Norma as a young woman on the back as she descended towards the audience, which also did exactly what melodrama is supposed to: shiver your timbers.

You've also adapted one of the most famous Gothic melodramas of all – Dracula *– again as a musical and again with Don Black.*

Don and I had wanted to do another show together, and when the composer Frank Wildhorn approached him to do *Dracula*, he said to me, 'Do you want to hop aboard?' *Dracula* is another of those books I read as a teenager, in search of the red meat of sensation. It's a bit chaotic, but the first seventy pages are absolutely riveting, and the thing as a whole is interestingly experimental, with all the different perspectives on the story. It's also *the* late nineteenth-century novel about repression, a subject which has always been of interest to me, so it joins a line of work which *Mary Reilly* belongs to – and *Liaisons*, in a way, which also deals with these mysteries of love and masochism and possession.

How easy was it to adapt?

It's actually rather difficult, because it's so long and rambling. Bram Stoker was a busy man and fitted in the novel when he could, so it doesn't really cohere. It's very poorly explained in terms of where Dracula comes from and what his game is and how many more of him there are. That's one of the things we're trying to iron out at the moment. We did a production in La Jolla which was very successful – packed out, in fact – but revealed questions that troubled audiences, like why Jonathan Harker gets bitten and doesn't turn into a vampire. We've done a second version in which all that is clarified, but I think we may have to pull back from it a bit. In other words, I think we've now got too much book – but, on the other hand, there's so much story to tell.

Are you aiming for quite a serious tone?

Yes, I think so – like the book. Bram Stoker was broken-hearted when, after the years it took him to write it, he showed the book to Henry Irving, whom he worked for, and asked him what he thought of it, and Irving said, 'Well, it's rubbish isn't it?' He was compensated by the fact that it was an enormous bestseller, but I don't think it is rubbish, and there must be some reason why the story has lingered for so long in people's psyches. Our version brings out the underlying theme of the book, which is, on the one hand, terror of sex, and, on the other, the fact that sex *is* quite terrifying. It's not camp at all.

Don Black told an interviewer that it took him thirty years to learn the craft of writing songs, but that you managed to pick it up in twenty minutes. Is that true?

The first time we met, he said to me, 'The thing I've learned about writing songs is that if you start at ten in the morning and you haven't written a song by six you feel like a fool,' and it's true, that's one of the most satisfying things about it. I'll go and see him, and of course there'll be a lot of pacing up and down and head-scratching and waving of rhyming dictionaries, but at the end of the day we'll have what we want. The danger is that you suddenly find you've written thirty songs and can't choose between them. There are already far more songs for *Dracula* than we can possibly fit in the show, so some good ones are going to have to be thrown out, which I understand is par for the course with musicals – although it didn't happen with *Sunset Boulevard*.

How does your working relationship with Frank Wildhorn compare to the one with Andrew Lloyd Webber?

With Frank, you have to supply your own critical sense, because he's such an affable man that his good nature tends to approve of whatever you might do for him. Not that Andrew disapproved; I don't remember being sent back to the drawing board at all on *Sunset Boulevard*. What disputes there were tended to be between me and Trevor, though never in an unfriendly way. On *Dracula*, there have been endless discussions between me and Don and Frank and Des McAnuff, who's directing it, but in this case the combatants are Des and Frank, because Frank's natural inclination is towards solo ballads, whereas Des – like Trevor – wants to nudge the show more in the direction of ensemble singing. It's tended to be Des saying, 'Can we have more of this kind of song?' and Frank wanting to do more of that kind of song, with Don and me sitting neutrally in the middle.

Have you enjoyed collaborating with someone at the writing stage?

Very much so. I usually get that experience of collaboration at a later stage, working with directors like Stephen Frears or Howard Davies or Richard Eyre, but it's very nice to have it at the writing stage as well. In the end, though, I'm probably too concerned about the shape of the writing to leave too much to chance.

Is that something you learned from Alice's Adventures Under Ground, *which is your only play to have developed out of improvisation?*

Again, that was a way of going down a path which I hadn't gone down before. I came up with vague ideas about what the structure should be, then the actors came in and acted out scenes from the books – which they then carried into scenes from life, as it were. Michael Maloney played the part of Lewis Carroll in the play, but the first time I worked with Ralph Fiennes was when he came in and played Carroll for a week in the workshops. As Alice we cast this amazing little girl, Sasha Hanau, who subsequently played the young Julia Roberts in *Mary Reilly*. Carroll is very specific that Alice is a girl of seven and three quarters, and only at that age are all her questions charming; in every other dramatization I'd seen she was much too old, and the questions seem moronic coming from a girl of fourteen. I'm glad I did it and I really liked the result, but you're right, I don't think it particularly suits me as a way of putting a play together.

What was the genesis of the play?

It was a proposal of Martha Clarke's, a choreographer who'd done some very interesting shows in New York, like ballets but non-linear and non-realistic, rich in imagery and suggestion. I wanted to work with her, and we kicked various ideas around, then she said that she'd always been interested in Lewis Carroll, who was the only children's writer whose work had really captivated me as a child.

Why do you think that was?

Because there's a melancholy at the bottom of it. I also wrote a screenplay version, and in that I went much further towards what I take to be the central wound of his life – and the source of all his work. In my opinion, he was hopelessly in love with girls of about seven or eight, but this sexual obsession wasn't something he could admit, even to himself, and the crisis in his life came when he couldn't see Alice Liddell and her sisters any more because their parents wouldn't allow it. Martha was going to direct the film for the BBC – until they discovered what it was about – and she and I went to Christ Church and discovered that from his rooms, where he had a telescope set up, he could see into the nursery of the Liddells' house across the quadrangle. I don't think he was a voyeur as such, just someone who waited for the lights to go on so he could watch the life behind the windows. I think he was a very unhappy man, and that twisted its way, like the word 'Brighton' in a stick of rock, through all his work – particularly *Alice Through the Looking Glass*, which is darker in tone than *Alice in Wonderland*.

Darker in what way?

There's more violence. There's more misunderstanding. And, as you work your way through the book, it becomes easier and easier to identify Lewis Carroll in these sad, strange characters. They're all evasive and melancholy and short-tempered, and they all have long conversations with Alice in which they seem to be trying simultaneously to educate and mislead her. I can't think of any other scenes in literature quite like that, where there's a strong sense of engagement with a child but at the same time an urgent desire not to tell the child the truth. In a crude sense, the books are about the way life doesn't have in store any of the things which you're told it does as a child – and also how, if you're a bright child, you'll understand that.

Life, of course, means growing up, which Carroll wouldn't have wanted Alice to do.

That's right. He was pretty open in his correspondence about the fact that there was a very narrow window of interest for him – between the ages of seven and ten – and that after that he didn't want to know these children any more. His letters to them are quite cruel, really, saying things like, 'I'm sorry, but you're too old for me now.' Frustratingly, on the day that whatever it was happened between him and the Liddells to get him banned from seeing Alice, the page is carefully torn out of his diary. He also had lots of photographic plates of nude children who had posed for him, and on or around that day – and this is included in the screenplay – he smashed them all, except for four which have somehow survived. It's as if he suddenly opened the door and saw the monster and said, 'I can't go there any more,' and if you read his later children's books they might have been written by another person. He became a fussy, moralizing old gentleman.

When the characters from the books appear in the play, they're dressed as Victorian ladies and gentlemen rather than as the Mad Hatter and the March Hare and so on. Why did you decide to do that?

Because I think the anthropomorphic approach sentimentalizes the books and makes them cute and false, whereas this was an interesting way of throwing some new light on them. I had the notion that they were more about life as an Oxford don than had previously been acknowledged, and that their surrealism was only a step away from the reality of Carroll's bachelor existence. We all know how eccentric those people are today, so God knows what they were like in the nineteenth century, when they weren't allowed to marry or anything. There must have been a lot of extremely clever, totally bonkers people wandering about. We went further in the screenplay, with the dons at the college playing the characters from the books, so in a sense the screenplay is less abstract than the play, but I still thought the play was very beautiful.

How was the play received?

Politely, I think, is the word. Some people were very struck by it when they saw it, but it was a slightly unexpected beast. It didn't have a linear narrative as such; it was more like variations on a theme. A lot of it was to do with the look of it, and the charge of certain images. I found it weirdly moving whenever I saw it, but it succeeded on a not particularly explainable level.

{8}

Hotel du Lac – The Good Father – The Wolf at the Door – Nostromo – A Bright Shining Lie – Mary Reilly – The Custom of the Country – The Secret History – The Day the Earth Caught Fire – The Night-Comers – The Cloak of Vice – Silent Witness – The Quiet American – Tulip Fever – Atonement – Chéri

The first two projects you worked on after Les Liaisons Dangereuses, *adaptations of Anita Brookner's* Hotel du Lac *for the BBC and Peter Prince's* The Good Father *for Film Four, are also concerned, in their different ways, with the battle of the sexes. Were you aware of wanting to pursue that subject futher?*

To be honest, I was pretty strapped for cash at that point in my life, because *Liaisons* had taken up part of 1984 and the rest of it was devoted to *The Price of Tea*; and, since *The Price of Tea* was not going to be made and *Liaisons* was only playing in a tiny theatre, when these offers came along I seized on them. But I wouldn't have done them unless I'd really responded to them. *Hotel du Lac* I adored, and I continue to be a great fan of Anita Brookner's. Sue Birtwistle and Anna Massey had the good luck – or the percipience – to acquire the rights before the novel won the Booker Prize, so there was a big buzz behind it which didn't do us any harm. I also liked Peter Prince's work in general and *The Good Father* in particular, because it dealt with something which I hadn't seen dealt with before: the fallout from the so-called women's liberation movement. I saw that it would be possible to make something along the lines of *The History Man*, about an interesting historical moment, but I also thought that it would be a chance to do a kind of *Kramer vs. Kramer* without the gush.

Reading both books and watching both films reveals something rather interesting about the way you adapt novels: rather than picking and choosing the scenes you like best and expanding those, you try to include as many scenes from the book as possible by boiling them down to their essence, thereby retaining not just the spirit but the substance of the novel. Would you agree with that?

I've never analysed it in that way before, but I'm sure you're right. I don't like to lose things from books, but, equally, if you pick the right image or the right line, you don't need to spend a lot of time expanding on them. That's the beauty of film, that you can convey those things in seconds. With *Hotel du Lac*, I thought it was simply a question of capturing the essence of the novel as best I could. Almost uniquely in the work I've adapted, the dialogue was so good, so clear and pointed, that I used it more or less verbatim. In that sense, the screenplay almost wrote itself. I wrote the first draft – or *the* draft, because there was only one – in about three weeks, then did some more work on it with Sue and the director, Giles Foster, later in the year, but there was really very little revision.

The *Good Father* was more complicated, because it has a more ragged, less shapely narrative, and there were certain aspects of the novel which I didn't pay much attention to and others I heightened, and so on. I remember asking Peter Prince why he wasn't adapting it himself, since he's a more than competent screenwriter, and his answer was that it was so personal he didn't really want to go there again. But, at a certain point, he panicked a bit and wrote a draft of his own, to highlight the things which I'd ignored and vice versa, and, faced with the two alternatives, Mike Newell was flailing about trying to see if he could combine them. I said to him, 'I think you'll have to do one or the other, really,' and, rightly or wrongly, he decided to do mine.

Mike Newell was originally slated to direct Carrington, *so presumably this was quite a happy collaboration?*

I hardly participated in the shooting at all, because Mike isn't particularly interested in having the writer around, but I'm very fond of him and also very grateful to him for inadvertently launching my career as a director. So I was very happy that he did this, and very happy with the result. The film was barely released in England, but there were reviews in America to die for. I remember a review in the *Village Voice* which said, 'I would suggest that there is no possible alternative to Anthony Hopkins for the Best Actor Oscar this year, if that would not be demeaning his performance.' I suggested Tony, actually; I had him in my mind while I was writing it.

I was struck by the length of Hotel du Lac *and* The Good Father: *the latter is ninety minutes and the former just seventy-five, and they still manage to be very faithful to the original novels. In other words, brevity really is the soul of wit.*

I think so, yes. And one of the things I'm pleased about when I look at those films again – although I haven't seen *The Good Father* for many years – is that they're pretty amusing. If you frame a line correctly, or put it in the right spot, or have the right actor deliver it, it will make audiences laugh – which, of course, is something I've always liked doing. Less so recently – or, at least, I've managed it less recently. There aren't many laughs in *Imagining Argentina*, God knows, or indeed in *The Secret Agent*, and I feel slightly regretful about that. There are subjects where it's just not appropriate, but my pleasure is to make an audience laugh. I've always got a buzz from that.

Interestingly, bearing in mind your adaptation of The Moon and Sixpence, *your next screenplay was about Gauguin.*

That was very interesting. I wrote *Hotel du Lac* and *The Good Father* back-to-back, very quickly, and at the end of it all, as I was breathing a sigh of relief, I got a call from Donald Sutherland in Paris, who said, 'Do you know anything about Gauguin?' I said, 'It's funny you should say that . . . ' It turned out that he'd been invited to play Gauguin in a movie by the Danish director Henning Carlsen, and that, having committed to make the film, he didn't really like the script, of which he'd only just been given a translation. Henning had directed a film called *Hunger*, based on a novel by Knut Hamsun, which I'd seen when I was knocking around in Paris in the late sixties, about a poor writer who's so starving that he starts hallucinating and eating his manuscript, and this film had struck a chord with me – to the extent that it's one of the few films I can remember watching and then sitting in the cinema and watching again, because I was so moved by it.

Anyway, I went to Paris and had lunch with Donald – who's absolutely charming – and after lunch I went back to the ghastly little hotel I'd landed up in – the same hotel from which Horváth sallied forth to meet his end – and I read the script. And I thought it was hopeless. But the idea was interesting: the story of Gauguin's return from Tahiti. He returned with sixty-six paintings and mounted an exhibition, thinking he was going to make his name, but the exhibition was a complete fiasco, with people pointing at the paintings and roaring with laughter, so instead he spent the next eighteen months scraping together enough money to go back. He eventually succeeded, by selling three paintings which had been given to him by Van Gogh – whose prices, after his death, were finally rising – and he left France, never to be seen again. Jean-Claude Carrière had written a very fanciful version of all this, full of heroic sexual encounters, and when I went back to have dinner with Donald – and Henning, who had arrived from Copenhagen – I said, 'It's a fascinating period in Gauguin's life, but I can't rewrite the script. I'd have to start from scratch and make it as close to Gauguin's actual life as possible.' This was Thursday, I think, and Henning said, 'There's a problem,' and I said, 'What's the problem?' and he said, 'We start shooting the Monday after next, and the sets have already been built.' They were the most expensive sets that had ever been built in a Danish studio, a whole street and courtyard from the Latin Quarter of Paris in eighteen whatever. So I said, 'What do we do?' and he said, 'We'd better go to Copenhagen and look at the sets.' And that's what we did. That was Friday, which left eight days to write the script.

So I wrote the script in eight days, and it was a fantastic experience. I was holed up in a hotel in the middle of Copenhagen, and I hardly left the room at all – except, at one point, to change my room, because the cinema next door was showing *Ran*, and, after two days of the sound coming through the wall, I could recite the dialogue in Japanese. The only other time I left the room was when Henning asked me to come to the studio and meet Max von Sydow, whom he'd asked to play the part of Strindberg. Strindberg, rather unexpectedly, was a friend of Gauguin's in that period, because Gauguin's landlady was a Swedish sculptress and used to hold Swedish evenings to which

Strindberg would come, so there were three big Strindberg scenes interspersed throughout the film. Anyway, I arrived at the studio and there's Max von Sydow, this great actor, and I said, 'You have three scenes. In the first scene, you meet Gauguin, who takes you upstairs and shows you his paintings, and you're impressed by them but don't really like them. In the second scene, he asks you to write the notes for the exhibition. And in the third scene, he comes and visits you in hospital, where you're laid up with psoriasis, and talks about how it's a necessity of art to suffer.' So I explained these scenes to him, and he said [*Swedish accent*], 'OK, I do it.' Then I went back to the hotel.

I finished the script on Sunday, and they started shooting it on Monday – which, in my view, is the ideal way to make a movie. And it's a very good movie. It was never released in England, but it got good reviews in America and did quite well in France. It was called *Oviri* in Denmark, which is the way Gauguin signed a number of his paintings – 'the savage' – but we called it *The Wolf at the Door*. Most of the minor characters were played by Danish actors, so for the English version we got the cast of *Liaisons* to come and dub the film. Alan Rickman played Degas, and Lindsay Duncan played Gauguin's Javanese model, and Juliet Stevenson played his French mistress, and so on, and it always amuses me when I hear it.

Whereas The Wolf at the Door *took you just over a week to write,* Nostromo *took you about a year. Is that right?*

August 1986 to August 1987. Peggy Ramsay did a brilliant contract, whereby I was contracted for six months and thereafter I'd have to be paid by the week – and I could have been on that weekly salary for another three years, because there was no reason for me to stop working on it if I hadn't excused myself to do the film of *Liaisons*.

Hadn't you already done some work on an adaptation of the novel before being approached by David Lean?

I wrote a detailed treatment for a seven-hour version, which Stuart Burge was going to direct for the BBC. He'd already done TV adaptations of Conrad's *The Secret Agent* and *Under Western Eyes*, so I thought I was in good hands; but there came a point, when we were talking to a Latin-American gentleman with extremely shiny shoes who told us that he could deliver the Venezuelan army no trouble at all, that a little voice in my head said, 'This is never going to happen.' And it didn't. I then got a call from Peggy, who said, 'Lean wants to see you.' I'd met David when I was younger and he was thinking of doing a film about Stanley and Livingstone, but he never referred to this meeting, so he may have forgotten it by the time we met again. I was summoned to this amazing house he had near Tower Bridge, converted from two warehouses, and I walked into the enormous study he had on the ground floor, with the river going by outside the window, and he looked up at me and said, '*Nostromo*!' I said, 'Yes?' He said, 'I gather you're interested in adapting it?' I said, 'Absolutely.' He said, 'Would you like to do a movie of it?' I said, 'Of course I would.' It took a few days for me to get used to his manner, which was quite scary, but like a lot of people of that kind it was just a carapace for shyness, and he was actually a very sensitive man. He went to see *Liaisons* at the theatre, for example, and he hadn't been to the theatre for years, so I was very touched by that – and he seemed to quite like it. He was also a man with astonishingly little confidence in his own talent. He hadn't seen *Brief Encounter* since the disastrous preview screening in Rochester when, about halfway through the film, a woman started to laugh and gradually the laughter spread until, by the famous ending on the platform, the entire cinema was in fits of laughter. He told me that he couldn't bear to watch it because it upset him so much, and having gone through something like this myself I can understand the feeling, but I said to him, 'Do yourself a favour: get it out and look at it. It's extremely good.'

Anyway, I was hired and went to work. He left me alone for the first six weeks – although he called two or three times a week to ask, 'How's it going?' – and after that the routine was that a taxi would come just before nine and trundle me across London to Docklands, and I would work with him all day – with a break for lunch, prepared by his wife Sandra – then finish at about six and get home about seven. And that was my life for a year – except for three months from January to March, when David went to stay at the Marbella Club, and I used to fly out to Marbella every Tuesday and come back every Friday. We always started at ten in the morning when we were there, and one day Sandra put her head around the door at ten in the evening and said, 'You haven't eaten all day!' The work was pretty intensive, but I thought we were very close to solving the knottiest problems, so I was feeling quite high at that point.

Then, in late spring, we went back to the beginning again – which was always slightly dispiriting – and, at the same time, *Liaisons* opened on Broadway. David very reluctantly gave me a week off to go to the opening; then Milos Forman announced his film of *Liaisons* and, because the agreement with Lorimar guaranteed that my version would be out first, I had to make a decision between *Nostromo* and *Liaisons*. And my decision was, because I'd begun to flail with *Nostromo*, that I'd go away and do *Liaisons* and then come back fresher. I said that to David, but he was very upset about it and kept me working until eleven o'clock on the last night of the last week of the contract. I then called him once a week, and one week when I called, while I was in pre-production in Paris, I felt some strange inhibition in his voice. I said, 'Is everything all right?' and he said, 'Actually, I'm sitting here with Robert,' and I knew then that he'd moved on to Robert Bolt. I had, probably foolishly, effected a reconciliation between them the year before, because it seemed ridiculous that they weren't talking to each other but were both professing that they wanted to – and, as it turned out, Robert was on the project for another three years. Several of my screenplays have assumed the proportions of the one that got away, but I think this was the one that got away most unexpectedly.

How different was the screenplay you wrote for Lean from the one you outlined for the BBC?

It was very different, because the amount of time you had on TV meant that you could go into the political ins and outs of the novel: the liberals and the radicals, the priests and the bandits, all the different factions Conrad deals with. And, towards the end, I imagined that you would be able to let fly with a tremendous amount of spectacle: sea battles and land battles and so on. But you had to chuck all that out if you wanted to get the story told in two and a half hours, and I was so enamoured of what we wrote that when the BBC eventually came back to me and said, 'We've got the money now,' I said, 'I'm sorry. I can't imagine doing a seven-hour version any more. You'll have to find someone else.' Which they did.

And how different was Robert Bolt's screenplay from yours?

The main grounds for dissent between David and me were the characters of Decoud and Hirsch. There are three principal characters in *Nostromo* – Decoud, Gould and Nostromo himself – and all of them are destroyed by money in one way or another: Nostromo because he steals it, Gould because he becomes a tycoon and winds up completely in thrall to it, and Decoud because he understands the damage it does but enjoys the privileges it provides. The story doesn't work, it seems to me, unless you present all three characters in all their fullness and show that these very different men are equally destroyed by the brute force of this money. It couldn't be a more resonant theme. But David wasn't at one with me on that. For a start, he couldn't get it into his head that Decoud wasn't a Frenchman, he was a Costaguanan exile who had spent a lot of time in Paris. He also wanted to despise the character, and wanted the audience to despise him as well, because he hated intellectuals. I remember him saying, 'He's a bit like Ken Tynan, isn't he?' and I said, 'In what way?' and he said, 'Too clever by half.' Decoud does have all the weaknesses of the intellectual, like mixing with the powerful people he condemns, but that's why he eventually commits suicide, to avoid a fate he takes to be worse than death. But by the time David and Robert got to where they were going, he'd become a complete caricature, a foppish dandy whom you were invited not to take seriously, which is a misunderstanding of the material.

Hirsch, on the other hand, they cut completely, which I just couldn't understand, because he's such a crucial character. The main sequence of the book – or what we took to be the main sequence – is the escape at night across the bay with a boatful of silver, and part of the tension comes from the fact that Hirsch stows away on board, and Gould and Nostromo discuss what to do with him to stop him giving them away. Finally, a shipful of soldiers crashes into the boat and Hirsch is borne away on an anchor as they go by – and winds up being tortured by them. But when he's being tortured, the torturer makes an anti-Semitic remark and, although Hirsch is a coward who stowed away on the boat because he was so scared of what was happening in the town, he spits in the torturer's face and the torturer shoots him, without getting any information about the silver. David was very worried about all this, and it turned out that he was worried because he'd been accused of anti-Semitism over the character of Fagin in *Oliver Twist* and he didn't want to be accused of it again. So he simply cut the character, which took the tension out of that whole sequence.

This is one of the dangers of working on a screenplay for a long time: you forget the basic principles you started with. The other thing which is hard to remember over a long period, which is always uppermost in your mind when you're writing something for the first time, is precisely how much information to give the audience and at what point. When you start rewriting it and changing it, all that tends to go out the window and fatal mistakes can be made. The besetting sin of commercial movies is that the film-makers either give the audience information at the wrong time because they've rearranged things, or else they've become so familiar with the information themselves that they forget to give it to the audience at all. You'd think that they'd have tumbled it by now, but time after time you go and see a movie and know that someone has said, 'What if we just changed this?' forgetting why they had the idea in the first place. David actually wrote the final draft of *Nostromo* himself, and it's hard to imagine an audience understanding it at all, because so much vital information had been glossed over. It was like a tone poem: impressionistic, very visual, hardly any dialogue. It was also a lot shorter – probably because, at his rate of shooting, if the script had remained the length it was when I turned it in, it would have been a five-hour film.

If he hated intellectuals, what was his attitude to writers?

He was very fond of writers. I think he responded to their artistic side, as opposed to their intellectual side – although he also hated the idea of people calling themselves 'artists' – and he talked very affectionately about all the writers he'd worked with: H. E. Bates, Noël Coward, Terence Rattigan, and so on. But he felt intimidated by intellectuals and thought his intuition was more valuable than their intellectualizing – and often he was right. There was an expression he would use: 'very wicker basket'. I never quite understood it, but it was a condemnation of fancy intellectuals. He thought Alec Guinness was 'very wicker basket'. In fact, he was ferocious about him. I said, 'You can't say these things. He's so great in so many of your films,' and he said, 'Oh, he's so difficult,' and I said, 'What do you mean?' and he said, 'He's the kind of actor who if you want him to sit down will always stand up.' He had every image of every film in his head before he started and didn't want people to disrupt the frame or move about when not requested to, so actors with ideas of their own were a kind of torment to him. I don't think that's the only way to direct films, but it was his way. I prefer to prepare very carefully and then leave certain things open to chance or improvisation on the day, but I think that notion was very alien possibly to that whole generation but certainly to Lean – and even more so to Zinnemann, who planned everything down to the inch. But they were good people to train with, because I've seen people turn up on set without any clear idea of what they're going to do today – and it's very destructive.

Given that Conrad's work in general, and Nostromo *in particular, is so thematically resonant, how did you manage to work so closely with Lean without any intellectual discussion of those themes?*

I just tried to keep all that under my hat – as much as I could. If you're told, out of the blue, that you've got to spend the next year writing an adaptation of one of the most difficult books of the twentieth century for one of the most demanding directors of the twentieth century, and you say yes, you can't really complain. And, in fact, I enjoyed it. I found David fascinating, and I learned an enormous amount from him. I was creating the skeleton and he was putting the flesh on the bones, and you knew from the way he was talking about it that it was going to be pretty spectacular flesh – so the whole thing remained exciting. He loved the scene where they rush the silver down from the mountain to load it onto the boat and get it out of the country; and the sequence which we called 'the day of dust', where all the armies converge on the town and there's this day of fighting and looting and confusion in the middle of a dust storm whipping great clouds of dust through the streets; and the love scene with Nostromo, where he and the girl are illuminated every few seconds by the beam from the lighthouse. You can see how brilliantly he would have orchestrated all that. I remember being so keyed up the night before we started working together – and this had never happened to me before and has never happened since – that I dreamed the opening of the film, the skeleton sitting on the bottom of the ocean with the silver spilling out of its coat pockets, and when I told him he was genuinely delighted – and, in fact, the scene was still there in the very last draft, although the detail of where you would cut to from there was much greater. I just wrote this image and then cut to Nostromo doing something or other, but David came up with the idea of rising from the body with an air bubble and emerging from the sea to reveal the geography of the Golfo Placido – which was brilliant, I think.

People think that the visuals were what really concerned David, but I think that what concerned him most was the editing. He was always very interested in the last image of one scene and the first image of the next. He once said to me, 'Should this be a cut or a dissolve?' I said, 'You're the director!' He said, 'But what do you think?' I said, 'I don't know.' He said, 'I don't know either.' So he got the storyboard artist to do three watercolours, two showing what it would look like if there was a cut and the third showing the dissolve, and he studied these and then decided whether it should be a cut or a dissolve. All the technical discussions were interesting. John Alcott, who died during the course of the year so wouldn't have ended up shooting the film, came for a fascinating discussion about the lighting of the escape by boat. At the start of the day David said, 'It's supposed to be absolutely dark and absolutely still. How are we going to see it?' and by the end of the day we'd come up with some very interesting ideas. I'd read somewhere that the seas around North and South America are much more phosphorescent than anywhere else in the world, so I suggested that we could use a lot of phosphorescence in the water; and because we were going to shoot it in a tank, John talked about how to make pencil light look like starlight; and David came up with the completely unrealistic but rather brilliant idea that the main lighting source should be the silver itself, the gleam of the silver. I'm sure making the film would have been fascinating as well, although no doubt it would also have driven me crazy – because, once David forged that relationship with Robert, he wanted the writer on the set all the time.

One of the producers on the project was Steven Spielberg. What dealings did you have with him?

Spielberg was originally the producer, but David had a falling out with him and he prudently withdrew. I didn't go to the meeting in Los Angeles where they fell out, but David came back and said, 'He gave me notes! Who does he think he is?' and I said, 'He thinks he's the producer, and he is.' He was scandalized, but I saw the notes and thought they were worth paying attention to. I only had one meeting with Spielberg, at David's house, and he said to me, 'I've tried to read this book and I can't, so I've got two very crass movie questions. Who's the hero?' I thought, 'Is this a trick question?' but I said, 'Nostromo.' He said, 'Yes, I see that. But it's about Nostromo going to the bad, right?' I said, 'Yes. Even the most heroic of characters can't stand up to certain pressures.' He said, 'That brings me to my second question: who's the villain?' I said, 'The villain is the money.' And he said, 'Ah,' and moved off in a thoughtful way. But I think, when he thought about it, he realized that it was the right answer.

You finished the script in 1987, and Lean died in 1991. Why didn't the film get made before the Bolt rewrites?

There was a certain point, about six months in, when Warner Bros. agreed to put up half the money and John Heyman undertook to raise the rest, and David said, 'If they don't have enough faith in it to put up all the money, tell them to bugger off.' And I think that was a mistake, because the film could have gone into production some time in that year, 1987, with a budget of $50 million. Then Serge Silberman became the producer and apparently had nothing but huge rows with David from day one; David died six weeks before shooting began, and there was an enormous insurance claim; and a year later, Serge, whom I'd never met, was going through all the material, found my script, which he hadn't been shown, called me and said, 'I think this is the script we should have gone with. Would you be interested in resuming work on it?' I went to Paris and met him, and thought he was a fascinating chap as well, with a body of work about as distinguished as any producer ever, including those French-language films by Buñuel and Kurosawa's *Ran*, so I was very interested.

He asked me whom we should get to direct it, and my slightly sentimental idea was Hugh Hudson, who was David's favourite of the younger English directors. Hugh had only made three films at that point, including *Revolution*, but Serge watched them and decided it was a good idea. So Hugh and I went back to work on it, which I enjoyed very much, and we produced the version that was published, which restored all the things I've been talking about – like Decoud and Hirsch. We also scaled the budget down, from about $45 million, which is what David had in 1991, to about $30 million. David was going to shoot all of it in the Victorine Studio in Nice and in the studio in Madrid where he did a lot of work on *Doctor Zhivago* – probably because he knew he wasn't well but also, perhaps, because the script had moved towards this abstract artificiality – but we went to the places in Mexico that he had originally earmarked as possible locations, and found that they were great. A piece of work as complicated as this is asking a lot, though, and we simply couldn't raise the money. Every now and then Hugh and I have a conversation about it, but the only way to make that kind of film now is to get a star attached.

What else did you do to the script after you resumed work on it?

I did some things which I'd always wanted to do but David had never let me do, like having a certain amount of dialogue in Italian. The story takes place in this imaginary country, Costaguana, and in it there's Decoud and his girlfriend and the high society of the town, who are South American but speak English in the script; there's Gould and Mrs Gould and Dr Monyghan, who *are* English; and there's Nostromo and the old man and his wife and their daughters, who are Italian; and it seemed perverse not to distinguish between them, because the audience would be less confused and the film would have more colour. So the draft I did for Hugh was my ideal draft, but I didn't feel disgruntled that the draft I did for David *wasn't* my ideal draft, because I was writing a David Lean film, and I fought with him as much as I could and then found a way which satisfied me to do the scene in the way that he wanted.

You've adapted two novels by Conrad, Nostromo *and* The Secret Agent. *Why do you admire his work so much?*

He seems to me to be the precursor of much of twentieth-century fiction. I don't think Graham Greene could have written a book like *The Quiet American* if Conrad hadn't blazed a trail first. Of course, he had no success at all for a long time. *Nostromo* and *The Secret Agent*, which were written back-to-back, are astonishingly innovative, but they both fell on stony ground. *The Secret Agent* was completely ignored, really, and it's hard to imagine that you'd be bored by it, so it must have dealt with subjects that people don't want to think about. Peggy used to say that the thing about original work is that it's always ugly in some way, and I think that, although Conrad was admired by other writers, the general public just couldn't get their heads around the harshness of the truths he was putting in front of them. And that's probably still the case.

Conrad is interesting, because he had a conservatively bleak view of mankind – derived from the fact that his father was a feckless radical who caused, as Conrad saw it, the death of his mother by getting the family into all kinds of political trouble – but at the same time a chivalrous belief in the importance of the individual. Also, he was so committed to telling the truth that he refused to allow his political views to overwhelm his stories. Although he's very clear-eyed about the hopelessness of the rabble in *The Secret Agent*, he does make distinctions between the ones he likes and the ones he detests. In the preface to *The Nigger of the 'Narcissus'*, he says that he tries to give you 'all you demand; and, perhaps, also that glimpse of truth for which you have forgotten to ask'. That seems to me as admirable an artistic manifesto as has ever been written, and I would say that I try to adhere to that myself.

I gather that your wife doesn't share your enthusiasm.

She says Conrad is a boy's writer; and, with the exception of Winnie Verloc in *The Secret Agent*, characterization of women was certainly not one of his strong points. I think he idealized women, though not in as distorting a way as Dickens. Dickens had no clue how to write women – which only goes to show what a great writer he was, because he managed to transcend that rather large defect. Mrs Gould in *Nostromo* is another woman Conrad had a good shot at, but she's more idealized than she should be. It's also to do with the subject matter: spies and policemen, and exotic climes and silver mines, and the ambitions and darknesses of men.

Another screenplay about the ambitions and darknesses of men – and another one that got away – was your adaptation of Neil Sheehan's epic history of the Vietnam War, A Bright Shining Lie. *How do you feel about that one now?*

I feel worse about that one. I had such an interesting time on *Nostromo*, and learned such a lot, that it compensated for the film not being made; whereas with *A Bright Shining Lie*, the amount of work involved was so colossal, and the result, it seemed to me, was so close to the best work I've ever done, that it was particularly embittering that it didn't get made – or, that it did get made, but only in an awful television version. *Nostromo* was vast enough, but *A Bright Shining Lie* was a thousand-page book with fifty other books in its wake.

In the introduction to your Collected Screenplays, *you quote from a letter which you wrote to one of the producers, Jane Fonda, explaining why you thought that the film should be made for cinema rather than television; and in it, you describe the central character, John Paul Vann, as being a symbol of 'both the conduct of the war and the reasons for its inevitable failure'. Could you elaborate on that?*

He was rather like Lawrence of Arabia. He was one of the only Americans in Vietnam who made an effort to find out who the Vietnamese actually were, but the more he got to know and love them, the better position he was in to betray and destroy them – and the knowledge of that finally unhinged him. When he first arrived in Vietnam, he was a typically unreflecting, patriotic, gung-ho American, but he had this strange urge to find out what was going on – which, by and large, his superiors didn't share. The conduct of the war was based on rotation: people would arrive, they would do their year and then they would leave. The entire energy of the army was directed towards getting to the end of your year so you never had to think about it again – which, of course, is no way to run a war. Vann saw that right away, and he also saw that the so-called 'hearts and minds' initiative to win the trust of the Vietnamese people was badly thought out and prone to corruption by Vietnamese officials. In other words, he saw that the war was not going as it was said to be going, and that came as a big shock to him. The general in charge at the time, and the people making the reports about how the war was progressing, were instructed to say that everything was going well and that so many people had been killed and so many bits of territory had been subdued, and it was all complete fiction.

Vann was the man who made people aware that the Vietnam War was something other than what they were being told. Although he was a react-from-the-gut, shoot-from-the-hip kind of guy, and by no means an intellectual, he understood that there was a fog of lies surrounding the war – just as there's a fog of lies surrounding Iraq. No one is asking soldiers to be imaginative on the whole, and if you plunge them into a situation they have absolutely no knowledge of – no knowledge of the terrain, no knowledge of the culture, no knowledge of the people or what they're thinking or why they might be thinking it – then the result is going to be an unimaginable cock-up, which is exactly what's happening in Iraq. That we should be proceeding in such total ignorance is absolutely staggering, and that was what Vann understood. It never seemed to cross anyone's mind in America that the Vietnamese weren't candidates for the 'Domino Effect', because they'd been fighting China on and off for a thousand years and they weren't about to succumb to Mao. It also never seemed to cross their minds that, just as with Allende in Chile twenty years later, Ho Chi Minh could actually be the clear, democratic choice of the huge majority of the population of Vietnam. They never even began to think in those terms.

There's a line about that in The Quiet American, *which is like the prequel to* A Bright Shining Lie. *The American of the title, Pyle, says that he wants to give the Vietnamese people the freedom to choose, and the English journalist, Fowler, asks what happens if they choose Ho Chi Minh.*

That was a line I kept putting back in, and it finally survives, almost as a throwaway, as the two of them are walking down the street. And I'm glad it survived, because it's true. It's unlikely that, if they'd had the freedom to choose, 80 per cent of the people of Iraq would have voted for Saddam Hussein – but the fact of the matter is that no one knows. I don't know what the nuances are between one set of political beliefs over there and another, but if people are being driven to strap bombs on themselves, there's obviously something going on which you ought to pay attention to, rather than saying, 'They're just terrorists.' It goes back to one of my most sincere beliefs, which is that one of the greatest enemies of mankind is oversimplification. People need to say, 'Love is this,' and, 'Death is that' – or, 'Freedom is this,' and, 'Terrorism is that' – and none of it makes any sense, because all of these things are infinitely more complex than people wish they were. Therefore, getting involved in a country that you know nothing about, for principles so simple-minded that you can inscribe them on a pinhead, is bound to end in profound suffering and unnecessary waste. If you aren't pursuing some ideological goal and you go and spend some time in these countries, it quickly becomes clear what's going on. But 95 per cent of the people who go into these countries go in to conform them to a CIA worldview – or a Foreign Office worldview – and pay no attention to what the people of those countries might be saying.

Or, they pay attention and then ignore it.

Or, they pay attention *in order* to ignore it. So it seemed to me, when I was working on *A Bright Shining Lie*, that although there was a corpus of movies about the Vietnam War, ranging from *The Deer Hunter* – which is despicable – to *Platoon* and *Born on the Fourth of July* – which are good – to *Apocalypse Now* – which is extraordinary – they were all about the American experience, and, apart from Marlon Brando rambling on in his temple, you got no sense of the characters having made the slightest attempt to understand the country they're in or what the fuck they're doing there. And it seemed to me a huge gap, that there hadn't been a film which analysed why they lost the war, because it's such an extraordinary thing to have happened, for the greatest power in the world to lose to a few blokes in black pyjamas. And they lost for a very simple reason: because they were incredibly dim-witted and narrow-minded about the whole thing – and, by the way, learned nothing from it, which is why we're all in it again. Can Americans really think that Bush is leading them in the right direction and that there's any kind of coherence behind what's going on at the moment?

Between Vann's realization that the war is a lie and his death, he, to use Spielberg's description of Nostromo, goes to the bad, and one of his Vietnamese girlfriends puts it very well: 'Before you looked at the power, your eye was clear . . . Now you are the power, you have gone blind.' In other words, power corrupts.

That's right. The poor boy from the wrong side of the tracks becoming the first civilian general in American military history. Vann did his year in Vietnam, then left the army; but, because of his fascination with the country, he went back as a welfare worker; and, when it dawned on the military brass that he knew an enormous amount more about Vietnam than most Americans, he was drawn back into being a combatant. And once he achieved his original ambition to be a general, all thoughts of the good he could do for the Vietnamese people were subsumed into winning the war. After the Tet offensive, he was one of the few people who thought that the war could still be won. Whereas, at the beginning, he was pretty well the only person who thought that they were losing the war, by the end he had transformed into this lonely fanatic who wanted to prosecute it as violently as possible, because it had become entangled with his self-image. He died in this curious, dramatically unsatisfying way in a helicopter accident, but by that time he was more or less barking mad, I think – hence the only scene I invented, where he's visiting bomb craters and machine-gunning dead bodies because he's in such a frenzy. Like Lawrence, he was one of those strange outsiders who felt that they had somehow come home – first in terms of his sexual tastes, and then in other ways – but was unable to shake off his own nature efficiently enough to stop him from turning on the people he had felt at home with.

In much the same way that the film of The Quiet American *uses Pyle and Fowler's relationship with the Vietnamese girl, Phuong, as a metaphor for western attitudes to Vietnam, you draw parallels in your screenplay for* A Bright Shining Lie *between the way Vann treats the women in his life and the way he ends up treating Vietnam and its people – starting with the betrayal of his wife, which he regrets not because it was wrong in itself but because he cheated on her with the wrong person and got caught, prompting her to say, in response to his assertion, 'There's such a thing as lying in a good cause,' that, 'A lie's a lie.' It's quite an uncompromising opening, and he's a pretty unsympathetic character, but it does set out the movie's stall.*

It does. And that's why I chose to open with it. But it was one of the things which, for some reason, Jane Fonda and others didn't seem to like. I think both of the directors I worked with on it, Phil Joanou and Oliver Stone, could see the reason for opening like that, precisely because it does set out the themes of the piece very clearly. He does exploit, walk over, take advantage of and generally mistreat all the women in his life in very much the same way as his country does to Vietnam. I went to see Vann's wife in Littleton, Colorado – where the Columbine High School massacre subsequently took place – and spent a couple of days talking to her. I talked to dozens of people in the course of hacking Vann's story out of Neil's book, and found it very exhilarating.

How did working with Phil Joanou compare to working with Oliver Stone?

Phil was my off-the-wall idea to direct the film – which, to my amazement, Warners went along with for a while – and he was particularly good to work with. He was very intelligent and argued his points very articulately, and for me that's the best kind of collaboration, because you know what they're talking about and they know what you're talking about and you can beat out some kind of consensus. Those six months of working with Phil got the screenplay to the place it is now – which was, I think, a very good place – and I was shocked by the way Warners got rid of him and brought in Oliver. They told me that they had discussed it and decided that it was too big a project for such an inexperienced director – although by that thinking Spielberg would never have done *Jaws* and Coppola would never have done *The Godfather*.

I didn't have that many meetings with Oliver. I first met him at his offices in Santa Monica, in a room lined with cartons of Vietnamese uniforms; then he came to London for another shortish meeting; then I went and stayed at his house in Telluride, and he listed about a dozen things in the book, sometimes just incidents, sometimes whole themes or characters, which I had missed out and he wanted me to incorporate. I subsequently heard that he wasn't very enamoured with our conversations, because he was used to writers doing what he asked them to do and I was putting my own views. For example, I refused to write a voice-over for Vann on the grounds that he was not a reflective person. Oliver said, 'Well, can't another character do it?' and then he said, 'Maybe the narrator should be me, Oliver, talking about my own experiences in Vietnam and how they relate to this,' and I said, 'Fine. You'd better write that.'

What prompted Warners to approach you in the first place?

It was the idea of a woman called Allyn Stewart, who was an executive at Warners at the time. I remember saying to her, 'I really want to do this, but why have you come to me?' and she said she thought it would be interesting to have an outside per- spective, that someone who wasn't American could be more objective. So she got me hired, and I then had to go and pitch to Lucy Fisher, who was senior to Allyn, and eventually Jane Fonda and the designated producer, Lois Bonfiglio, came into the equa- tion. Lois Bonfiglio was the one who finally produced it for HBO, by which time battle fatigue had set in and getting the thing over and done with was more important than whether it bore any resemblance to the original set of ideals. It played so fast and loose with the truth – because the director wrote it in no time at all – that they had to dub on fictional names at the last minute. The whole thing was a disgrace, I thought. If it had been done properly, it could have been both popular and thought- provoking in a way very few films are – the kind of film which would have been impossible to ignore.

The film you wrote immediately after A Bright Shining Lie *was thought-provoking but not popular –* Mary Reilly. *Why do you think such a good film was so badly received?*

Stephen Frears gave an interview not long ago, which someone kindly pointed out to me, and when he was asked about *Mary Reilly*, he said, 'We never got the script right.'

Do you agree with him?

Stephen is so clever that from time to time he outsmarts himself, and the crucial thing that happened to *Mary Reilly* was that he thought it would help him steer the film through a big studio if he had a big studio producer to protect him; but the big studio producer, Ned Tanen, came with his wife, Nancy, who had a very fixed set of opinions and turned out to be more keen to impose studio values than the studios. That was the first problem. The second problem was that I was directing *Carrington*, so Stephen didn't have the writer on the set all the time, and I think that unsettled him. Then there was all the nonsense about the ending, even though the ending we wound up with wasn't that different from what I wrote in the first place; and finally there was the whole business of post-production, where he came out of all those fights with the producers with a film pretty close to the first cut he had nine months before. And, in fact, it's a film I like very much – obviously more than Stephen does.

It was originally going to be directed by Tim Burton, wasn't it?

That's right. I'd spent more than a year writing *A Bright Shining Lie*, so I just fell on this and wrote it in about a week. I've never written a script so quickly, and I've never received such messages of congratulation. Directors and actresses were phoning the studio trying to get in on it, but the rights had been brought to Sony by Tim Burton's producer, Denise DiNovi, and he was going to direct it. We only had a few sessions together, and he wasn't particularly coherent in terms of saying, 'I want this, this and this,' but he would talk about scenes in a very expressive, eloquent way which was somehow more inspiring than if he'd said what he wanted. Then he had a row with Sony about *Ed Wood*, because they wanted him to shoot it in colour, so he took it to Disney, who agreed to finance it in black and white, and Sony were so annoyed that they took him off *Mary Reilly*. And the next thing I knew the phone rang, and it was Stephen, and he said, 'They've offered me your film.' Norma Heyman came on board as producer, because Denise DiNovi had left with Tim Burton, and we went and met Julia Roberts, who seemed absolutely right for the part. Stephen said to her, 'You're not allowed to smile,' and nor does she. The critics said that she looked gloomy and depressed throughout, which just means, 'Wait a minute, she's trying to do something outside her normal range.' None of them said that she was doing it very well. Instead, they sneered at her Irish accent, which can't have been that bad because Neil Jordan, who is Irish, proceeded to hire her for *Michael Collins*. They just picked on the most abjectly simple things to write about.

What kind of film do you think Tim Burton would have made?

I don't know. I suppose it would have been quirkier, but I have no sense of where he was going to take it. I did have a sense that a lot of the longer dialogue scenes made him a bit uncomfortable, because they were so outside the frame of what he normally does, but I don't know whether the goodwill that existed between us to try and move our respective styles towards some kind of coherent apex would have succeeded or not. We found that we were both very enthusiastic about *Mrs Beeton's*, which I'd read as part of my background research to find out what it would have been like to be a domestic servant at that time; and somewhere in there is an account of how difficult it is to kill an eel, so that's where that scene comes from.

In adapting Valerie Martin's version of the Jekyll and Hyde *story, did you go back to* Jekyll and Hyde *itself?*

Oh, yes. I read a lot of Stevenson, and came to like his work very much. There are some things in the film which are from *Jekyll and Hyde* and not from *Mary Reilly* – the murder of Sir Danvers Carew, for example, which was one of the violent scenes I was prevailed upon to add. I'm very fond of Valerie's novel, but as it proceeds, particularly towards the end, it leaves so many thoughts hanging in mid-air that you're obliged to complete them – and often I found that you could complete them by going back to the Stevenson. Things that were hinted at in her book you could hook up with things that were hinted at in the Stevenson and make something concrete out of them rather than just a poetic suggestion.

Surely the whole point of the novel, which takes the form of Mary's diary, is that the story is told from her point of view? In order to make the film more violent, you have to add scenes she couldn't possibly have witnessed – like the murder of Sir Danvers.

I think you're right. And I suspect the first draft was told from her point of view. But the more money you spend on a film the more noise you're obliged to make, otherwise people don't notice you've spent that money, so if a film is all atmosphere, that tends to go out the window – although I think the film is pretty atmospheric, actually. I've always said that the biggest mistake that was made with the film was the amount of money that was spent on it. I remember Ned saying, 'We've got Julia for $8 million, which is much less than her usual salary,' and I thought, 'If you'd offered her $1 million and said, "I'm sorry, we can't pay you any more than that," 'she'd certainly have done it.'

There's more of Hyde both in your screenplay and in the film than in the novel, and you've also brought out his sexual desire for Mary and vice versa. In fact, what your screenplay and the film seem to be saying is that she's in love with Jekyll . . .

. . . but is attracted to Hyde. And in some vile way her attraction to Hyde is connected to the abuse she received from her father, which is the subtext that everyone was keen to avoid in the film but is the central psychological observation in the book. Something which didn't work in the film, which should have been the simplest thing in the world, was the fact that the peculiar way Hyde walked reminded her of her father; but you're not aware of it, even though you've got the scene of her father walking back with the bag of rats, and pretty soon after that you have Hyde coming into the house for the first time. It's like the moment in the film when he smells her on the stairs. That didn't come across, either, and I don't understand why.

The cyclical nature of victimhood is a theme which the film shares with Liaisons, *and another is the redemptive power of love.*

The ending we wound up with had to do with Hyde being unmanned by this girl who isn't frightened of him, isn't even resistant to him, because he so closely resembles something she understands from her past. The fact that she understands him rather than reacting with total horror, which is what everyone else he came across must have done, causes him to save her by sacrificing himself. What was interesting about the story – or what Valerie Martin had done with it – was that it narrowed the gap between Jekyll and Hyde and said that Hyde was in some senses a wish fulfilment for Jekyll. Of course, Stevenson says that as well, but the idea had been obscured by the many versions of the story, especially the two movies in 1931 and 1941 where Jekyll is portrayed as a pillar of the community. That isn't there in the original story. The original story is a brilliant metaphor for repression and what it does to people; and what it does to Jekyll is make him unable to gratify himself, so he transforms himself into someone who thinks about nothing *except* gratifying himself. And that's there in the film.

Jekyll talks about having a sadness which 'comes in like the tide' and a desire 'to be the knife as well as the wound' – lines which I don't think are in the novel.

As a matter of fact, the two lines you've just quoted are both from Baudelaire, because it seemed to me that the atmosphere of the book, and this hinterland of outrage and desire which comes sweeping over him, was very much like what I remembered to be the atmosphere of Baudelaire. He also says at the very end, 'I wanted the night, and here it is,' which is another quotation from Baudelaire.

The novel ends with Jekyll as Jekyll. The film ends with Jekyll as Hyde, in line with Hyde's comment that 'I am the stronger.' Were you trying to say that, in the end, evil is more powerful than good?

That's also going back to the Stevenson. In the Stevenson, Jekyll commits suicide, but when they find the body, it's Hyde, and I thought that was very strong, because it's his true essence coming through. One of the objections raised by people who didn't like the film was that it was ridiculous that Mary couldn't tell that Jekyll and Hyde were the same person. In fact, the objection was raised before the film was even made, and I added a line where she says, 'How could anybody possibly guess?' Because, in reality, it wouldn't cross your mind, would it? You might think two people were slightly similar, but you'd never think they were the same person. But that's an example of where you can't reason with an audience. An audience will think, 'I know Jekyll and Hyde are the same person, so how come she doesn't?' and then feel patronizing towards her – and you can't legislate for that, really.

What kind of working relationship did you have with Julia Roberts?

My working relationship with Julia wasn't extensive, but we got on very well. I thought that the points she brought up in the course of making the film were very intelligent, and some of the rewrites had input from her. She was also large-spirited enough not to think that the failure of the film was a failure in the wider sense.

In addition to the scripts for Mary Reilly, Carrington *and* Dangerous Liaisons, *which have all been made, you included two unmade scripts in your* Collected Screenplays – A Bright Shining Lie *and* The Custom of the Country. *Out of all the scripts you could have chosen, why did you choose the latter?*

It's the other unmade script, apart from *A Bright Shining Lie*, which I'm most pleased with. I loved the book. When the producers, Joan Kramer and David Heeley, sent it to me, I read the first hundred pages and thought, 'I don't suppose I'll do this,' but then I became more and more gripped as it went along. Firstly, its plot is so unpredictable. Secondly, it's about people behaving badly, which is always enjoyable to watch. And thirdly, it lends itself to dramatization much better than the other Edith Wharton books that had been filmed. *The House of Mirth* and *The Age of Innocence*, which are her other two masterpieces – and *Ethan Frome*, which is slightly out on its own – have all been filmed, and they're all tremendously sombre affairs; but in this she seems to be kicking her heels up and having a bit of fun, and I like it for that, although that's not to say I dislike the others. It is a serious book with a serious point, to do with America giving up on Europe, but it could be done in a way which would be very entertaining. It was Edith Wharton's biggest success at the time, but like Conrad's big bestseller, *Chance*, it's not very well known any more.

The theme of America giving up on Europe is very contemporary.

There was a time, around the turn of the century, when America stopped emulating Europe, and this was something which Edith Wharton, being a close friend of Henry James, was very aware of. Henry James kept looking to Europe until he died, but Edith Wharton realized that wasn't a relevant subject any more, because something new was happening in America. The giant was awakening and stretching its limbs and saying, 'I don't want what I'm supposed to want. I want something different.'

And the character of Undine Spragg represents that?

Yes, she does, and she can't understand why everyone's getting so upset about it. Basically, she just wants to gratify herself. Not gratify herself in a sexual way – I sense that she's not particularly interested in sex – but gratify her whims and desires. Uma Thurman has been keen to play the part for some years, but it's hard to raise money on an actress, however eminent or successful she may be, and it's hard to find actors prepared to accept secondary roles in a film about a woman. This is something I've experienced many times, particularly with *The Custom of the Country* but also with *Carrington* – and even with my screenplay of *Hedda Gabler*: the difficulty of getting a film off the ground if the central character in it is a woman. People are astonishingly reluctant to fund them, and you can't believe that they could be so retrograde. Look at the strength of the Hollywood film industry in the forties, when they made all those pictures about women and their stories. Or just look at *Carrington*. Women's stories are so often more powerful and more interesting and more sympathetic than men's stories. I simply can't understand what the problem is.

People also had problems with your screenplay of Donna Tartt's novel The Secret History, *didn't they?*

That's right. I read the novel when it came out and enjoyed it very much, and called my agent and said, 'Is there any prospect of being asked to write the screenplay?' And the answer came back that Warners had bought the rights for Alan J. Pakula and he would be happy if I did it. So I did a draft and delivered it and everyone seemed very pleased; then I did a second draft and delivered that; then, after a long silence, Alan called me and said he thought there was a big problem with it, which was that the central character was so passive. I said that, as far as I could see, that was what the story was about – an outsider longing to be part of this charmed circle of people, and becoming complicit with them in an essentially passive way – and I didn't really know how to solve that problem. So he said that he would do a draft, and we could discuss it; and he did; and when I read it, I thought it had taken all the sense out of the story. Throughout all this, he was making *The Devil's Own* with Harrison Ford and Brad Pitt, which had its own difficulties. And soon afterwards, he had this horrendous accident driving home from his office, in which he was killed. So silence descended again. Occasionally, I heard vague stories about other writers having a crack at it. Then I heard that Warners had sold it to Miramax for Gwyneth Paltrow to star in and that her brother was going to write the screenplay and direct the film. And most recently, I heard that the option had reverted to Donna Tartt, so who knows what might happen in the future.

What was it about the novel which you enjoyed enough to ask about adapting it?

I was looking to do contemporary subjects, which I don't get offered very often. And I thought it would be good fun, which it was: I enjoyed writing it and I liked working with Alan, who was extremely shrewd and sympathetic. But mainly, I thought it was very original; there was a real sense of a new, distinctive voice. It reminded me of F. Scott Fitzgerald, because it dealt with the kind of privileged east-coast characters who don't get written about much any more. I was also interested in the idea of the bad teacher, the guy who takes all these impressionable intelligences and deforms them and then disclaims any responsibility – which is a figure we can all recognize. The structure of the book was very original, too, and that was another great discussion point. I stuck to the structure, which has the murder right at the beginning – like a teaser, telling you which direction the story is heading in – but this was endlessly debated, because it didn't follow the rules of what was supposed to happen on page thirty-three and so on. It's like an esoteric religion which these executives cling to: I don't know what they're talking about, and I suspect *they* don't know what they're talking about, but it gives them a *way* to talk about whatever it is they're talking about.

My view is that if you take a book that you like – and why, on the whole, would you take a book that you didn't like? – I don't see any reason not to be faithful to it. There is such a thing as being too faithful, but if you take a book that's been a success you'd be quite stupid to change it, and this book was an immense success. Yes, it's about a bunch of students studying Greek literature and it does assume that the audience has half a brain, but it's also a thriller and the public did buy it in vast quantities. This perpetual underestimation of the audience's intelligence always angers me. Audiences are looking for something stimulating, something which will engage their minds, not a lot of bloody explosions all the time. So I went into it, as I usually do, thinking, 'They're bound to make this film, because it'll be very successful and very interesting.' I mean, what's the problem?

The novel is divided into two parts of almost equal length, but in your screenplay the first part occupies roughly ninety of the 135 pages. Why did you diverge from the original structure in that way?

I've always been in favour, both in plays and in films, of what I call plot acceleration, of upping the energy as you go along and getting from the climax to the end as quickly as possible. It's particularly extreme in *Imagining Argentina*. The climax of both the novel and the film is the death of the daughter, but in the novel there's quite a lot left after that, and in the film we get from there to the end in about ten minutes. Once that terrible event has happened you just want to get out. *The Secret History* is rather like that. The first half is the fascinating bit, getting to know this group of people through the eyes of the central character, Richard Papen, and the slow unravelling of what it is they're up to as he becomes more accepted into their circle. The bickering and the infighting after the murder has taken place you can get through more quickly, it seems to me, because if you've set up the characters properly you can simply watch how everything plays out. In fact, the screenplay is still too long as it stands, and I guess the next stage would have been to do some weeding out and cutting down – some quite difficult weeding out and cutting down, because it's already quite tight.

You subsequently signed a three-picture deal with Fox, who are unlikely paymasters for someone with your views on studios. How did that come about?

I think it was the idea of Peter Chernin, who was one of the executives on *Liaisons*, and I was given a huge amount of freedom. I agreed to consider anything they asked me to do, but I wasn't made to do things I wouldn't normally have done.

One of the three projects, though, was a proposed remake of The Day the Earth Caught Fire *for the age of global warming, which* doesn't *seem like something you'd normally do.*

That was one of their many suggestions, and I particularly liked the original – which I remembered seeing as a schoolboy at the Hammersmith Odeon, in the days when there were still 3,000-seat cinemas. It was a marvellously imaginative film, given that they obviously only had about seven-and-six to make it, and it created the world of the newspaper very vividly. My thinking – naive as ever – was: 'They're making all these disaster movies one after the other. Wouldn't it be great to make one which actually had something to say about the way the world was going?' I liked the idea of doing a blockbuster action movie with a message, as opposed to a blockbuster action movie where the message is that you should have bigger weapons than everyone else. I was interested in the whole business of global warming, and how no one gives a fuck that the world is in serious jeopardy. I didn't realize how serious that jeopardy was until I went to the Global Warming Conference in Oakland, California, where speaker after speaker stood up and reeled off these terrifying predictions. I worked with a scientist at Columbia University to get the science as accurate as possible, and I was given a week's pass to Fox Television to get a sense of the television newsroom. I had a really enjoyable time writing it, but it had a quintessentially Hollywood denouement.

I arrived in Los Angeles for a big meeting with the producers and Jan De Bont, who was going to direct it, and the mood of the meeting was very positive until Jan walked in, sat at the head of the table and said [*Dutch accent*], 'I think we make a big mistake with this script,' at which point everyone looked stricken, as if they'd all just heard about a death in the family. Over breakfast the next morning, he tried to explain what the problem was, and what it boiled down to was that the two huge hits of the previous summer had been *Independence Day*, in which the central character worked in TV, and *Twister* – directed by Jan – in which the central character was a maverick scientist, and he thought it would be better if the central character in our movie was not a television journalist but a maverick scientist, because this year the maverick scientist was going to win out over the guy who worked in TV – i.e. *Twister* was going to gross more than *Independence Day*. It was completely absurd. So I wrote him a long memo – to which I received no reply – explaining why it was better to have an enquiring central character who explains all the science to himself and thus to the audience, and why we should keep the urban milieu.

Why did you think the milieu should remain urban?

Because the scale of the damage would be much easier to project. One of the things I learned from the Global Warming Conference – which we saw when that hurricane hit Washington not long ago – was that, as global warming proceeded, hurricanes would move further and further up the east coast of America, and therefore it was only a matter of time before one hit New York. That's the middle act of the script: when the hurricane hits New York and knocks over the Citicorp Building, which I discovered had been built without whatever they put in to resist high winds. And the final act, when people can't go out in daylight, also seemed a very interesting situation to set in New York – much more interesting than some bloke living in a log cabin in the forest sending emails saying, 'You've got to stop this!' which seemed to be what Jan was suggesting.

The fact that the central character was an alcoholic also horrified the studio, as it turned out. They said, 'Tom Hanks is waiting to read this. We can't ask him to play an alcoholic.' I said, 'What are you talking about? Actors adore playing alcoholics.' I once proposed writing a film for Tom Hanks in which he would play Roy Cohn, Joseph McCarthy's right-hand man and probably the most unsympathetic American figure of the twentieth century, and Tom Hanks was delighted by the idea. We didn't do it because someone else did it, but still. Anyway, they said, 'We can't show it to him. He won't want to play an alcoholic.' The last time I enquired, they said that they had no plans to do anything with it, because they felt that if they did do something with it, that would upset Jan De Bont, which they had no wish to do. I can't think why. Why should it make any difference to him?

A project which came closer to getting made was your adaptation of the novel The Night-Comers *by Eric Ambler, for producer Philippe Carcassonne and director Alain Corneau. Was that to be a French- or English-language film?*

The screenplay they had was in French and they wanted an English version of it, and they also wanted some more input because they were a bit stuck with it, so I was hired for two weeks to translate and rewrite it. I then did another draft, which took it further away from what it originally was, and then – we're talking about a time span of at least five years here – Alain decided that he didn't want to direct it, and Philippe asked me if I'd like to. He sent me and a couple of production executives to Thailand to look for locations, and I did yet another draft, which updated the story to 2001 and moved it to Sumatra, where a similar power struggle was taking place between Islamic moderates and fundamentalists. And then events overtook us, because the real world changed in such a way that it became difficult to envisage financing a film which dealt with the subject of Muslim politics – or that's what Philippe felt. We had some conversations about starting again and resetting the film in Phnom Penh in 1975, around the time of the Khmer Rouge, but I never got around to writing that draft.

The atmosphere of the novel, and its theme of a man forced to take sides, reminded me of The Quiet American, *although the story is set in a fictional country rather than an actual one.*

What the novel has in common with *The Quiet American* is that it is extraordinarily prophetic. The historical details indicate that it's supposed to be set in Indonesia; and, years before the Suharto coup which occurred in Indonesia in the sixties, here's Eric Ambler writing about a character called Suparto doing pretty much what subsequently happened. It's another example of a writer being so on the ball that he predicts the course of history. Unlike Greene, though, Ambler makes certain generic assumptions about political developments in that part of the world which don't bind you specifically to one country. It might be seen as an advantage to give yourself the elbow room of inventing the country, but in fact I read a stack of books to see if I could twist the story to mirror more exactly events in Indonesia and actually call it Indonesia.

What attracted you to it as a director?

I found the idea of making a simple adventure story very attractive, and I liked the characters. I liked the character of the girl, whom everyone looks down on because she's Eurasian, and the character of the villain – as I suppose you could call him – the unprincipled political intriguer who, like Suharto, wriggles his way through the middle and winds up on top. I also loved the physical side of the story, in which the central character has to use his expertise as an engineer in order to save their lives, and I thought the business of him and the girl being confined at the top of this building was quite sexy. It's the kind of film that people don't make any more, so I don't know how it would be received if you did make it, but I got very excited when I was in Thailand looking at the locations. I felt that, at the very least, you could make a film which would be great to look at.

You later collaborated with another French producer, Pascal Houzelot, on another English-language project, The Cloak of Vice, *this time for Stephen Frears to direct. How did that come about?*

There's this famous and very interesting nineteenth-century French play by Alfred de Musset called *Lorenzaccio*, about a political assassination committed by a disturbed young man, and Pascal's idea was not to adapt the play but to use the core of it and write a screenplay on the same theme: that in order to get close enough to someone to kill them, you have to adapt to them in some way, and the fonder you become of them, the harder it is to follow your principles and do what you think is right. The play is very literary and very romantic and plays fast and loose with history, and the only line I took from it was a line I also used in *Total Eclipse*, about putting on the cloak of vice and finding that it's stuck to your skin. It always takes me for ever to come up with plots, but Pascal had definite ideas about how it should be plotted – because he'd done lots of research into the historical background of the play – so we sat down and thrashed out the simple business of what happens, and I was happy to abide by that in writing it. It was rather a big job, actually. There's a lot of French literature about the period, and Pascal had found a contemporary account published in France in the sixteenth century, so I had an enormous amount of material to draw on – although, of course, I also had a grounding in the whole period from working on *The Florentines*.

It could almost be a companion piece to The Florentines.

The Florentines is set at the turn of the sixteenth century, and this is set twenty or thirty years later – after the Medici, who had been thrown out a couple of times at the beginning of the sixteenth century, were restored for a second time. At this point, the Pope was a Medici, Clement VII, and he was a very bad pope, because all he was interested in was getting Florence back. The Musset play doesn't deal with the Pope at all; it starts just before the assassination of his illegitimate son, Alessandro, and ends with Lorenzaccio being killed; but the most interesting thing in the historical sources is the fact that, at sixteen, this boy was forcibly made the lover of the Pope and fled from Rome as a result of an impotent act of revenge against him – smashing all the statues which the Pope adored so much. He then had this relationship with Alessandro, which turned from friendship and complicity into genuine horror, because the man was like Caligula, absolutely brutal and completely irrational. There were also other interesting characters, like Cosimo, the overlooked, ill-favoured eighteen-year-old who grabbed his chance, slipped through the gap and became Duke for the next fifty years; and Hippolito, who should have been Duke but was too good for his own good and got rubbed out along the way. I actually started the first draft with a race between these four cousins, which pre-figured what was going to happen to them, but Stephen felt it was too on-the-nose.

How many drafts did you do?

I did a couple of drafts, and then I felt that Stephen didn't really want to do it – but I couldn't get him to say that he didn't want to do it. He just said, 'I can only do it if it feels right, and I can't tell you what would make it feel right.' We started reworking it together, and we'd got to about page twenty when he said, 'I can't do this. It's too difficult. I'll give you my impressions of what I don't think works and you'll have to do it on your own.' He finally brought in a chap who teaches screenwriting at the National Film and Television School to talk to me about the plot, and this chap had some very good ideas; but I still sensed that Stephen didn't really want to do it, and I didn't have it in me to go on doing draft after draft when I had no idea what was wrong with it in the first place. Pascal is very anxious to do it, but it's a big undertaking, and UGC, who were putting up the money, didn't want to do it without a big director: a Frears or a Forman or a Bertolucci, someone able to make films on that scale.

There's a similar relationship to the one in The Cloak of Vice *at the heart of a very different screenplay, your adaptation of Richard North Patterson's courtroom thriller* Silent Witness, *which represented something of a departure for you in that the novel is a contemporary genre piece.*

I'm very fond of a certain line of films, which I think started with *Shadow of a Doubt*, a film written by Thornton Wilder for Alfred Hitchcock. Joseph Cotten plays a serial killer who comes to a small mid-western town and proves to be a much more com-pelling figure than the seemingly normal people who live there – so much so that his niece, played by Teresa Wright, adores him, precisely because she senses this aberration and is attracted by it. It's a line which goes all the way down through *Blue Velvet*, to do with America representing itself as the ideal in the world, with the picket fences and the clapboard houses and the high-school reunion – all that stuff which we know is merely the thinnest canvas stretched over a seething mass of bloodthirstiness and dissatisfaction – and it's something which I responded to in the plot of *Silent Witness*. The characters are less straightforward in the screenplay than they are in the novel, but the plot is very carefully followed.

The novel was sent to me by a producer called Lester Persky, who had a hand in a lot of interesting seventies films like *Taxi Driver*, and I agreed to adapt it if I could also direct it – partly because I wanted to make a contemporary film after *Carrington* and *The Secret Agent*, and partly because I thought it could be a non-clichéd addition to a rather clichéd genre. So I plunged into it, and I had one of the most interesting experiences I've ever had in preparing a film: attending a trial in Cleveland in which the accused, a dandy-ish black guy in his late twenties, was found guilty of a murder which he plainly didn't do. I was very shocked by this, and also by the fact that it was only because one member of the jury dissented from the verdict that he escaped an automatic death sentence. It was a very strange experience sitting in the courtroom watching all this going on, and the reason I did it was that I wanted to see if it would be possible to shoot the trial scenes in a way which was not like a thousand other trial scenes. I hadn't realized that it was all so casual and laid back. It didn't take place before a gallery of gasping people, it took place in a shabby little room where you had to break off for five minutes while someone from a completely different case was brought in to be sentenced.

The novel is basically a whodunnit, but the answer to that question is pretty obvious. Did you think that was a problem, in terms of maintaining suspense?

No, I didn't. In *Shadow of a Doubt*, you know throughout that Joseph Cotten is the killer, and it's not a problem there. I don't think suspense is to do with whodunnit; whodunnit is a rather uninteresting question. I think *why* the person did it is much

186

more interesting, and the *kind* of person who did it, and the kind of person who is *liable* to do it – psychological realism, in other words. That's what makes *Psycho* such a brilliant film, because it explains why that particular man was in that particular place doing those particular things, whereas when, in something like *The Bone Collector*, it turns out that the killer is a bloke in a white coat from reel one-and-a-half, you think, 'What's all that about? I'm interested in the people the story is about, not in some mad axe-wielder who turns up at five to twelve.' There's a twist which you don't see coming at the end of *Silent Witness*, but you do see that the killer is the killer, and that was something which worried New Line, who were preoccupied with how to pull the wool over the audience's eyes. I was never interested in that. I was interested in the way the central character talks himself out of what *is* pretty obvious to the audience: that his friend is the killer. That seems to me a psychologically very realistic observation, how readily people delude themselves. In the novel, the central character, Tony, is more conventionally sympathetic, but I wanted to make him more ambivalent and his friend more charming, so that the virtuous hero turns out to have a frightening amount in common with this psychopathic liar. One of the things which interested me most about the project was showing what happened in four different ways as the killer constantly modifies his story, so you only see what really happened at the end, but the trouble with ambiguities in films is that teams of highly trained idiots do nothing but point them out to you when you've put them in deliberately in the first place.

Did you get as far as casting the film?

We did quite seriously try to cast it at one point. In the first draft, the characters were seen at the ages of seventeen and forty-five, as per the novel, so it was necessary to cast two sets of actors, and there were a number of responses to the effect that young Tony was a more interesting part than old Tony. I eventually cast Dennis Quaid and Patrick Swayze. Patrick Swayze I knew very little about but was very impressed with, and I thought he'd be rather interesting as the killer. But the studio wouldn't finance it with those actors, even though I'd cast them within the parameters of whom I'd been asked to cast, so I thought the way around this was to be radical. Rick Patterson says that in reality you wouldn't be a leading criminal lawyer at the age of thirty, but there's a Hollywood reality of young actors playing lawyers, and it seemed better to have one actor play both the older and the younger characters, so I rewrote it to conform to that possibility.

Then Lester died, and that threw everything up in the air. I still could have made it, for USA Cable, shooting somewhere like Melbourne, but it was very much a second-best solution; so, given a straight choice between making *Silent Witness* and making *Imagining Argentina*, I chose to make *Imagining Argentina*. They wanted to go ahead with another director, and I said, 'I can't stop you from doing that,' but somehow Rick stopped them from doing it – which was very kind of him, and perhaps rather rash. Two of his novels have been televised and they were both emasculated – the plot of one of them turned on the sexual abuse of someone's daughter and all that was just taken out – so he was very bruised by his experiences and very anxious for this to be done properly. I get on well with Rick, and he recently sent me a list of his worries and objections and suggestions – which I asked him for, because the relationship between adaptor and adaptee can be very helpful. I certainly found Malcolm Bradbury and Peter Prince very helpful, and I anticipate that Ian McEwan will be very helpful with *Atonement*.

The perfect example of a novel being emasculated is Joseph L. Mankiewicz's 1958 version of Graham Greene's The Quiet American. *What do you think he would have thought of your adaptation?*

Presumably he would have thought it was an improvement on that, because that was a shocking betrayal of the novel: turning it upside down and making the character of Pyle an all-American hero – played by the all-American hero, Audie Murphy. Michael Redgrave gives a fine performance as Fowler, but it's still a travesty. I don't know how Greene would have felt about the changes I made, though.

When were you first approached to adapt it?

I heard through my agent that Sydney Pollack and Anthony Minghella were interested in making *The Quiet American*, and that Phillip Noyce wanted to direct it, but that they needed some work done on the script. I said, 'I happen to know the book very well. I'll start from scratch and do my own script.' So I wrote the first draft quite quickly at the end of 1999, and at the beginning of 2000 I went out to Los Angeles and worked very intensively with Sydney Pollack, Phillip Noyce and the producer, Bill Horberg, and did several more drafts. Their main concern was that the character of Pyle should be less two-dimensional than he was in the book, to provide an effective foil to Fowler rather than being a straw enemy who could be easily demolished. They felt that Greene's anti-Americanism had pushed the character into caricature and that it would be more interesting if he were more rounded. I also felt that the girl, Phuong, was much less interesting than she should have been and had been portrayed by Greene in a rather frivolous way which didn't take into account the reasons she was doing what she was doing. In fact, the only fully rounded characters in the book are Fowler and Vietnam – the rest are functional, really.

Probably because there's a lot of Greene in Fowler and he loved Vietnam.

Exactly. I also did a lot of research around the novel – into the character of General Thé, for example, a real character who's merely alluded to in the book. I discovered an incident at a press conference where he pulled a gun on someone who was asking him a question, and I put that into the story – although it didn't survive in the final film. Anyway, it was rather a good process, four of us around a table. I hadn't been through that kind of collective bargaining before. Sometimes these things become antagonistic and hence uncomfortable, but this was done with a view to finding the best solution. However, I was clearly more stubborn than they would have liked me to be, because, in the nine-month gap after I handed it in and before shooting began, Phillip had other drafts done by other writers. He had a draft done by Paul Schrader, certain elements of which remain in the film – like drawing out the suspense of whether Fowler will be called back to England and combining the characters of Fowler's assistant and the mysterious Communist who asks him to betray Pyle. That was a very good idea, but somehow the character hadn't been made into a character, so I found myself hastily writing those scenes after shooting had started, with the help of the actor who played the part, Tzi Ma.

So having been rewritten by others, you subsequently rewrote them?

Yes. Phillip called to tell me he'd had this done, and said that there were interesting things in the Schrader draft but he still considered me to be the principal writer, and asked if I'd come to the rehearsals and the shooting. I said I would, because I thought it was nice of him to ask. Then, on the day before rehearsals began, in February 2001, I was startled to be given yet another draft, written by Richard LaGravanese, which had been rustled up in the last few weeks. The principal thing of his which remains in the film is a scene I really don't like now: the climactic scene between Michael Caine and Brendan Fraser. There was a moment in the rehearsals when Phillip made them read my scene and then made them read LaGravanese's, and he plumped for LaGravanese's – which I couldn't understand, because it was so crude. He had Brendan making an explicit parallel between Phuong and Vietnam, which I thought was very on-the-nose and too heavy a weight to put on her character.

The principal thing which had been changed overall, which I'd resisted and they'd obviously decided had to be there, was the whole notion of maintaining the mystery about the identity of Pyle, so there comes a moment in the middle of that scene when Fowler reels back in astonishment and says, 'You're with the CIA!' Now, if you take the process of script development and compare it to being at the wheel of a ship, when you keep making small adjustments you end up steaming in the opposite direction; and, as I pointed out to Phillip, in order not to make Pyle look naive and stupid they'd made Fowler look naive and stupid, because this experienced *Times* journalist hadn't twigged what was clearly obvious. One of the jokes in the novel is that *everyone* knows Pyle is CIA – even Phuong knows he's CIA, before she's even met him – which I take to be the truth of that kind of situation. So the business of Pyle successfully pretending to be a trachoma worker, and Fowler playing detective to unmask him, is movie language rather than book language. I can see why they did it, and maybe they were right, but I didn't much care for it.

I carried on rewriting until about two weeks into shooting, when it occurred to me that nothing I'd said in the last two weeks had made much difference, either to Phillip or to Michael. Michael was focused, as he should have been, on doing whatever the director wanted him to do, and since the director wanted him to do a number of things which I didn't want him to do, I thought the best thing would be for me to proceed directly to the airport – which I did. I wouldn't like it to be thought that I'm harbouring resentment about *The Quiet American*, though. On the contrary, I like the film and I found the process of summoning every shade of opinion very interesting. I didn't find it demeaning or humiliating. What *is* demeaning and humiliating is when the studio does what they did with *Tulip Fever*, where you get fired because they've told you a lot of things which make no sense at all and you can't translate into any sensible modifications to the work that you've done. I did find it weird that the person I shared the screen credit with on *The Quiet American* was the only person who had none of his draft in the film – the previous writer, Robert Schenkkan – but that was probably Phillip's nod towards the fact that a lot of his ideas about the film had come out of their discussions.

Did you ever read the previous draft?

Only afterwards, when there was talk of an Oscar nomination and there was a big interview in the Writers Guild magazine with the two of us – at which point I had to admit to him that I hadn't read his script. Then you get into diplomatic areas. Phillip was upset when I said at the London Film Festival screening that Anthony Minghella had written the voice-over, because Anthony had written the voice-over on the strict understanding that no one would be told that he had written the voice-over. I didn't think it needed one; I couldn't see anything which needed explaining. I'm not saying it was badly done, just that it should only be used in films which have been planned around a narrator's voice.

Is it the case that in the finished film most of Michael Caine's dia-

logue was written by you and most of Brendan Fraser's was writ-
ten by Richard LaGravanese?

I don't think that is the case, but I do think that a lot of the stuff which was kept from LaGravanese was Brendan's stuff – including a lot of stuff which drove me crazy. He kept saying, 'No way,' and I'd say, 'They didn't use that expression in the fifties,' and people would look at me as if I was absolutely insane. That kind of pedantry is only of interest to me, it seems. Some of these things I managed to cut out and some of them I didn't manage to cut out – and some things which I didn't want to cut out were cut out. Various lines and speeches which I felt were central to the characters were taken out on the grounds that they were too bookish – decisions which, to my great surprise, Anthony Minghella completely endorsed. One of the things I most missed, which was cut out after the first draft for economic reasons, was the scene from the novel when Fowler goes up in a plane and the French pilot blows up a sampan and says, 'We've got the bombs, so we might as well do it.' That little sequence, when Fowler is trying to come to terms with the fact that he's lost Phuong and sees at first hand the meaninglessness of war, I liked very much.

The scene I most missed, which particularly struck me reading both the novel and your first draft, was the scene in which he tags along with a French patrol and sees them shoot a mother and child, mistaking them for the enemy.

Funnily enough, I spoke to Phillip about that, and he said, 'We've got the scene in the square at the end where there's a mother covering her dead baby with her hat. We don't need to have it twice,' and I thought, 'Fine' – although, of course, the reason you have it twice is to drum it home. One of the things I fought for, and kept whining on about until they shot, was Pyle getting blood on his trousers in the square, because that really is the clearest indication of the human cost of what he does – something which, in the exhilaration of war, people tend to forget. Phillip shot the explosion in the square for a week, and it was the first thing he did. In order to do it, they closed the main square in Saigon, and, because I could speak French, I had the extraordinary experience of chaperoning the wife of General

Giap, the Napoleon of Vietnam, who had expressed an interest in watching the shooting that particular week. She was absolutely fascinated. She had on her face the look of a woman thinking, 'This is just like old times!'

It seems a shame that the scene in the square is now seen partly in flashback as Fowler washes the blood off his hands back at the office. It lessens the horror of it.

I can see why they did that. Their priority was to show the penny dropping for Fowler. You didn't need to do that in my version, because the penny had already dropped hundreds of pages before. Nevertheless, I think they did justice to the scene. It wasn't as horrific as the way I described it in the original draft, but it was still pretty startling. Whenever anyone turned to me and showed the slightest sign of listening to what I was saying, I would say, 'It's absolutely vital that at the end of the film you don't think that he kills this boy because he's jealous of him and wants his girl back. That's not what the book is about. The film won't work unless the audience understands that he has him killed because he loves Vietnam and wants to prevent all the ghastly things which this young man's plans will do to the country.' And I'm pleased to say they got that. The extra irony, which I think Phillip brought to it – it certainly wasn't emphasized in my original draft, which had a more romantic ending – was that he avoids having to go back to England precisely because all these ghastly things he foresees do happen, and Vietnam becomes an important place for a journalist to be.

I gather that Miramax, who distributed The Quiet American, *were very nervous about releasing the film in the wake of 11 September.*

The first public preview was in New York on 10 September – Anthony Minghella was staying in the Mercer Hotel, pretty well next to the Twin Towers – and it was clear that whatever had happened would have an impact on the film. The story was that Miramax were so nervous about it that they wanted to consign it straight to video, and it therefore fell to Michael, who rightly felt that he'd given a sensational performance and didn't want it to be overlooked, to sail into battle and persuade Harvey Weinstein to allow it to be shown at the Toronto Film Festival – where it received tremendously good reviews. So Miramax were obliged to release it. And what could have been more timely than to bring out a film which said, 'Don't send your troops into countries which you know very little about, because it's a stupid thing to do and will end in tears'? But I suppose for that very reason everyone did their best to ignore it.

You've since written three more screenplays, two of them adaptations of bestselling novels: Deborah Moggach's Tulip Fever *and Ian McEwan's* Atonement. *Did you find those experiences equally interesting?*

In the case of *Atonement*, I read it and was very moved by it and let it be known that I wanted to do it and, although it turned out that lots of other people had done the same thing, Richard Eyre and I were eventually given the job of directing and writing it. With *Tulip Fever*, I'd already read the book when Paul Lister of DreamWorks approached me, and I thought it was very entertaining and would be great fun to adapt – which it was. As you know, I'm very interested in painters, and I liked the idea that the painter at the centre of this story only becomes good because the disasters which befall him somehow toughen him. I also like the look of Amsterdam in that period. Those Dutch paintings are so specific that you just want to animate them and go into them. The visualization of emotion is obviously one of the things that you try to do in films, but it's much more difficult for a painter to do that and fascinating when they succeed.

You weren't the first writer on the project, were you?

No, I wasn't. I think Deborah Moggach herself was the first writer on the project, and then Lee Hall had written a draft – which I subsequently read and which seemed to be mostly about the collapse of the stock market. It looked like one of those classic Hollywood misunderstandings, where they've said, 'This is interesting: it's like the bursting of the dotcom bubble!' When executives start saying things like that, you think, 'If you *want* a film about the dotcom bubble then *make* a film about the dotcom bubble, don't make a film about tulips, since, if you read the book carefully, you'll notice that the collapse of the stock market doesn't happen until after the story is over.' So I went back to the book and did a first draft, which they thought was so-so, and then I did a second draft, which they were much more pleased with.

What did you do to the screenplay to make them much more pleased with it?

Not a lot. I just did the work I'd normally have done, because the script meetings were the usual waffle. After they professed themselves delighted with the second draft there was a lot of hanging around, because they were busy working on some big, important film like *Lara Croft: Tomb Raider*, and they kept saying, 'Can we have the meeting tomorrow?' then calling to change it. Eventually, we did have this meeting, during which we all ate steak sandwiches in someone's office; and, when I got back and looked at my notes, I saw that nothing of interest had been said by anyone. So I did a little bit of work on it, sent it in and then there was a long silence. Finally, Paul Lister called me and said, 'They're very disappointed with the third draft, because you did so little.' I said, 'It was a forty-minute meeting, during most of which people's mouths were full!' But he said, 'They still feel you haven't really done anything, and they think they'll look elsewhere.'

Which they did.

Yes. And subsequent enquiries indicated that the thing which had displeased them was that I'd been so faithful to the book. But why buy it for a million dollars if you don't think it's any good? The brilliant climax of the book, and the main reason I wanted to adapt it, is the scene where the painter's unreliable servant is coming home with this incredibly valuable tulip bulb, which is going to buy the hero and heroine onto a boat and into the sunset, and in a drunken fit of absent-mindedness eats it, thinking it's an onion. That seems to me an absolutely brilliant scene, but Lee Hall had taken it out, and although I haven't read the Tom Stoppard version, I bet he's taken it out as well.

Atonement is much more ambitious than Tulip Fever. *Was it more difficult to adapt?*

It was technically more difficult – although, to be fair, I found *Chéri* even more difficult – partly because it doesn't fall into the usual three-act structure. It's really a two-act structure, with the two acts pretty much equal in length – or, if anything, the first act a little longer than the second – which means that you have to manage a tremendous gear shift, from country house life in 1935 to the retreat from Dunkirk. I thought the best way to do that was the way *The Deer Hunter* did it, where you just go – bam! – from one world to another. I think *The Deer Hunter* is a more than dubious film, but it does have this brilliant effect in it: an extreme change of direction which galvanizes the audience so that they trust you to bring the whole thing together again at the end. You also have to thread into those two acts the very short last section of the book, which reveals that it's been written by this character called Briony, who's a thirteen-year-old when the story starts, and that she wrote it to atone for this crime which she inadvertently committed as a girl. It's further revealed that she's been as truthful as she can in 75 per cent of the story but, unable to come to terms with all the facts, she's invented a kind of happy ending for the lovers which she has to confess is not what actually happened. Although this last section of the book is a real revelation, there are discussions and observations throughout about the nature of fiction which make it retrospectively logical, and you need to reproduce that so the ending doesn't just come out of nowhere. So that's the other technical difficulty.

How did you set about overcoming that?

You have to find a cinematic way of dealing with it, and my way of dealing with it was to start with this old lady and the manuscript on her desk called 'Atonement', without explaining who the old lady is. You don't know whether it's Briony or Cecilia – in fact, you're slightly misled in that respect – until halfway through the film, when you finally want to say, 'This is all seen from Briony's point of view.' In addition, I thought that this atonement of writing the book was not quite dramatically big enough, so I added the notion that she's led an entirely self-denying and celibate life to make up for what she did to her sister and her sister's lover. Everyone seems pretty pleased with the first draft, but it's early days yet. I think the thing to do is to write a second draft which is radically different in the way it deals with that particular problem, because the more different you can make the two, the more clearly people who are reading them can see which of the approaches works better.

Why did you find Chéri *even more difficult?*

The book is exquisitely written but very impressionistic: everything is implied. It's the first time ever that I've written an adapted screenplay which is longer than the original book, because everything which is hinted at in the book has had to be teased out. Things which are glossed over in a line or two you need a page or two to deal with in the screenplay, so it took me longer to write than any screenplay for quite a while.

Who are you writing it for?

It's for Bill Kenwright and Jessica Lange, but I've been interested in Colette in general, and *Chéri* in particular, for some time. I had the notion of writing a screenplay about Colette and talked to Lester Persky, the producer of *Silent Witness*, about doing it. Then Pascal Houzelot, the producer of *The Cloak of Vice*, said, 'What about doing a film of *Chéri*?' but we discovered that the rights had been bought by Jessica Lange's company and a script had already been written. Then, by coincidence, they decided that they weren't satisfied either with that script or a previous one and came to me, and, thinking it would be rather an easy one, I said, 'I'll do it!' I then discovered it was horrendously difficult, but Bill and Jessica are very pleased with the result and we're just beginning the process of finding the finance. Bill wants to make it for $8 million, which might be slightly tricky because it has to look absolutely exquisite. Colette wrote the novel in the twenties but it's set in 1912, harking back to that golden age before the First World War, and takes place entirely in what's known as the *demi-monde*. All of the characters are either courtesans, ex-courtesans or relatives of courtesans, and courtesans made fortunes during the *belle époque*. There was an enormous amount of money sloshing around towards the end of the nineteenth century, and one of the traditional ways of spending it was on these famous courtesans, so you need to create that world of country houses and luxury hotels and coaches and servants. I think you could make it for $10 million – although $12 million would be more comfortable – but we'll have to see whether the money is raisable at all on such a strange subject.

When did you become interested in, first of all, Colette in general?

I'd never read any Colette, because the French Literature course at Oxford ends in 1914, but Laura would often say to me, 'Collette is very interesting.' Then one day I was having lunch with Philip Roth, and he started talking about *Chéri*, and, when I told him I hadn't read it, he said, 'Colette is one of the greatest writers of the twentieth century!' So I read it and was knocked out by it, and then I read a lot more Colette, and then I became interested in her life, which is rather an intriguing subject. When she was eighteen or so she married an incredibly dissolute middle-aged writer, who encouraged her to write and then put out these huge bestsellers she'd written under his own name. She eventually left him, but without her royalties she was obliged to hit the road as an actress – in fact, as a kind of striptease artist in those touring *tableaux vivants* – which gave rise to another set of books, about provincial theatre in France. I get the impression that she's fading off the radar now, but she's a wonderful writer.

And Chéri *in particular?*

Chéri is like *Carrington*: it takes place in a very self-contained world but its concerns are universal. It deals with the relationship between a fifty-year-old ex-courtesan and the twenty-five-year-old son of another courtesan, and is basically about the demands and limitations of the body. They've been having this relationship for about six years, but at the beginning of the story the bombshell is dropped that his marriage has been arranged to the daughter of another courtesan, and at the end she lets him go and he leaves her for the last time. It's a tiny tragedy, and very touching. She backs out in the most graceful way, but you understand that she has no future because she's thrown away the last thing which ties her to life – and, in fact, in a much later sequel, Colette reveals that *he* never recovers either and winds up committing suicide because he's never been able to get back to the Garden of Eden. The main job is to find the right actor to play

Chéri, because otherwise the story won't make sense. The thing about him is that he's unreflective and unselfconscious, and the only way you can make him sympathetic and comprehensible to the audience is to convey that he doesn't know what's happening to him; so I want someone with an animal quality, someone who's comfortable with themselves and their sexuality, someone who lives a physical life and doesn't think about things very much and therefore, when faced with this huge decision about which woman to commit to, is completely baffled by his feelings and the fact that he can't control them. That requires a particular kind of actor, I think.

You're hoping to direct Chéri. *Do you think scripts benefit from being guided by one person throughout?*

If you write one lot of scripts which aren't buggered around with, and you write another lot of scripts which are endlessly buggered around with, you do get a sense that the ones which aren't buggered around with are the ones which work better, because the people who bugger around with the others do so with an imperfect understanding of why you've done what you've done. It's not that you're arrogant about these things; it's just that if you take a play like *Les Liaisons Dangereuses*, which was put on stage in the shape of its first draft, and you compare it to *Mary Reilly*, which squads of well-intentioned buffoons put their oar into, experience tells you that you have some innate ability to get it right first time. In Hollywood, the notion of getting it right first time and sticking by what you've done seems to be completely outlandish. You spend however long it takes researching it and writing it and changing things and polishing things, and then they say, 'We like this very much and are really looking forward to the next draft,' so you say, 'What do you want in the next draft?' and they have no idea. It's a kind of mania, and unfortunately the theatre has been infected by it as well. Of course, when you collaborate with people you respect and admire, good things can come out of it, but if you look at *Imagining Argentina*, it's more or less the script I wrote when I sat down to do it for the first time, and the same is true of *The Secret Agent*, for better or worse, and of *Carrington*, except that it's half the length it was. It's a strange thing, and it came up on

Imagining Argentina as it's often come up in the past, that the things which people most object to, the things which make them most uncomfortable, are the things which are most characteristic of you and therefore most original – so it's always those personal things which get smoothed away in the collaborative process.

That doesn't mean I've become so proprietorial about my work that I'm not happy to be writing *Atonement* for Richard Eyre, but with some of the more personal scripts, it does seem like a better idea to direct them yourself because at least you know what they're about. The other good thing about directing is that it's a way to avoid being shut out of the film-making process, which is almost inevitable if you're only the writer. If you're also the director you can enjoy the entire process – which is not to say that I haven't had many enjoyable experiences working with directors, simply that as the writer you're much more disconnected from a film than you ever would be from a play, where the impression is that the aim of the people involved is to try and realize your vision. That's seldom the case with movies. Most of the time they don't even make the movie, which means that far from trying to realize your vision they just pour it down the nearest gutter. The wastefulness of that is something I've never been able to come to terms with. It breaks my heart that I've done a lot of extremely good work which has not progressed beyond the script stage. On the other hand, to have had twelve films made, all within hailing distance of the original intention, isn't too bad. I'm looking for wood to touch now, but there are no genuine horror stories. There have been some tough times – *Imagining Argentina*, for example – but so far nothing catastrophic.

Carrington – The Secret Agent – Imagining Argentina –
The Talking Cure

In the introduction to your Collected Screenplays, *you say that you were 'shaken and haunted' by Michael Holroyd's biography of Lytton Strachey, on which you based* Carrington. *Why did the book move you so much?*

It's one of the few books to have had a really profound effect on me, in the sense that, when I got to the end of it, I couldn't stop thinking about it for days. I was really upset by it, to tell you the truth, so there was obviously something fundamental there which I responded to. I don't know what that is or why, but I did feel very moved by that story. It's an instance of something I've often talked about, which is that you take on subjects without really knowing what they're about, and they tell you what they're about while you're working on them. The first draft was called *Lytton Strachey*, and it actually took me some time to figure out that the story was about Carrington – the exact opposite of *The Talking Cure*, where I thought that the story was about Sabina Spielrein and then realized that the central subject was Jung.

So what is the story of Dora Carrington about?

It's a story about the irrationality of love and the fact that it's a different thing from sex, and how sorting out those differences is one of the most difficult tasks that anyone can face. Some people are lucky enough to combine the two in a satisfactory way, but Carrington worked out that although this person was and always would be her love object, that didn't necessarily have to cut across any other aspects of her life. As her life went on – and you see this in the little part played by Jeremy Northam – she found that the best solution was to have fleeting sexual relationships with people she had nothing in common with. The proprietoriness of someone like Partridge was not at all congenial to her. That's why, six weeks after finally agreeing to marry him, she made a pass at his best friend, Brenan. But she found Brenan equally impossible, because he wanted to be emotionally entangled with her. She was happy to meet him, or spend an afternoon in bed with him, but when he started to say, 'Come to Spain,' or, 'I must tell Lytton,' she just didn't want to know. She loved Lytton and wanted to stay with him, and nothing could be allowed to threaten that. In fact, in the end, she couldn't live without him, which I found tremendously moving. It was that unique, individual aspect of the story which interested me. The first draft had a much greater sense of literary society, and included people like Virginia Woolf and E. M. Forster, but, once I started refocusing on Carrington, I realized that she was not a part of all that: she was this strange creature who had fallen in love in this impossible way, and simply wanted to express that as best she could and get on with her work. I sort of fell in love with her, really. I just thought she was an enchanting woman.

How did the process of refocusing the script work?

It was really a question of going through it and stripping away anything that wasn't new information in terms of her character. For example, there was an elaborate comic sequence where she and Lytton and Ralph Partridge went on a disastrous excursion to Spain to visit Gerald Brenan, which was easy to take out. There was a section about her lesbian affair with a woman called Henrietta Bingham, which was by way of an experiment for her and therefore seemed rather peripheral. There was a second love triangle, apart from her and Lytton and Partridge, between her and Lytton and a sculptor called Steven Tomlin, which felt redundant. And, as I say, I took out all the scenes with Virginia Woolf. Virginia and Leonard Woolf were the last people to see Carrington alive, and there was a scene towards the end where they came to visit her, but it seemed more important to have that final scene between her and Partridge after Lytton's death. Because the whole story has the untidiness of reality, I could have left those things in and taken other things out, but I kept on trying to figure out what the essentials were. There's a scene I liked very much which I took out of the film, where Carrington and Partridge and his wife Frances are sitting around in paper hats eating Christmas dinner, and Partridge tells Carrington that Brenan is back in town, because he wants to get rid of her by restarting the relationship which he stopped; but it felt too late in the film to do that, to take a step backwards instead of pressing on to the end.

The film is divided into six chapters covering consecutive time periods, four of them titled with the names of the men in Carrington's life: Gertler, Partridge, Brenan and Lytton. Do you feel that by dramatizing her life in relation to the men in it, something of her own character gets lost along the way?

No, I don't feel that. I do feel that, in the editing, I tipped the whole thing slightly too much in the direction of Lytton. I cut some material at the last minute, mostly from the 'Brenan' section, to do with her growing desperation at trying to have a satisfactory sex life as well as her life at home with Lytton, and I feel that those scenes would have pushed the film back in Carrington's direction. But I don't feel that Carrington is less vivid a character than any of the men. She's obviously less flamboyant and aphoristic than Lytton, because Lytton was like an Edwardian Oscar Wilde and said all these hugely witty and memorable things, but you have to make Lytton an immensely vivid character to explain why she was so besotted with him, because it's quite mysterious. Certain people who read the script would say, 'I don't understand. Why does she fall in love with him if she was going to cut his beard off?' And I would say, 'That's what's fascinating about human nature: it's inexplicable.' It's why all these screenwriting rules are such a load of bloody rubbish. What makes people interesting is their irrationality, their bursts of strangeness, when they do things which aren't in the bleeding manual.

Why did you cut those scenes?

I made the film for PolyGram, who were exemplary to work for and didn't interfere in any way. The only thing Michael Kuhn said when I delivered it was: 'If it were five minutes shorter, I'd be happier.' Then the film was shown to the Cannes committee, and they said that in principle they'd like to accept it but they felt it was five minutes too long. So I thought, 'I'll just see if I can take five minutes out.' Ronnie Shedlo, who was the prime mover among the producers, was violently opposed to what I'd done and very vociferous about the fact that I shouldn't have done it; but PolyGram were happy, and the Cannes committee were happy, and I felt that the film was tighter and that the scenes I'd cut were moments when I'd felt the audience drifting slightly, so it seemed like the right thing to have done. But I would have liked the chance to put the scenes back for the DVD release – because they're not in the published script, either.

One criticism of the film was that Carrington's work doesn't feature very heavily in it. How do you respond to that?

I don't agree with that. One of the interesting things in making a film about Carrington is that her work wasn't just painting, it was the whole design of their lives. She painted the doors, she painted the walls, she painted the cups, she painted the fireplaces, she painted the Welsh dresser. She made an artwork out of their house, created a living environment at a time when people didn't do that. Her whole life had a kind of artistic imperative, which I think we were able to show without discussing it because it was there on the screen. I don't think artists talk about their art; they just do it. They're not very comfortable talking about it, really. That was certainly the case with Carrington, who was one of those English artists to whom the idea of being 'an artist' was rather scary and pretentious. She didn't want to be recognized as an artist. She refused to deal with galleries and just gave her paintings away to friends, and if she wanted to earn some money she would go and paint a pub sign. She sidestepped the business of marketing art in a very interesting way, I thought, and was exemplary because she wasn't doing it for anything except itself.

There were a lot of period films being made in the mid-nineties, and I read that you were concerned about your film opening in Britain first because you were worried it would get tarred with the 'heritage' brush. Is that true?

I think it is, yes. In no way do we suggest in the film that times were better then, but 'heritage' is an easy shorthand, and if your film slides into that category you're liable to find it pre-judged.

When we took the film to Cannes, against all possible expectations Jonathan won Best Actor and the film won the Special Jury Prize, and this baffled the British press, who had been very tepid about it during the festival – so much so that they reported it was a screenplay prize, or didn't report it at all. It seemed largely of no interest to the British press that a British film had won a couple of prizes at Cannes. If a British film won a couple of prizes at Cannes now, I think it would be better reported – but then, it's almost impossible to get a British film into Cannes any more. So that fed into my feeling that the film would not be particularly well received in Britain, and nor was it. I thought we'd be better off opening in America, but that was ignored. For me, the most significant statistic was that *Carrington* took more money in Argentina than it took in Britain. In fact, it did quite well around the world. It cost just under $6 million to make and it took about twenty.

Why were you so reluctant to direct before Carrington?

I just found the idea very scary. I'm not really shy but I'm quite reticent, and I've never felt that I've been able to be particularly eloquent about my work. Also, I've always thought that if you work with a good director, their objective eye will bring a different perspective. For all those reasons I didn't feel qualified to do it, although I'd spent a lot of time on sets watching other people do it, sometimes with pleasure and sometimes without. But it was back-against-the-wall time with *Carrington*, so there was no other choice but to take on the direction, and I had absolutely no idea how enjoyable it was going to be. It was one of the happiest summers of my life, making that film, next to sitting in the hammock writing it. I hadn't imagined that every morning you could get up and think, 'Oh good, we're doing so-and-so today.' I remember appearing on stage with Tom Stoppard and Stephen Frears for some BAFTA event; I hadn't directed at that point, but Tom had just made *Rosencrantz and Guildenstern are Dead*, and he spoke very eloquently, in a way I subsequently came to feel myself, about how nice it was to go to work every day, and he ended by saying, 'I can only tell you that I found it much easier than the daily grind of being a writer,' at which point Stephen leaned forward and said, 'That's because you're not a director.'

I've always remembered that. I kept thinking during *Carrington*, 'This shouldn't be as enjoyable as this. Why isn't it as miserable as struggling with a piece of paper?' and then I'd hear Stephen's voice saying, 'That's because you're not a director.'

Strachey says in Carrington, *'I've heard rumours to the effect that there are people who actually enjoy writing. Can this be true?' Does that reflect your own feelings about writing?*

Absolutely. Completely. That whole speech is very much my own struggle. One of the things about Strachey is that, even allowing for the fact that he died when he was only fifty-two, he wrote very little, and I think that was because he was one of those writers who was endlessly struggling with the process. And it really doesn't get any easier. It sometimes takes me until two or three in the afternoon to start writing, and even then I'm very weak in respect of the phone – in that if it rings, I want to pick it up. That's why now, when I have to finish something, I bugger off somewhere, because it's only by walling myself up in a hotel and saying, 'This is costing you two hundred quid a night, so you'd better get on with it,' that I can do it. It's one of those things where the more you know about it the harder it is, and possibly that's true of directing as well. I found a quantum leap in difficulty between *Carrington* and *The Secret Agent*, and I realized while making *The Secret Agent* that the reason it was far more difficult was because I knew much more than I'd known at the time of *Carrington*, when I just blithely sailed in with a kind of beginner's euphoria. *Imagining Argentina* was physically a very difficult film to make, because of shooting at night and in the cold and all the stuff to do with cars and animals, but because I hadn't done those things before, I enjoyed it as much as I enjoyed either of the other films. It's very exhilarating directing a film, because life sort of takes care of itself. In fact, it's rather like being a dictator: your only job is to articulate what you want, and you're surrounded by extremely skilled people who can give it to you.

Equally, they're there if you don't *know what you want.*

That was the other good thing about not directing until my late forties: I didn't have that arrogant insecurity of youth, where you have to know better than everyone else. I didn't have a problem saying to the costume designer or the director of photography, 'What do you think?' because these people have been doing their jobs for years and I'd chosen them because I admired their work. Likewise with the actors – although, of course, it's a bit more delicate with the actors. I think in that respect it's tremendously helpful if you've worked in the theatre, because I suspect that one of the problems that young American directors have, coming out of USC knowing all about blue screen and so on, is that they've never met an actor in their lives and don't know how to talk to them.

Given the number of actors you'd worked with in the theatre, how did you set about choosing your cast for the film?

I read a review of a documentary about Ken Loach in which he was quoted as saying that if you don't cast a film yourself you can't possibly pretend that you're the director, but I have to admit that, in the case of *Carrington*, Mike Newell cast Emma Thompson and Jonathan Pryce. I think he cast Emma a bit reluctantly, because I'd badgered him to do so, but I just knew that she was the right person for the part. Mike had wanted to go with Juliette Binoche, who's a great actress but, as I kept saying to him, is French – although, of course, I later cast Emma as an Argentinian. Jonathan, though, was his idea, and obviously a very good one. The rest of the casting was done with Janey Fothergill, who'd cast the TV version of *Tales from Hollywood*, and we went through the usual process of seeing people. Steven Waddington I had in my head as being physically exactly right for Ralph Partridge, so I offered him the part without even asking him to read – to his complete amazement. For the other parts I saw lots of people, but the thing about casting films as opposed to casting plays is that everyone tends to say yes to films. I'm not talking about really big stars, but, in general, if you ask people to be in a film they'll agree, and, if you have a fairly clear idea of who you want, it's an easier process than casting a play, where everyone is balancing whether they want to be in the play against what television series – or film – they've just been offered. So the casting process was relatively straightforward.

Were you receptive to contributions from the cast and crew – dialogue changes, for example?

We didn't make any changes to the dialogue at all. In *Imagining Argentina*, there was much more liberty for people to say what they wanted, because it has a naturalistic surface, but *Carrington* is not a film where you could do that, because the dialogue is very specific. In fact, all the way through – and this relates back to what I was saying about not knowing enough – the film was pretty much shot and edited in the shape of the script, with very few differences. For me, one of the ace contributions to the whole thing was the eye of Denis Lenoir, the director of photography, whom I became aware of when I saw, within a short space of time, Patrice Leconte's film *Monsieur Hire* and Bertrand Tavernier's film *These Foolish Things*, both of which he shot exquisitely. He reminded me of Philippe Rousselot, whom I'd thought of as DP but wasn't available, because he was doing some big film in America.

Actually, he was doing Mary Reilly *at Pinewood.*

So he was. Well spotted. Anyway, Denis was brilliant in terms of giving each section of the film a slightly different look, which he did by 'flashing' the negative – exposing it a little bit in the lab, so the image isn't as sharp as it would otherwise be. It's a technique which was used a lot in the seventies, in films like *McCabe and Mrs Miller*, to achieve a kind of pearly effect. In *Carrington*, the first section is quite considerably flashed, which makes the actors look younger – which is useful – and gives the film a soft, gentle, slightly nostalgic feel. Then, as the film goes on, the flashing is reduced and reduced until, in the last section, it's not used at all, so you get a subliminal sense of the scenes looking harsher and harsher. The other thing we did was to use an ochre-ish filter known as a 'tobacco filter' for all the scenes in which they were happy together; and, although none of this is necessarily discernible when you watch the film, I think it gave it a distinctive look which was particularly suitable to that story. That was the reason I chose Denis, really, apart from liking him very much: I'd noticed that all his films were shot in different styles, depending on what was appropriate.

The camerawork itself is pretty straightforward, though.

I wanted to avoid what I'd often observed in first films, which is
that the director throws everything but the kitchen sink at it.
Apart from what I've described in terms of treating the film, we
only did a few complicated shots. The most notable is obviously
the scene at the end where she's sitting out in the garden, which
took us two days to complete, but the scene where they're walking through the woods was pretty elaborate as well. There was
also a steadicam shot which I clashed with John McGrath over.
Perhaps not clashed, but he surprised me by how rigorous he
was about staying on budget, because he was a writer and therefore the one you least expected to be lecturing you about using
too much film. The shot I wanted was Gerald Brenan, sitting
abandoned on White Horse Hill, disappearing out of the top of
the frame, and the only way I could think of to do that was to
get a steadicam operator to walk backwards down the hill. John
said it was impossible, but the riggers did it very simply in the
end, by driving two stakes into the ground and roping the
steadicam operator to them, so he could walk down the hill like
abseiling down the side of a building. So we did try to make the
film look original in some ways, but mostly we told the story in
a straightforward way.

*Your production designer and editor also made important con-
tributions to that. Why did you choose Caroline Amies and
George Akers for those roles?*

I interviewed a lot of editors and I liked the cut of George's jib.
He'd done a lot of quite interesting but rather underappreciated
films, and he had an encyclopaedic grasp of old movies – which
reassured me, because so many modern films suffer death by a
thousand cuts. I think that scenes should be allowed to breathe,
and I sensed that he was on the same wavelength. As for Caroline,
she was suggested by John McGrath and Ronnie Shedlo, who'd
worked with her on the Beryl Bainbridge adaptation, *The Dress-
maker*. I liked the fact that her sets – and this goes for Penny
Rose's costumes as well – looked real and lived-in. When you see
characters in films sitting in freshly decorated, recently constructed houses wearing brand new clothes, it distracts you

because you think, 'Don't these people ever wear anything twice?'

Did you learn anything from editing this film which you were able to apply to writing and directing subsequent films?

I don't think I really got the measure of what you can do with editing until I did *The Secret Agent*. I was much more flexible in the editing of *The Secret Agent*, whereas with *Carrington* I thought, 'Well, that's it.' And that process has continued. For a lot of *Imagining Argentina* we had two cameras, so there was a vast amount more material, and it was also the first time I'd worked on Avid, so we were able to summon up that material much more quickly, but I still feel I'm only just starting to understand all the possibilities of editing. In fact, there are certain aspects of making films which I feel I haven't grasped at all. I find the dub extremely difficult and stressful, because sound is so important in a film yet it's relegated to the end of the process, and you have so little time and the decisions you make are so final.

To put it another way, when you're writing now, are you more aware of things which, even if they're shot, will probably end up being cut?

I think that's always been a consideration, even before I started to direct, but certainly, once you have directed, you start to think much more in terms of the best way to move from one scene to the next or how to begin a scene as late as possible so the first minute of it doesn't get chopped off. Then, if you are the director, I think you have to do a final director's draft in which you say to yourself, 'What's he on about here?' or 'How does he imagine I'm going to do this?'; all those things you have to think through before you get on the set.

You chose the same creative team – director of photography, editor and production designer – on both Carrington *and* The Secret Agent, *except that you used Michael Nyman for the first and Philip Glass for the second. Why did you make that choice, and that change, of composers?*

I like that style of music and I came to it through Philip Glass, but I didn't think to ask Philip to do *Carrington* and I was very happy to get Michael Nyman. I liked one of his string quartets very much, so we used a chunk of that as the basic theme, but he also wrote music for each character, which worked extremely successfully. In both cases, they were a pleasure to work with, but Michael wasn't available for *The Secret Agent*, so I approached Philip and he accepted. When I went to see him in New York and he played me the main theme, the theme which runs beneath the opening credits, I just thought, 'This is exactly what I'm looking for.' It's nice to have a team of collaborators whom you have a shorthand with, but I now think that a composer needs to be cast a bit like an actor. I can see that if you're Alfred Hitchcock, and you make a certain kind of film, you'd thank your lucky stars that you had Bernard Herrmann, but if you make different kinds of films, you might be wise to find different kinds of composers.

Having been forced to direct Carrington *after the withdrawal of Mike Newell, I gather that you actually offered to direct* The Secret Agent *in place of Bob Hoskins.*

Bob had just directed a film in Canada called *Rainbow*, which he'd had an absolutely awful time on, and he said that he was all directed-out. We then had a conversation, brokered by Norma Heyman, in which he said, 'If you want to do it, you do it.' I think I did it very differently from the way he would have done it, but, even though he was one of the producers, he was very generous in terms of going the way I wanted to go.

How do you think he would have done it differently?

I think my version was probably much more severe. I have a feeling Bob would have humanized it more, given it an earthier touch, whereas I thought it had to be done very sombrely, as true to the novel as possible – because to me the novel is a masterpiece, one of the most influential books of the twentieth century, and it seemed necessary to keep it as dark as it is.

It is a very dark film, both thematically and visually.

Yes, it is. There's a lot in the novel about the thickness of the darkness in the streets of Soho, and, like Philippe on *Mary Reilly*, Denis was interested in getting as close to darkness as he could without the scenes actually becoming invisible. I think Caroline did another magnificent job, too, because those streets all had to be built at Ealing Studios. We went all over the country – and even to Ireland – to try and find towns and cities with the quality of nineteenth-century London slums, and everywhere we looked the cobblestones were too modern or the roads were too wide. I wanted to get a real sense of these tiny alleyways, so that when Verloc goes to meet the Russian delegate at the end of the first act, it's as if he's stepping out into a different world.

You were also true to the structure of the novel, which is quite an unusual one.

Yes, it is, particularly in the sense that there's no single character whom you follow all the way through. There are two central characters, Verloc and his wife Winnie, who dominate the first act and the last act, but the middle act is like a relay race, where one character takes the baton and passes it onto another character, who then appears in the next scene with the next character, and so on, so that all the minor characters have their day. I'd never seen anything done like that before.

The intent being to show how all the characters are connected to each other.

That's right. Conrad seems to be saying, 'There's this central event, which culminates in an explosion, but I'm not going to tell you anything about that explosion, or who's died in it. Instead, I'm going to unreel the story until suddenly, hours later, Verloc turns up having survived the explosion. Finally, I'm going to tell you what really happened in this central event, and I'm leaving it until this point because the account of what really happened is going to unleash the final holocaust in the last part of the story.'

In the novel, the connections behind Verloc lead first to Scotland Yard and then to Parliament, taking the reader from the bottom of society to the top, but you omit the scenes involving Parliament.

I think that section of the novel is the least successful. It doesn't feel as authentic as the rest; it feels satirical. It works very well when you're reading it, but I thought that dramatizing it would expose some cracks. That's the principal cut I made to the story.

There's also more suspense in the novel about whether the policeman, Heat, will pin the explosion on the hapless anarchist, Michaelis.

Conrad actually wrote a play of *The Secret Agent* in which Michaelis and the other anarchists had a much bigger role, but I largely disposed of them in the first scene of the film. I thought all we needed to do was establish that milieu, with all these different shades of opinion – some of them opportunistic, like Ossipon; some of them idealistic but unrealistic, like Michaelis; and some of them old-style revolutionaries, like Yundt – because to me it isn't a story about shades of opinion; it's a story about betrayal and cowardice and selfishness and the victims of those things. Therefore, I wanted to shift the focus as much as possible onto Winnie and her brother, Stevie – and onto Verloc himself. That said, the longest scene in the film is the scene between Jim Broadbent and Julian Wadham in Scotland Yard. It took something like seventeen or eighteen set-ups to do this one scene – I remember Jim saying at the end of the day, 'Got that covered, did you?' – because we needed to deal with all the jostling which happens in the novel between the rather idealistic Assistant Commissioner who wants to establish the truth and the cynical policeman who just wants to put someone away – in a sense, the mother and father of ten thousand such scenes in police procedurals ever since.

There are two major structural changes between the novel and the film. The first is that you shifted the section where Winnie's mother moves out of their house to the beginning of the film rather than the beginning of the third act. Why did you do that?

As a way of introducing the characters. In stories where a certain amount of exposition is unavoidable, I always feel that it's best to say at the beginning, 'Look, this is quite complicated, but I'll set it out for you as clearly as I can and then you can watch the consequences unfold,' because an audience is much more prepared to be patient with you at the beginning than anywhere else. When you're still giving out exposition an hour in, it can be very destructive to an audience's concentration. The beginning of *The Secret Agent* is the bit you have to get through, really; before Verloc is asked to do this disastrous thing by the Russian delegate, I wanted to get everyone in position. I also wanted to plant the significance of this awful fellow, the Professor, so I devised this tremendously elaborate opening shot which used just about every inch of the set. It was about four o'clock in the afternoon before I could do the first take, and I only had time to do about seven takes, of which the one we used was the best – although, if you look closely, you can glimpse the first assistant director in a white T-shirt reflected in a plate-glass window.

The implication at the end of the novel is that sooner or later the Professor will set off the bomb which he carries around with him, but at the end of the film you actually have him do it – or, rather, have him squeeze the detonator prior to a freeze-frame.

That was simply irresistible. And it's interesting, isn't it, what a central position in our consciousness is now occupied by the suicide bomber? In fact, the most successful screening I went to was at the Jerusalem Film Festival, where they absolutely loved it, and I could see that the film spoke directly to all sorts of concerns in that part of the world.

The second major structural change you made was to shift Winnie's suicide on the cross-Channel ferry from the end of the story to just after she murders Verloc, and to show her escape with and desertion by Ossipon in flashback from his point of view.

I recut that at the last minute. If you were to read the script as it was, you'd find that her escape with Ossipon, him deserting her, her suicide and the final scene were all in sequence, much as they are in the novel. But I was watching a screening with the continuity supervisor, Penny Eyles, and I said, 'There's something about this ending which doesn't work,' and Penny said, 'Why don't you think about compressing it?' The sequence with Winnie and Ossipon was originally much longer and didn't end with him jumping out of the train; we had him running through the streets and counting his money, too. So what we thought we should do was have her committing suicide, then have him sitting on his own, reading the newspaper and looking upset, then have the flashback of events leading up to her suicide, and then have the final scene. Firstly, it compressed the whole thing so we got to the end that vital three or four minutes faster, and secondly, it seemed to situate the whole thing in Ossipon's guilty mind and point up that important last speech where the Professor says, 'Remorse is for the weak.'

Do you think that by showing Winnie's suicide before her desertion by Ossipon you lessen the impact of his betrayal?

It's possible. It was one of those decisions where if you gained this you lost that, and if you lost that you gained this. I just found that when I was watching it over and over again – as you have to – my heart sank as we got to that bit where they run out of the shop and go off to escape together. It went on and on, and then it got to the ship and then it got to the suicide – and then you had the last scene, which seemed like a bit of an anti-climax – whereas, by enfolding the two scenes into one another, we made it clearer what the end of the film was supposed to be saying. And as soon as we did it, I thought, 'That's much better.' I may be wrong, but it seemed like a huge problem had been solved. The interesting thing about editing is that the images always give you more information than you expected, and therefore you can reorganize them in a more eloquent way than you imagined.

Carrington *is a two-hour film, whereas* The Secret Agent *is only ninety minutes – and there's a lot more plot in* The Secret Agent, *so that's quite an achievement.*

Yes, I thought so. I was very chuffed by the despatch of it. I was very happy with the performances, too. I thought it was a really well-acted film.

I was interested to hear you say that Bob Hoskins's version would have been less severe, because one of the things which struck me from reading the novel and then watching the film is that his Verloc seems a lot more sympathetic than Conrad's.

It's true that there's something you warm to in Bob, and if you compare him with Oscar Homolka in Hitchcock's version of the story, *Sabotage*, it's certainly a more sympathetic performance, but I wouldn't necessarily attribute the effect that you're describing only to Bob. In the novel, Conrad says that Verloc is like an unmade bed, and it seems to me that his behaviour is morally careless rather than morally wicked, so the softness which Bob brings to it is absolutely right. He's sympathetic but he's not playing for sympathy, and he doesn't hesitate to show the pathetic thoughtlessness of the man. I remember talking to him about this and saying that the thing about this man is that he's lazy. He's taking money from one side to do this and money from the other side to do that, but actually he doesn't give a fuck about anything except his own comfort – which I think is a more widespread condition than one might imagine. There are huge squads of people out there of whom that could be said, and therefore the more sympathetic Verloc is and the more common-place his failings, the more appalled you are at what he does and the more terrible his punishment seems.

Patricia Arquette is an unusual choice to play a nineteenth-century Londoner. Why did you decide to cast her as Winnie?

We screen-tested four or five actresses – Ashley Judd was one, Embeth Davidtz was another – but Fox Searchlight were very keen to get Patty, so I met her and I liked her and I cast her. I think she's very good in the latter half of the film, but there are certain scenes where I feel I wasn't able to make myself as clear to her as I wanted to be, and consequently I think she's slightly at sea in the earlier parts of the story. She's very instinctive about scenes which require emotional investment of one kind or another, so in all the scenes towards the end where she's in a state of distress she knew exactly what to do. The reviews all criticized her accent, which I thought was very good. The only problem with it was that she was sometimes worrying about it when she should have been worrying about the scene.

Robin Williams, as the Professor, doesn't even bother with an accent.

When I first met him, he said to me, 'What accent do you want?' and put on all kinds of Scottish accents and Cockney accents; but it isn't clear in the novel where the Professor is from, so I saw no reason why he shouldn't be an American. Then he said, did I want someone from New Orleans or someone from the Bronx?, and I said, 'What I'd really like is just your regular voice.' That startled him a bit, but that's what he gave us, and he was very good. He's so talented that what you have to do is tie that talent down, and I spent proportionally more time with him than with any of the other actors. He was very meticulous about everything: should he put the rubber bulb to detonate the bomb in his left pocket or his right pocket, and should he take his glasses off or should he keep his glasses on, and when should he have a hat and when shouldn't he have a hat. I like all that; it shows that the actor is tremendously engaged. And it was a wonderful, restrained performance – although at the end of each series of four or five takes, which is what I regularly do, he would ask if he could do one for himself, and then improvise wildly, saying things like, 'Are you feeling the heat, Heat?' Most of it was completely unusable, but every now and then some mad bit of energy would come into his eyes and he would do something great, like that sideways leap onto the sofa in the middle of talking to Jim Broadbent, so it was certainly worthwhile letting him have his head – quite apart from the fact that he had the crew in stitches every single time. He was terrific fun to have about, and I liked him very much. I felt he was very vulnerable, and I responded to that. He just gave us an enormous amount, and brought a colour to the film which was very valuable. It's an important character – and, in fact, the character Bob wanted to play when he was thinking of directing the film.

Whose idea was it to cast him?

It was Bob's idea, and I thought it was brilliant – except for this condition Robin made, which was that he was not to be credited. I wouldn't do that again, because it feels as if the actor is distancing himself from the film. His view, which I could well understand, was: 'If you want me to publicize the film, pay me my usual fee. If I'm going to do four days for $25,000, you can have me anonymously.' But I found that the first question in interviews was always, 'Was that Robin Williams? Why wasn't he given a credit?' and I had to spend ten minutes explaining it.

Gérard Depardieu also had a small but important part, as Ossipon.

Bob made the initial contact with Gérard, too. We first spoke when we were both in Los Angeles, and he spent a good ten minutes telling me how he couldn't play the part because he was doing one film in Mauritius and another film in Texas; then five minutes later the phone rang again and it was him and he said, 'What the hell, I do it.' We had him for about twelve days, and he was absolutely wonderful. I adored him, actually. I think he's a great actor. At the end of the film, when Robin does a long exit, I kept the camera on Gérard and stood behind the camera and gave him a sign as to when he should drink his drink, and for the few seconds that he sits there the whole story of that character is written on his face in the most eloquent way.

Eddie Izzard, as the Russian delegate, was another interesting piece of casting.

Eddie was my idea. I just had a brainwave one day: 'Eddie Izzard would be great in this role.' Apart from his act, which is amazing, I'd seen him in a David Mamet play, and I had an instinct about him. It was a two-day role, and he came in and did his big scene at the Russian Embassy on the first day and then he attached himself to the production for the rest of the shoot – out of curiosity, really, to see how it was done.

Even allowing for your three-picture deal with Fox, it's still a pretty surprising project for them to have taken on.

Yes, it is. But at that point, because *Carrington* had been such a success – in its own terms – there were any number of things I could have done, so I suppose they were indulging me. When I entered into negotiations with them, I said, 'I know about these three-picture deals. You never make any pictures. So can we at least do one which is already there?' and it's hard to imagine the film being made otherwise. It's not an easy film to watch, and it's no surprise that in the year the novel was published Conrad's earnings were about five pounds, seven and six, because it's as tough a story about the murkiest corners of human nature as you could hope to find. We had a preview in Los Angeles, in a cinema on Wilshire Boulevard, and it scored below the radar. I think at that stage Fox decided that there was nothing they could do to improve the scores, because no one ever said to me, 'You'll have to make some changes.' I made those changes which we were talking about myself, then it went to the Toronto Film Festival, where it was extremely well received, and it was finally chucked out in November in about half a dozen cinemas. It got a very warm review in the *Los Angeles Times*, so it did quite well in California, and a very cool review in the *New York Times*, so it did very badly in the east – and that was it, really. It ran for two or three weeks and was withdrawn, then played in London the following February, where it was dismissed or pissed on by all the critics – all except Alexander Walker, who said that it was the most atmospheric British film since *Brighton Rock*, which was fantastic because I'd never had particularly good reviews from him in the past. Apart from him, no one engaged with it as a film; they just quoted the American grosses or said, 'God, this is so dreary.' But I'm extremely proud of it.

Do you feel that its perceived failure hurt your directorial career?

Box-office jail, it's called. I was put into box-office jail. And it took several years to get out.

And after Imagining Argentina, *you might be put back in again.*

I could be, especially as that film was quite a bit more expensive than the other two. But that's the way it is these days. Nothing is any good unless it's been endorsed by a hundred million dollars' worth of audience. If you've delivered a hundred-million-dollar film, people will stick with you while you dish up all kinds of unconscionable rubbish.

On page one of Lawrence Thornton's novel, the narrator says, 'We have long been hostile to the things of the spirit . . . the mere mention of the unknown and unknowable occasions peals of bitter laughter,' which is true of the reviews the film has received.

I'd forgotten that was in the novel, but it seems apposite. There is something about the film which is difficult for certain people to take on board.

Did you discuss the adaptation with Lawrence Thornton before starting work on it?

No, I didn't. I did the first adaptation in 1989, and it was only fifty-three pages long. I had in mind a film rather like *Vertigo*, where the guy just sits in his car and drives and drives and drives, trying to find what he's lost. I didn't think it needed a lot of dialogue, and I cut things like the old couple in the pampas; but I timed it in my mind as I was writing it, and it ran about ninety minutes. I'm then summoned to the Columbia offices in Los Angeles, and Gareth Wigan, a nice British executive who's been at Columbia for ages, walks into the room weighing the script on the tips of his fingers and says, 'We can't accept this.' I said, 'What do you mean?' He said, 'We've never received a script of this length before.' I said, 'I think you'll find it runs to about ninety minutes.' He said, 'I don't care how many minutes it runs to. We can't pay you for a script of fifty-three pages.' I said, 'Well, what do you need?' and he said, 'About twice this.' So I went back to England, worked on it for a few weeks and sent back a script of 106 pages. Interestingly, one of the many people who were involved in the project along the way was Anthony Minghella – before he became, as it were, Anthony Minghella – and he said that he much preferred the first draft to the second. Another person who liked the original fifty-three-page script was Larry Thornton. The only reason the film got made in the long run was that, although I'd only spoken to him on the phone, we kept in touch through the project's various vicissitudes, and one of the things which pleased me was how delighted he was with it. He absolutely loved it.

What were those vicissitudes?

To start with it was Richard Gere's project, and he began working with a director called Randa Haines – whom I met a couple times and who couldn't wait to see the back of me. Other writers were brought in, then the whole thing was shelved and Larry got the rights back. Two or three years later, Disney bought it and a new script was written – which I've never seen but Larry says wasn't too good – and it was almost financed with Kenneth Branagh, directed by a woman called Lesli Linka Glatter. Then that also fell through, and the option again reverted to Larry. So I said to him, 'Sell it to me,' and I bought the option in about 1997.

Were you originally approached to write it because of working with Richard Gere on The Honorary Consul?

It came in the spate of offers after I won the Oscar, but the fact that we'd already done this film about Argentina may have been why I crossed Richard's mind. Unfortunately, he wanted something much more mystical or metaphysical than I did. In other words, he wanted a European movie – or what he would have thought of as that – with dream sequences and so on, and I wanted to make it as plain as possible.

Given that the novel is a fine example of magic realism, why did you want to lessen the magic and heighten the realism?

I suppose because I felt that it was a very grave situation, and that it would be better served dramatically by making the hero as bemused by what's happening to him as any member of the audience might be. He's not a man of a mystical bent; he's just a man on whom this second sight descends, and he has to cope with it as best he can. The other reason was that I'd always liked those Buñuel movies where some strange scene occurred, in precisely the same style as everything that had gone before, and you realized from the subsequent context that it was a dream sequence. I eventually included a lot of those and specified to the DP that I wanted them shot in exactly the same way as the rest of the film. That was the subject of one of my big disputes with the producers, when they took those eighteen minutes of visions or dream sequences or whatever you call them and dunked them in the bleaching bath – which succeeded only in driving the DP mad with rage, because to him the scenes now looked ghastly and to general audiences the difference was hardly noticeable. It's most noticeable in the scene by the river, which was the scene it was least necessary to do it to. I said to them, 'If you must do this, don't do it to that scene, because it's a flashback, not a vision,' but of course they ignored me.

You weren't worried that if you didn't use a different style for the visions, audiences would be confused by this mixture of past, present and future, even allowing for the fact that the story came from the magic-realist tradition?

I never came across anyone who was confused by it. That was one of the interesting things about the first preview in California. The producers were all saying beforehand, 'People won't understand what's happening,' and in the question-and-answer session afterwards it was plain that everyone had understood everything. If you tell the story lucidly enough you don't need to use any distancing devices. I never really thought of the story in terms of magic realism; I thought of it much more in terms of Buñuel – and Costa-Gavras, whose movies I also liked. It's a fusion of those two influences, I think. However, something which didn't really occur to me when I was writing the first draft but was very much in my mind when I was making the film is that, although I decided to do it in a realistic style, the story isn't realistic; it's actually a metaphor for the fact that in those circumstances, a military dictatorship, the only power you have is your imagination, and that because imagination is the one thing the other side does not possess it will, for reasons beyond logic, eventually prevail. In that sense, it's a very optimistic story, which is what led me to do the ending in the frankly fantastical way I did: this extravagant carnival scene at which, like in Carlos's rewriting of the *Orpheus* myth, these two people come together for a strange bittersweet reunion. There is one thing I regret about the ending, though. In the novel, the two brothers who shelter his wife after she escapes from prison say, 'You'd better lie low for a couple of weeks, and when we next go to Buenos Aires we'll take you in.' Now, I was interested in being elliptical at the end, so I never wrote that and never shot it, and lots of people have said, 'I don't understand. Why didn't she just phone him up?' It's one of those things you could have explained in two lines of dialogue, but I didn't feel it was necessary.

I don't think it is. The absence of that explanatory dialogue suggests that the ending might be in his imagination, because the penultimate scene ends after she looks in at the brothers playing cards, and you don't know whether they took her to Buenos Aires or turned her in to the authorities. It's a fruitful ambiguity.

It's like the one scene in the film which was imposed on me, in the sequence when Emma Thompson is thrown off the roof of the presidential palace. How it played before was that Antonio Banderas goes to see the minister, then he leaves the palace, hears a commotion on the roof, turns around and sees her being thrown off – and then wakes up, eliding his return home. And the producers absolutely insisted that, between the scene with the minister and the scene where he leaves the palace, I insert five seconds of him tossing and turning in bed so everyone would know it was a dream. But I didn't want everyone to know it was a dream, I wanted people to think, 'Did he just dream that or did he dream the entire scene with the minister?' The Argentinians who saw and disliked the film in Venice apparently said it was ridiculous that he should have been allowed into the presidential palace at all, but I'd always imagined that it was a sadistic whim of the minister's. He makes it clear when the guy gets up there that he knows exactly who he is, but I can see that it probably is unrealistic that someone could have walked in during that regime and said, 'I want to see the minister.' But the premise of the story is that, while they bump off everyone else in the vicinity, they keep him alive, to punish him worse than if they actually took him.

You mentioned the Orpheus *myth. That was something which you introduced into the story, wasn't it, along with a provocative production of* The Masque of the Red Death, *in which Death removes his cloak to reveal an Argentinian army uniform?*

The Carlos character still runs a theatre in the novel, but I came up with the plays he puts on: *Orpheus* and the Poe. There was also a third one, a nativity play, and various scenes in the Garden of Gethsemane kept appearing to him, but it just seemed like an extra confusing element, so I took it out. In fact, the producers also cut the *Masque of the Red Death* sequence at one point, and I had to fight to put it back.

I'm surprised that in your original script you cut out the old couple in the pampas, Auschwitz survivors whose pet birds represent the souls of their dead friends, which is my favourite sequence in the film and sums up so much of what the story is about.

I agree, and it's my favourite sequence as well – and one of the first things there were rumblings about: 'What's all that stuff in the pampas? It slows the film down. You have to cut it.' When I wrote the first draft, it seemed tricky to correlate the Holocaust with what had happened in Argentina, but I subsequently changed my mind – particularly, of course, because vast numbers of Nazis escaped to Argentina and were warmly welcomed there. I also didn't know at the time I was first writing the script – and you have to remember that when I was writing it all this was very fresh in people's minds – that the military dictatorship had called some of these Nazis out of retirement and employed them as consultants on torture and so on. That's why I included another scene which people begged me to cut: Hitler's birthday dinner, where the minister is entertaining various people wearing SS uniforms.

Presumably you did a lot of research beyond the novel?

Once I knew the film was likely to be made, the first thing I did was go to Argentina, because, although I'd written two films set there, I'd never actually been there. Larry Thornton had never been there, either, so his Argentina was as imaginary as mine, and, once I did go there, I started to reimagine the film in terms of what the country actually looked like. For example, the pampas, which I'd always imagined as being rather interesting, looked like bloody Lincolnshire: hundreds of miles of featureless flat landscape. The pampas around Olavarria, the town where the women's prison camp was, was marginally more interesting than elsewhere, but it was five hours south of Buenos Aires. We went and saw it on an absolutely horrible winter day – pissing with rain, mud up to your knees – and when I said, 'Sorry, chaps, I think this is the one,' a great groan went up, because it was so far out of the way. But when we were shooting there, the first AD was having a drink in town – which itself was forty minutes from this location – and someone said to him, 'It's very clever of you to have found that place,' and he said, 'What do you mean?' and they said, 'It really was a prison camp.' It had a very scary atmosphere, and one thing I did not do was shoot in the basement. There was a series of five-foot-high cells, with rats in puddles and bars on the windows, and the DP said, 'Let's shoot here!' and I said, 'I really don't want to make everyone come down here.' In the end, Emma got a rather luxurious cell on the ground floor.

Even so, shooting on location does give the film a real immediacy.

There was tremendous pressure to shoot it in Spain, and we actually went and looked at locations there, but I kept thinking, 'This is crazy. We ought to do as much as we can in Argentina.' And it coincided with a new regime which was anxious to air these issues, and they gave us the presidential palace and the main square and closed off great chunks of Buenos Aires whenever we wanted. When we were shooting Emma being thrown off the palace roof, the DP said, 'There's a nasty shadow,' and I said, 'What is it?' and it was the flag of the nation. So I went over to the liaison officer and said, 'Do you think we could take that down?' and he said, 'That's the flag of the nation!' and I said, 'Yes, but it's casting a shadow.' He said, 'How long do you need it down?' and I said, 'An hour should do it,' and he said, 'Let me make a phone call.' And about five minutes later, he came back and said, 'You can take it down.' The most extraordinary thing was being able to film those women in the square. Every Thursday afternoon at three o'clock these women go there and demonstrate about the fact that their loved ones disappeared and were never accounted for; and, in the course of our research, we spent an afternoon with one woman called Laura Bonaparte, a psychoanalyst who lost six of her family, and I said, 'Do you think your colleagues would like to be in the film?' So she read the script and talked to them, and some of them said no but most of them said yes, and we used them in as many scenes as possible. Shooting the scene in the square when Antonio has the vision of his daughter being killed, with all those women walking around and chanting while the scene was going on, was incredibly moving, an unforgettable experience.

Was Antonio Banderas your first choice to play Carlos?

I talked to Andy Garcia about doing it, and he very much wanted to, but I couldn't raise the money on Andy, so we were forced to move on. I had to phone him and tell him, and that was a very difficult conversation. In the end, Antonio Banderas seemed like an inevitable piece of casting – even though it took us an age to get the script to him. Despite the fact that we're both represented by CAA, sixteen months went by before the producer, Geoff Lands, met someone at a party who was able to give the script to Antonio. They gave it to him on a Friday, and on the Monday he said, 'I'll do it.' I went over to meet him and that went well, and we had a conversation about how we could make him look different from the way he looked in his other films, and he said, 'Do you want me to grow a beard?' and I said, 'What a great idea!'

A Spaniard playing an Argentinian makes sense, but, as you said earlier with regard to the idea of casting Juliette Binoche as Carrington, you also cast Emma Thompson as one. Why?

I put this notion to Antonio rather diffidently and he loved it, but I suppose if he'd said, 'Are you out of your mind? We have to cast a Latin-American,' then we would have. In general, I wanted to cast as many Latin-Americans as possible: Rubén Blades is from Panama, María Canals is from Cuba, Kuno Becker is from Mexico – so we had quite a broad Spanish, Hispanic and Latin-American contingent. But I knew that Emma had written a script about Victor Jara, the Bob Dylan of Chile, who was murdered in the national stadium in Santiago, and I also knew that she spoke Spanish, so that's why she crossed my mind, and I think she raised everyone's game when she arrived.

She did a little bit of writing on this, too, didn't she?

Yes, she did. She felt that there wasn't really enough of her character – although there was much more than there had been. The fifty-three-page script didn't show you what happened to her from the time she disappeared to the time she came back again, so it wasn't really a role. There's a certain amount in the novel about what happened to her, but, as a result of all the research I did on how the prison camps were run and how the prisoners were treated, I added quite a lot for the film. But Emma still felt that there wasn't enough, so we had a conversation about putting in two extra scenes. One was the scene in which she fights with her husband about whether or not she should print this article, and the other was the flashback scene by the river. I said to her, 'You won a screenwriting Oscar. You write the scenes, and I'll write the scenes, and we'll meet this time next week and see what we think.' And the following week, I read her scenes and she read my scenes, and I said, 'Your scene by the river is much better than mine,' and she said, 'Your argument scene is much better than mine,' and I said, 'Done! A pleasure doing business with you.' So the scene by the river was written by Emma, and, other than the fact that it was dropped in the bleaching bath, it's great.

Your desire to cast as many Latin-Americans as possible obviously extended to the crew, who, with the exception of editor George Akers and composer George Fenton, were mostly Spanish-speaking – like the director of photography, Guillermo Navarro.

I thought we needed a Spanish-speaking DP. It wasn't that I didn't want to work with Denis again; it just seemed to be a requirement. I'd particularly liked *Jackie Brown*, which Guillermo shot, and was then very taken with another film he shot, *The Devil's Backbone*, which had exactly the look I wanted. Guillermo is Mexican, and he came with a Mexican first AD, Sebastián Silva, who was fantastic. The second assistant was also Mexican, so we had a Mexican team, an Argentinian team and a Spanish team, because we did five weeks on location in Argentina and four weeks in the studio in Madrid. I did ask Penny Rose to do the costume design, but we lost her to the final three-week delay, and instead I was lucky to get Sabina Daigeler, a German living in Spain who did John Malkovich's film, *The Dancer Upstairs*. Bárbara Pérez Solero was also a last-minute replacement, for another Spanish designer, Benjamín Fernández, who we again lost to the delay, because he had a Tony Scott movie to do. So the crew was a bit cobbled-together, but I was very happy with all of them.

Compared to the problems you encountered in pre-production – never mind the ones in post-production – the actual shoot seems to have gone pretty smoothly.

We only had nine weeks to shoot it, but we still managed to finish on time and under budget. Most of the time Guillermo uses two cameras, one of which is a steadicam, and he works with a brilliant operator called Joaquín Manchado, so Guillermo would operate one camera, and Joaquín would operate the other, which enabled us to work with terrific speed. The first week of shooting was the scenes in the pampas with John Wood and Claire Bloom, and they got us off to a fantastically powerful start. Usually at the end of the first week I'm thinking, 'Oh, my God, I'm going to have to reshoot this,' but this time I felt very good because they were both so strong. John said that it was the first time he'd ever felt really comfortable in front of a camera, and his performance is one of the highlights of the film, I think. All the scenes involving the birds had gone well, too. Flamingos: I can recommend them. They do exactly what they're told.

Unlike you, who argued continuously with various producers about the finished film. Could you put those disputes in context, starting with who the key players are?

After I bought the option, this marvellously exuberant fellow Geoff Lands came across the script, liked it and proceeded to hustle the thing into life. He and I went to Cannes and tramped the Croisette, having meetings with everyone we could think of, and the only positive response came from Kirk D'Amico, the head of a company called Myriad. But Kirk couldn't get the required amount of money together in time, so a producer called Santiago Pozo, and his company Arenas, put $5 million into the film in return for the US, UK, Spanish and Latin-American rights. However, the first objections were made by the woman who runs Antonio's company, Diane Sillan Isaacs. We had a first cut very quickly but Diane had all kinds of problems with it, so I did something which was a bit of a risk but I thought was worth it. I said to her, 'Since we're a bit ahead, why don't you re-edit the film exactly as you want it and we'll see what it looks like at the end of the week?' and she did, and it was absolutely incomprehensible. I don't know exactly what she had in mind – something to do with giving it a thriller pace and trying to make Antonio's character more sympathetic, I think – but whatever it was it wasn't reflected in the version she prepared.

We then had a screening of the original cut in early November, and Kirk was very pleased with it. He said, 'Instead of having the first preview in London after Christmas, I think we should have it in Los Angeles at the end of November.' I said, 'There's quite a way to go yet. We haven't even got a score,' but he said,

'No, I think that's what we should do.' So I turned up for the preview and found that Santiago had chosen to hold it in a multiplex in the desert in Ontario, California, and had asked for half of the audience to be under twenty-five and half to be Latino. And it was very interesting, because, although the film didn't score well, the audience, who were rather restive to start with, settled down and seemed to get into it – and the focus group afterwards was more positive than any I'd been to before. The guy leading it said, 'I want someone to raise their hand and tell me the first word that comes into their head about this film,' and a young man put his hand up and said, 'Original,' and the woman sitting next to him said, 'Unique.' The film then got a good review on aintitcool.com, which said that the temporary score sucked – which it did, because we put it on in about seven minutes – but that it looked like one of the more interesting films of the year.

I wasn't in a bad mood after all this, but I was then summoned to a meeting with Kirk and Santiago and told not to bring Geoff Lands or Michael Peyser, who had both been with me all the way through shooting and had done the physical production of the film. I go to this meeting and I'm told that the film is in terrible trouble and I'm to come back to Los Angeles after Christmas to continue editing with a different editor. I wasn't best pleased about that, but it was a *fait accompli*, so I came back to London and consulted Stephen Frears, who said, 'The best editor in the world is Anne Coates. Why don't we show her the film?' So we showed her the film, and she liked it and said she'd do it. I called Kirk and he hummed and hawed, then Anne called me and told me she'd been interviewed and they'd said to her, 'In the event of a dispute between the producers and the director, whose side would you tend to favour?' Of course, she said, 'I normally work for the director,' and they said, 'Thanks, but no thanks.' Instead, they hired Claire Simpson, who edited *Salvador* and *Platoon*. I said, 'I don't approve of that,' and they said, 'We don't give a fuck if you approve of it or not.' So I arrived in Los Angeles two weeks after Claire had started, saw what she'd done and said to her, 'If this is the way the film is going to be, I'm off home and you can do what you like – but I can't put my name on it.' She was very startled and said, 'What do you mean? I thought this was the direction we were all moving in,' and I said, 'Well, no.'

What had she done to it?

She'd decimated it – on their instructions. The first cut was just over two hours, and it was about forty minutes shorter. Now, since there were so many executives involved, she'd insisted on only having one of them in the editing room at any given time, and the designated executive was a chap called Lucas Foster, Kirk's second-in-command, whom I'd only met once prior to the making of the film, when he'd candidly explained that it was being made against his advice. I thought, 'Blimey! On top of everything!' but the next day, when I was summoned to go back and watch it with him, he gave her pretty well all the notes I had. I said, 'This is very strange. You just said all the things I was going to say,' and he said, 'We'd better not let anyone know. I'm supposed to be in here beating you up.' He then became my staunchest ally over the next few weeks, but towards the end of this period, having just about got everything in order, he had to go off and do something else. We then got Santiago's assistant, a guy called Jordi Ros – the one who said to me, 'Do we have to have all these Nazis?' – who started making all sorts of objections which no one had made before.

Everyone was getting very panicky by this stage. The savings which I'd made on the shooting were now exhausted, so there was no money left. There were two people working at immense expense putting on a temporary score – and George Fenton was out there at his own expense trying to be helpful – and the title sequence was costing $50,000, which no one had budgeted for. Then Santiago came in on the very last day and insisted that the opening sequence be re-edited and *The Masque of the Red Death* be removed. Kirk and Santiago slugged that one out and Kirk somehow had the edge, so the following week we re-edited it again in the way I wanted it. By this time, they'd had to re-engage George Akers back in England to do the sound dub, and when he saw the film after all these months, he was astonished at how little it had changed. I said to Claire, whom I came to like very much, 'Am I exceptionally stubborn?' and she said, 'Yes, you are. Most directors do as they're told.' I was amazed by that, but I think the notion of the director having creative control is very much the exception rather than the rule these days.

Why had no one budgeted for the title sequence?

I'd planned to go straight into the film, but Kirk said, 'I don't want my name to appear at the end of the film, I want it to appear at the beginning, otherwise everyone will have left by the time it comes up.' As a result of that, I had a series of meetings with a titles company in Los Angeles, and they put together this title sequence of newsreel footage. I then had the idea of putting on the voice-over about Orpheus, because it became clear in the preview that a lot of people had no idea who Orpheus was, and encapsulating that story at the beginning and relating it to the historical situation in Argentina turned out to be quite helpful. George Fenton put it very well when he first saw it. He said, 'It tells you in the first minute what kind of film you're in for.'

And after all that there was the Venice Film Festival.

By the time the film was finished, it was too late for Cannes, so the next possibility was Venice, who accepted it straight away. Everyone was very pleased about that – except Santiago, who said that we shouldn't open it in Venice, because Venice could be quite dangerous, but should open it at the Latino Festival in Los Angeles, where it would be better received. He was probably right, as it turns out, but he was overruled, because in certain areas, Italy being one of them, Kirk has the final say. Santiago had the power to withdraw it from Toronto, which he did, but he didn't have the power to withdraw it from Venice, which he would have liked to. The press screening was on Sunday night, and Michael Peyser and I went in and stood at the back for five or ten minutes, thought that everything looked hunky-dory and went out to dinner. Then, an hour or so later, one of the organizers called and said, 'I'm sorry to tell you that your film has been booed.' I said, 'Oh, dear. That's rather disturbing,' but he said, 'It often happens in Venice. The Bertolucci film was booed as well. Don't worry about it.' So I didn't worry about it, and the public screening the next day passed in rapt silence, followed by what they say was a six-minute standing ovation – broken only by Emma saying, 'I can't stand this any more,' and hurrying out.

The following evening Myriad gave a very nice dinner, and that's when we started to hear that there had been all this bad press. The *Evening Standard* had printed a picture of Emma crying at the standing ovation and captioned it, 'Emma Thompson responds to boos.' It also said that Antonio Banderas had been in Venice but cannily left town, which wasn't true: he was appearing in a play on Broadway and couldn't come. There were lots of other bits in other British newspapers, and in American ones as well, and before we knew it the film was being described in *Variety* as the worst-received in the history of the Venice Film Festival. But I went to the public screenings of *Intolerable Cruelty*, which was politely but not enthusiastically received, and *Lost in Translation*, which was very enthusiastically received, so we were on a par with Sofia Coppola's film in terms of the audience response. As you can imagine, I was very depressed for a few days after all this happened, but it soon passed. There isn't any point, really. You just have to think, 'Is this the film I wanted to make? Yes, it is. Is it regrettable that certain people think the film is no good? Yes, it is. But, in the end, it's much more important what Judge Baltasar Garzón, who had Pinochet arrested, thinks of the film than a lot of cynical hacks in Venice.' What does worry me is that after this I may not be allowed to make another film, and there seems to be a deeply felt conviction among the British press that I shouldn't be.

Another film you do want to make is The Talking Cure – *which, in fact, you wrote as a screenplay,* Sabina, *before turning it into a play.*

That's right. The story of Sabina Spielrein and Jung had been in the back of my mind since the late seventies, when a book called *A Secret Symmetry* by Aldo Carotenuto gave the first inkling of this special relationship between them; but although I thought how interesting their story was, and how interesting it would be to write something about psychoanalysis, perhaps the defining intellectual notion of the first half of the twentieth century, I did nothing about it. Then, in the mid-nineties, when I signed that contract with Fox to do three projects in two years, it surfaced as something that Julia Roberts's company was interested in, and I went for it. I had, in the meantime, read a lot of Freud – although not much Jung – but it took me a tremendous amount of time to do the research, and quite a lot more has come out about all this since then. Julia's company had taken an option on a very interesting book by John Kerr called *A Most Dangerous Method*, but he hadn't managed – as I did, by befriending the curator of the Jung museum at the Burghölzli Clinic in Zürich – to get hold of the case notes. So he didn't know, for example, that Sabina was a patient of Jung's for six months; he thought that her treatment only lasted a few weeks and concluded that they weren't lovers – an assumption I was perfectly prepared to make myself until another bunch of her letters to Jung were published, followed by Jung's letters to her, the tone of which seemed conclusively to contradict that assumption.

Was Julia Roberts interested in playing the part of Sabina?

Yes, she was – although I don't think it was the kind of part that anyone was about to *let* her play. I was dealing mostly with her development person, a man called Pliny Porter, so things were largely filtered through him, but I had a lot of conversations with them about it, and I think Julia liked the screenplay. It was one of those projects where people said, 'We're looking forward to the next draft,' without saying what they thought the next draft should contain, so I just let it ride and didn't do another draft. Eventually, they produced a load of notes – and Fox also produced a load of notes, because they were still interested in it as something Julia wanted to do – and, boiled down, these notes seemed to be saying that there was too much Jung in it and not enough Sabina. However, what was gradually dawning on me was the exact opposite: that the central character was Jung, because it was Jung who was torn between his wife and Sabina, and between Freud and Sabina, and that he had to be even more at the centre of it. I let various friends of mine read the screenplay, and they all encouraged me to follow my instinct, which was to reorganize the material as a play, so that's what I did. Of course, the reaction of Julia's company was to say, 'No, no, no,' and to demand this, that and the other, but she just cut through all that and said, 'Give it back to him,' and wrote me a very nice letter saying, 'Good luck with it.' In fact, both she and Fox were exceptionally generous about it.

Do you think the screenplay did things which the play couldn't, and vice versa?

The only thing I really miss from the screenplay is the sense of landscape, because there's something about the contrasting landscapes of Zürich and Vienna that tells you a lot about the characters of Jung and Freud, but I don't think there was anything essential in the screenplay which didn't make it into the play. I think the play is more effective than the screenplay – crucially the shift in focus from Sabina to Jung – but I'm actually reworking the play for America, because neither it nor the screenplay gave the Freud–Jung relationship its full weight. I originally set that up a bit like the Brecht–Horváth relationship in *Tales from Hollywood*, an ironic comic battle between people of huge ego and great vanity; I don't want to lose that, but I do want to get more of a sense of how excited they both were by their initial contact, in order to make the final split between them seem like a more momentous intellectual fracture. At the moment, their final argument is about the expunging of the names of Egyptian kings from their monuments by their sons, so the whole thing happens at one remove, and I think it would be better to have a scene where the gloves are off and they go for each other.

I'm always being asked, in relation to screenplays, 'Why don't the characters just say what's on their minds?' and I usually feel that it's more interesting if you're able to see what's on their minds without them saying it, but in this case I probably erred in the direction of indirection. I think that's accurate, because I don't think Jung and Freud ever did say what was on their minds – and I was trying to respect that, because I've always been well served by being faithful to the facts – but perhaps, in this instance, I ought to respect the principles of drama more than the principles of history. At the end of the play, the audience should feel that the breakdown that Jung is beginning to suffer is caused by having both chocks knocked out from under his wheels, one being Freud and the other Sabina. Subconsciously, he knows that Sabina is right when she says, 'It's important that you go forward together rather than undergo this damaging split,' and the last letter she wrote to Jung was about that very subject. In other words, a constructive movement became factionalized, which happens in progressive politics as well and is one of the more distressing tendencies of the human race – or of men.

The reason I asked whether the screenplay did things which the play couldn't is that the former starts with Sabina being brought to the Burghölzli Clinic in a carriage and kicking and screaming until she gets inside the building, where she sees Jung descending the main staircase like some kind of god and immediately falls silent – a scene which, in the play, Jung simply describes, to less effect, in my opinion.

Funnily enough, the first change I've made to the play is to set the first scene, which is Jung casually discussing the case with his wife at breakfast, against Sabina arriving and being gagged and tied into a chair in the treatment room. In the production at the National, that energy went into creating a web of sound which evoked Victorian lunatic asylums, with clanking doors and people screaming, but I don't think the Burghölzli was like that, so I want to start the play in a completely different way. Another problem with the play, which I don't know how to solve, is that the first thirty pages, with their intense concentration on this one case, are so powerful that the rest of it struggles to keep up. You have the scene where the dam is breached and Sabina finally admits everything about her father, and then you have the first scene with Freud, and I don't know how to get around the sense of anti-climax and regroup.

One benefit of turning scenes which were dramatized in the screenplay into scenes which Jung describes in the play is that the character he describes them to, his wife Emma, becomes better developed and therefore a more effective rival to Sabina.

I think that's right, and I think she's the character who could stand more development on this pass and in the film. There's a new biography of Jung by Deirdre Bair, and Emma has really caught Bair's imagination and seems to be the person she feels most sympathetic towards. She's also quite ambivalent about whether Jung and Sabina had an affair, which I'm surprised by. It seems clear to me that Jung had a whole series of affairs after Sabina left, but she's much more cautious about that. She doesn't deny that Antonia Wolff was Jung's mistress throughout his life, but she does imply that sex wasn't terribly important to him, which I find hard to accept. She also spends an awful lot of time talking about whether he had Nazi sympathies, because there have been a number of books in recent years claiming that he was a closet fascist. I don't think that's true. He wasn't ambivalent about them; he just didn't make his views known as decisively as he might have done.

A theme of the play seems to be the way in which women, unlike men, are willing to set aside their egos for the good of others.

I think that's a truth which extends beyond the particular circumstances of this play. In general women are infinitely more generous-spirited than men, and men tend to take advantage of that as much as they possibly can. Sabina really behaved as well as it's possible to behave in those circumstances, and you can see how much it cost her, when it finally got on top of her, by the violence of her reaction. She stabbed Jung in the face with a letter-opener, which is not the kind of thing that happens every day in Switzerland. And he was only able to nurse himself through his nervous breakdown – five years of not taking any patients and just trying to grapple with his depression – through the support and generosity of Emma. She was the one with all the money. Men also spend much more time than women worrying about unimportant things like their reputations. Freud was always asking Jung why he hadn't mentioned him in this or that essay or article, which is the opposite of how you imagine scientists ought to be. I suppose it's a very human trait, but it's not one I particularly sympathize with. In fact, the play implies that this disturbed adolescent girl is more balanced and sensible than these two giants, and that she's just as formidable an intellect as them but isn't recognized as such because she dedicates herself to others rather than herself.

When we were discussing Total Eclipse, *you said that the facts in* The Talking Cure *were extremely inconveniently organized. You've solved structural problems in other plays by using mathematical devices –* Treats *and* Liaisons, *for example – and in this case you set up several parallels: the parallel love–hate relationships between Jung and Freud, and Jung and Sabina, and the parallel triangular relationships between Jung and Freud and Sabina, and Jung and Emma and Sabina. Was that deliberate?*

Yes, whilst leaving the door open for a bit of inspiration – like showing the death of Sabina. That was an impulse which came on me in the middle of writing the play, at what was going to be the end of the first act, and you have to decide whether to give way to those impulses or corral them. The challenge is to come up with a structure that feels aesthetically right to the spectator while respecting the anarchy of real life and the spontaneity of the imagination.

Was the flash-forward from one of Jung and Sabina's trysts to her murder by German soldiers in Russia in 1942 meant to echo Jung's premonition, at the end of the play, of rivers of blood sweeping over Europe?

Yes – although, in the rewrite, the whole scene unfolds in the bedroom and a double plays her in the future, so the two scenes happen simultaneously in the same way as the two scenes at the beginning. Some people really hated that scene, but, as I've said, it's always the original things which people tend to hate, and it is original to say to the audience at the halfway point, 'This is what happens to her.' It means that you have that knowledge in your head throughout the second half, especially since the second half deals with issues of anti-Semitism. David Cronenberg was very interested in making a movie of it, and when I told him that the original screenplay didn't have that scene, he said, 'It's absolutely vital, and in a movie I'd put it exactly where you've put it,' which was interesting. It just seemed like the right thing to do, but unfortunately in the staging – which is not to blame the staging, because the staging did what the play asked it to do – it became distanced and looked tacked on rather than organic.

Something else you said when we were discussing Total Eclipse *was that the play was your first treatment of a subject which you've dealt with over and over again, the clash between a radical and a liberal, and that in the case of* The Talking Cure *you come down on the side of the radical, Freud. Could you expand on that?*

The real radical is Otto Gross, who radicalized Jung to such an extent that he had an affair with Sabina, so the story is much more complicated than that statement would imply. Nevertheless, it operates in the same area as the conflict between Carlos and West in *Savages* or Brecht and Horváth in *Tales from Hollywood*, and in those terms I do think that Freud's ideas were much more radical than Jung's. You could argue that Jung's fascination with the occult and his theories about life after death made him more radical than Freud, in the sense that Freud remained narrowly rationalistic about everything, but I think that in the field of psychoanalytical thought Freud's ideas were the more radical, and I also think that from the beginning Jung bucked against that. In the simplest terms, Jung felt that Freud's determination to reduce everything to sexual motives was limiting – and wrong. The great surprise of the Bair book is how intolerant of dissent Jung became during the later flourishing of his career, because when he was young he was prone to vacillation and confusion and all the things we normally associate with liberal woolliness. At the same time, as a young man he was also supremely self-confident, and in the course of the play all that falls away, leaving him completely bereft. He's taken from Freud and taken from Sabina but hasn't yet made his own distinctive contribution, and he knows that and feels unworthy because of it, and is on the verge of this illness which he'll have to forge his way through. The bricks are lying all around him, and he has to put them back together himself.

You said that the split between Jung and Freud was damaging to the psychoanalytic movement, but if they hadn't gone their separate ways Jung might never have made that distinctive contribution.

That's one of the questions that the play poses: is it a requirement of originality to be buffeted by some self-destructive force? The production of ideas often seems to require a bedrock of weakness or illness – what is often called, in the case of Jung's breakdown, a creative illness – but what is the exact relationship between the debility and the creativity? Funnily enough, when I was writing the play – as usual, in a hotel in Paris – I collapsed three days before the end, which had never happened to me before. I often feel a bit spaced-out as I move towards the completion of a piece of work, but I've never had to walk out of a restaurant in the middle of a meal and go to bed for two days. It was quite startling.

Would you say that you come down on the side of Freud because Jung's treatment of Sabina proves that everything does have a sexual motive?

It's partly that, and partly the fact that Freud was much more scrupulous than Jung. I'm not saying that Jung was unscrupulous. I don't condemn him for yielding to these temptations; but he knew that he shouldn't, he knew that sleeping with patients wasn't consistent with his theories. On the other hand, his patients found him more helpful than Freud's patients found him, precisely because of his all-embracing philosophy. Whereas Freud ploughed a straight furrow, Jung tended to proceed in circles. That's why his books are so hard to read, because you have to surrender to this circular motion as he tries out one theory and then flirts with its complete opposite and so on. They're much more spontaneous than Freud's books, which are long and considered – and classical, I suppose. So it's another old clash, between the classical and the romantic, and in those circumstances my sympathies tend towards classicism rather than romanticism, which tends to be irrational and destructive – or self-destructive.

Perhaps Jung's patients found him more helpful than Freud's not just because he'd surrendered to those temptations but because he wouldn't condemn them for doing so – as he says to Sabina at the end, 'Only the wounded physician can hope to heal.'

I think that's right. And I think the sense at the end of the play is that he's going to come through all this, because he's now aware that there are certain problems in life which can't be solved and therefore have to be accommodated. What he said in later life, what he finally came up with, was that we're all a mass of contradictions and we won't be well until we understand that we're a mass of contradictions, and the road to being well is to understand your own particular mass of contradictions, because your own particular mass of contradictions will be different from the next man's. That's who you are, and what you need to do, and what it takes you twenty years of adult life to do, is to figure out who you are, accept it and get on with it. But he's not in a position to say that when he's in the middle of all this, because he's busy defending his corner. He thinks that Freud will think less well of him if he admits sleeping with a patient, so he denies it; then later on he admits it and apologizes for it, which makes him resent Freud and makes Freud resent him. So Sabina was really the crack down the middle of the Jung–Freud relationship. She brought them together and she drove them apart.

In other words, she's the pivotal character without being the central character.

Yes – like Lytton in *Carrington*. Sabina precipitates all kinds of intellectual as well as emotional developments in Jung by making him understand that he has instincts other than those of a bourgeois Swiss, something unreleased in him which she can release and no one else.

With a little help from Otto Gross, a character who you said unlocked the play for you.

The notion that Otto Gross somehow liberated Jung came from John Kerr, but there's not much about him in the book so I had to do quite a lot of side research. There's a book about the Von Richtofen sisters, one of whom became Freda Lawrence and both of whom had affairs with Gross, and there's a very good account of him in that – and from there I moved on to the German sources. I've never actually read anything that he wrote, which is frustrating because I'd like to know more about him. He seems to have vanished into the mists of time, but he was clearly a fascinating character. He's one of those characters, like Braham in *The Philanthropist*, whom you want to run with a bit longer. I remember Charles Gray saying, when we offered him the part of Braham in the first production, 'Why hasn't the foolish author brought back this wonderful character in the second half?' and the answer is: you can't, because their whole dramatic function is to come in and tilt the proceedings and then disappear.

When James Hazeldine, who was originally cast as Freud at the

National, died after three performances, Howard Davies made the decision to double the roles of Freud and Gross. What was your reaction to that, and what do you think the dramatic and thematic implications were?

I was absolutely opposed to it, but I was overruled by Howard. Dominic Rowan, who played both parts, was remarkable and did an amazing job as Freud, but it was still a mistake. Freud was twenty years older than Jung and saw him as his son and heir, so that didn't come across, even on the simplest possible visual level; and in the second half of the first act, which literally alternates between Freud and Gross, each character wiped off on the other in ways which weren't particularly helpful to the unfurling of the play. It was just ill-advised.

On the other hand, it did throw the spotlight more on Ralph Fiennes and Jodhi May as Jung and Sabina, who were both very powerful.

They were wonderful casting. Ralph doesn't do very many modern plays, but the part of Jung requires all the skills you learn as a classical actor. There's a lot more subtext than text, and it's great to get an actor who can convey what's going on in his mind without resorting to tricks or exaggerated behaviour. His nervy quality, that sense of troubled depths, was very appropriate, because you could see the constant state of tension which the character was in all the way through to his final nervous collapse – or the state just prior to nervous collapse. He's also a very unselfish actor. It's a long march as far as the part of Jung is concerned, because the first half of the play really belongs to Sabina, and he dealt with that very straightforwardly and successfully. He knew when to do something which made you focus on what Jung was thinking and feeling, but he also knew how to make you concentrate on what Sabina was thinking and feeling. Of all the characters I've written, Sabina is probably the one who has the longest and – even though I show what happened to her in the end – most optimistic journey to make, and Jodhi was totally committed to that. She's a remarkable actress, and the two of them did make a powerful combination.

How did you feel about the first production as a whole?

The circumstances of the first production were so unhappy, and the play itself was so demanding, that what I'm trying to do now is start again and rethink the whole thing, because there's no doubt that it didn't land with the impact it should have. But then neither did *Total Eclipse* or *Tales from Hollywood* in their first productions. If you deal with a complex subject, the task is to do it in such a way that an audience, which is only going to watch it once for two hours, will grasp some of that complexity. That's a big thing to hope for, because people don't apprehend all kinds of things, so to expect a piece to land perfectly the first time out is asking too much, really. It often takes a play a while to find its way. Of course, if it doesn't make much impact in the first place it's never going to get a chance to find its way, which is something else you have to grapple with, but it can take a period of consideration and a production or two to teach you what it was you were trying to say. So I suppose I'm finally doing what I was originally asked to do, which is write another draft.

Do you think that the reason why you found The Talking Cure *so demanding is the same reason why, with the exception of* Total Eclipse, *you've never revised a play to this extent: that although you're dealing with many of your favourite themes, you're dealing with them directly rather than obliquely – going to the source, as it were?*

It hadn't occurred to me in those terms, but you may be right. *The Talking Cure* and *Total Eclipse* both go back to basics: *Total Eclipse* is about the basic issues behind being a writer, while *The Talking Cure* is about the basic issues behind being a social animal. It's the same kind of fundamental subject, and I suppose the reason why I'm so interested in psychoanalysis is that it's turned out to be fertile ground for all my work.

Who's going to direct the play in America?

It's being done in Los Angeles in April 2004, directed by Gordon Davidson, which is hopefully when we'll get a chance to try out this new version. Gordon is retiring from the Mark Taper and this will be his last production, which closes a chapter in my life. He did *Savages* in 1974, then *Tales from Hollywood* in 1983, so it's thirty years. It'll be nice to do it there, and having remounted it,

I want to go on and make the movie of it, incorporating all the lessons I've learned. That's the plan, anyway.

Do you ever worry about spreading yourself too thinly?

I'm sure I do too much, but I can't see any way not to. I was pretty lazy in my twenties and waited for inspiration to strike in a way I don't now. Now I feel the die is cast. I'm a writer so I might as well get on with it, and history will judge how good I was at it – although how good you are at it isn't really important; what's important is that you do it. You see, I don't think all these forays in different directions are very successful in producing what they're supposed to, which is objective art. I always attempt to erase my own petty concerns from the work I do, but in the end you always leave something of yourself on the barbed wire. In fact, the stuff of mine which works best is probably the confrontations between autobiography and history, like *Tales from Hollywood*, so perhaps that's what I should be doing – but I haven't got around to making those kind of decisions yet.

How different do you think the theatre is now to when you started writing?

I think the theatre has its periods of heat, and the sixties was one of those periods. There was just something in the air, and a number of playwrights were lucky enough to be around to breathe that in. My sense now is that there are still plenty of talented people around, but it's a much more difficult time to be trying to establish yourself. When the Royal Court accepted *Total Eclipse*, Bill Gaskill actually said that he would prefer to put it on as it was rather than my trying to improve it, so I could see what was wrong with it and avoid making the same mistakes again, which is an inconceivable attitude in these corporate times. It's becoming more and more difficult to put plays on at all in the West End unless you have big stars in them, and we're only just coming to terms with the fact that you can only run a play for as long as the star is available. Occasionally a play will overtake the actors, however eminent they might be – as *'Art'* did – but by and large it's the event which the public wants to see – Kevin Spacey in *The Iceman Cometh* or Ralph Fiennes in *The Talking Cure* – and the perception is that, if you don't have those people, you're not going to be able to sustain the life of the play. As a corollary to that, you can put on terrible plays with big stars in and people will flock to see them, which is equally regrettable. Even so, I get very exercised about the way, every two or three years, some opinionated bore in the *Evening Standard* or the *Sunday Times* will come out with a piece about how it's not worth going to the theatre any more. It's hard to believe that anyone can be so ignorant. It's like writing an article saying, 'I love going to the National Gallery, but why do they bother with all those sculptures? Goodness me, sculpture is boring!' It's an art form, you know what I mean? And if you don't understand it, then shut the fuck up!

Credits

Theatre

When Did You Last See My Mother? (Royal Court, 1966)
Isaac Babel's *Marya* (Royal Court, 1967)
Total Eclipse (Royal Court, 1968)
Chekhov's *Uncle Vanya* (Royal Court, 1969)
The Philanthropist (Royal Court, 1970)
Ibsen's *Hedda Gabler* (Stratford Festival Theatre, Ontario, 1970)
Ibsen's *A Doll's House* (Playhouse Theatre, New York, 1971)
Molière's *Don Juan* (Bristol Old Vic, 1972)
Savages (Royal Court, 1973)
Treats (Royal Court, 1976)
Ödön von Horváth's *Tales from the Vienna Woods* (National Theatre, 1977)
Ibsen's *Ghosts* (The Actors Company, 1977)
Ödön von Horváth's *Don Juan Comes Back from the War* (National Theatre, 1978)
Ibsen's *The Wild Duck* (National Theatre, 1979)
The Portage to San Cristobal of A.H., from the novel by George Steiner (Mermaid Theatre, London, 1982)
Tales from Hollywood (National Theatre, 1983)
Molière's *Tartuffe* (RSC, Barbican, 1983)
Les Liaisons Dangereuses, from the novel by Choderlos de Laclos (RSC, Stratford, 1985)
Ödön von Horváth's *Faith, Hope and Charity* (Lyric Theatre, Hammersmith, 1989)
White Chameleon (National Theatre, 1991)
Sunset Boulevard, book and lyrics by Don Black and Christopher Hampton, music by Andrew Lloyd Webber, based on the screenplay by Billy Wilder, Charles Brackett and D. M. Marshman Jr (Adelphi Theatre, London, 1993)
Alice's Adventures Under Ground, adapted from the writings of Lewis Carroll, in collaboration with Martha Clarke (National

Theatre, 1994)
Yasmina Reza's *'Art'* (Wyndhams Theatre, London, 1996)
Ibsen's *An Enemy of the People* (National Theatre, 1997)
Yasmina Reza's *The Unexpected Man* (RSC, Barbican, 1998)
Yasmina Reza's *Conversations after a Burial* (Almeida Theatre, London, 2000)
Yasmina Reza's *Life x 3* (National Theatre, 2000)
Dracula, book and lyrics by Don Black and Christopher Hampton, music by Frank Wildhorn, based on the novel by Bram Stoker (Belasco Theatre, New York, 2004)
The Talking Cure (National Theatre, 2002)
Chekhov's *Three Sisters* (Playhouse Theatre, London, 2003)

Film

A Doll's House, play by Ibsen (Patrick Garland, 1973, UK)
Tales from the Vienna Woods, co-written by Maximilian Schell, play by Ödön von Horváth (Maximilian Schell, 1979, Ger/Aus)
The Honorary Consul, novel by Graham Greene (John MacKenzie, 1983, UK)
The Good Father, novel by Peter Prince (Mike Newell, 1986, UK)
The Wolf at the Door, original scenario by Henning Carlsen, Jean-Claude Carrière (Henning Carlsen, 1986, Fr/Den)
Dangerous Liaisons, play *Les Liaisons Dangereuses* by Christopher Hampton, novel *Les Liaisons Dangereuses* by Choderlos de Laclos (Stephen Frears, 1988, US)
Carrington, book *Lytton Strachey* by Michael Holroyd (Christopher Hampton, 1995, UK/Fr)
Total Eclipse, play by Christopher Hampton (Agnieszka Holland, 1995, Fr/UK/Bel)
The Secret Agent, novel by Joseph Conrad (Christopher Hampton, 1996, UK)
Mary Reilly, novel by Valerie Martin (Stephen Frears, 1996, US)
The Quiet American, novel by Graham Greene (Phillip Noyce, 2002, US)
Imagining Argentina, novel by Lawrence Thornton (Christopher Hampton, 2003, US/Sp)

Television

Total Eclipse, play by Christopher Hampton (Peter Cregeen, 1972, BBC)

The Philanthropist, play by Christopher Hampton (Stuart Burge, 1975, BBC)

Savages, play by Christopher Hampton (Alan Bridges, 1975, BBC)

Able's Will (Stephen Frears, 1976, BBC)

Treats, play by Christopher Hampton (John Frankau, 1977, YTV)

Marya, play by Isaac Babel (Jack Gold, 1979, BBC)

The History Man, novel by Malcolm Bradbury (Rob Knights, 1981, BBC)

Tartuffe, play by Molière (Bill Alexander, 1985, BBC)

Hotel du Lac, novel by Anita Brookner (Giles Foster, 1986, BBC)

The Ginger Tree, novel by Oswald Wynd (Tony Garner, 1989, BBC)

Tales from Hollywood, play by Christopher Hampton (Howard Davies, 1992, BBC)

Uncredited Screenwriting

Ned Kelly (Tony Richardson, 1970, UK)

The Great Gatsby, novel by F. Scott Fitzgerald (Jack Clayton, 1974, US)

Agatha (Michael Apted, 1978, US/UK)

Unproduced Screenwriting

When Did You Last See My Mother?, play by Christopher Hampton, for Bryan Forbes/Ronald Shedlo (1966)

Edward II, play by Christopher Marlowe (1970)

A Temporary Life, novel by David Storey, for Barry Krost (1974)

The Tenant, novel by Roland Topor, for Paramount (1975)

The Moon and Sixpence, novel by Somerset Maugham (1976)

The Last Secret, book by Nicholas Bethell, for Fox (1979)

The Florentines, original teleplay, for Franco Zeffirelli (1982)

The Price of Tea, original teleplay, for the BBC (1984)

Nostromo, novel by Joseph Conrad, for Warner Bros./Serge Silberman (1987/1993)

Ghosts, play by Henrik Ibsen, for Eric Abraham (1987)

A Bright Shining Lie, book by Neil Sheehan, for Warner Bros. (1990)

White Chameleon, play by Christopher Hampton, for Norma Heyman/John McGrath (1991)

The Custom of the Country, novel by Edith Wharton, for TriStar (1992)

The Secret History, novel by Donna Tartt, for Warner Bros. (1994)

The Day the Earth Caught Fire, screenplay by Wolf Mankowitz and Val Guest, for Fox (1996)

The Night-Comers, novel by Eric Ambler, for Philippe Carcassonne (1996)

Alice's Adventures Under Ground, play by Christopher Hampton, adapted from the writings of Lewis Carroll, for the BBC (1997)

Hedda Gabler, play by Henrik Ibsen, for Universal (1997)

Sabina, book *A Most Dangerous Method* by John Kerr, for Fox (1998)

The Cloak of Vice, original screenplay, for Pascal Houzelot (1999)

Silent Witness, novel by Richard North Patterson, for New Line (1999)

Tulip Fever, novel by Deborah Moggach, for DreamWorks (2001)

Atonement, novel by Ian McEwan, for Working Title (2003)

Chéri, novel by Colette, for Bill Kenwright (2003)

Theatre Awards

The Philanthropist (Evening Standard Award, Best Comedy, 1970)

Tales from Hollywood (Evening Standard Award, Best Comedy, 1983)

Les Liaisons Dangereuses (Olivier Award, Best Play, 1986; Evening Standard Award, Best Play, 1986)

Sunset Boulevard (Tony Award, Best Book of a Musical, 1994–5; Tony Award, Best Original Score, Lyrics, 1994–5)

'Art' (Olivier Award, Best Comedy, 1996; Evening Standard Award, Best Comedy, 1996; Tony Award, Best Comedy, 1997–8)

Film Awards

The Good Father (Prix Italia, 1986)

Dangerous Liaisons (Academy Award, Best Adapted Screenplay, 1988; BAFTA, Best Adapted Screenplay, 1988; Writers Guild of America, Best Adapted Screenplay, 1988)

Carrington (Special Jury Prize, Cannes, 1995)

Index

Gero, Frank, 115–16
Gertler, Mark, 203
Ghosts, 42–3, 47–9, 245, 248
Giap, General, 192–3
Gill, Peter, 41–2, 85
Ginger Tree, The, 128–30, 247
Glass, Philip, 140, 210–11
Glatter, Lesli Linka, 220
Glenny, Michael, 35
Go-Between, The, 11
Godard, Jean-Luc, 12
Godfather, The, 170
Gold, Jack, 247
Good Father, The, 152–4, 188,
246, 249
Gossett, Lou, Jr, 37
Granada, 106–8
Gray, Charles, 240
Great Exhibition, The, 33
Great Gatsby, The, 90–91, 96,
247
Greene, Graham, 101, 103–4,
165, 183, 188–9, 246
Grégoire, Hélène, 41
Griem, Helmut, 33
Griffith, Eva, 43
Griffiths, Richard, 35
Grillo, John, 19–20
Gross, Otto, 81, 238, 240–41
Grossman, David, 110–11
Guest, Harry, 2, 5
Guest, Val, 248
Guinness, Alec, 86, 161
Gulf + Western, 91–2, 102
Guthrie Theatre (Minneapolis),
37

Haggard, H. Rider, 1
Haigh, Kenneth, 37
Haines, Randa, 220
Hall, Lee, 194–5
Hall, Peter, 76
Hamilton, Nigel, 80
Hamlet, 38
Hampton, Christopher: educa-
tion (Alexandria), 1, 135–6;

(Lancing College), 2–3, 5, 29,
42–3; (New College, Oxford),
2–3, 5–10, 15, 18, 29–30,
35–6, 43, 72, 112–13, 137,
198; (prep school), 1–2, 136;
family (brother), 4, 88, 133,
136, 138; (father), 3, 5,
133–40; (mother), 133–5,
138–40 (see also Laura Hamp-
ton)
Hampton, Christopher (poet),
6–7
Hampton, Laura, 32, 56–9, 101,
116, 127, 165–6, 198
Hamsun, Knut, 154
Hanau, Sasha, 148
Hands, Terry, 115
Hanks, Tom, 182
Hanson, Barry, 69
Hare, David, 3, 18–19, 21, 29,
33, 68, 82, 85, 132
Harris, Jared, 116
Hawthorne, Nigel, 32, 117
Hazeldine, James, 240–41
HBO, 171
Hedda Gabler, 34, 41–4, 47–8,
177, 245, 248
Heeley, David, 176
Hellman, Lillian, 98
Henry V, 89
Henry, Victor, 8, 10, 19–20
Herrmann, Bernard, 211
Herzog, Werner, 23–4
Heyman, Norma, 101–2, 140,
163, 173, 211, 248
Hickox, Douglas, 89–90
History Man, The, 70–71, 152,
188, 247
Hitchcock, Alfred, 185–7, 211,
215–16
Ho Chi Minh, 167–8
Hoffman, Dustin, 96–7
Hogg, Ian, 21
Holland, Agnieszka, 23–7, 246
Holroyd, Michael, 201, 246
Homolka, Oscar, 215–16